KT-392-302

3

333.9532 CRO

LEARNING services

01209 722146

Duchy College Rosewarne
Learning Centre

This resource is to be returned on or before the last date stamped below. To renew items please contact the Centre

Three Week Loan

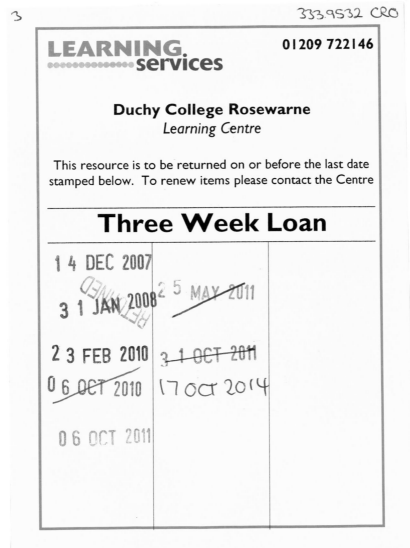

1 4 DEC 2007

3 1 JAN 2008   2 5 MAY 2011

2 3 FEB 2010   3 1 OCT 2011

0 6 OCT 2010   17 OCT 2014

0 6 OCT 2011

Cornwall College

141656

PEOPLE AND PLANTS CONSERVATION MANUALS

Manual Series Editor
Martin Walters

Manual Series Originator
Alan Hamilton

People and Plants is a joint initiative of WWF,
the United Nations Educational, Scientific and Cultural Organization
(UNESCO) and the Royal Botanic Gardens, Kew.

Other titles in the series

Applied Ethnobotany: People, Wild Plant Use and Conservation
Anthony B Cunningham

People, Plants and Protected Areas: A Guide to In Situ *Management* (reissue)
John Tuxill and Gary Paul Nabhan

Forthcoming titles in the series

Biodiversity and Traditional Knowledge: Equitable Partnerships in Practice
Sarah A Laird (ed)

Ethnobotany: A Methods Manual 2nd edition
Gary J Martin

*The Management and Marketing of Non-Timber Forest Products:
Certification as a Tool to Promote Sustainability*
Patricia Shanley, Sarah A Laird, Alan Pierce and Abraham Guillén (eds)

*Uncovering the Hidden Harvest: Valuation Methods for Woodland and
Forest Resources*
Bruce M Campbell and Martin K Luckert (eds)

Plant Invaders

The Threat to Natural Ecosystems

Quentin C B Cronk and Janice L Fuller

Earthscan Publications Ltd, London and Sterling, VA

Published in the UK and USA in 2001 by
Earthscan Publications Ltd

Originally published by Chapman & Hall in 1995

Copyright © WWF, 2001

All rights reserved

A catalogue record for this book is available from the British Library

ISBN: 1 85383 781 4

Bound in the UK by
Cover design by Yvonne Booth
Cover photo by Alan Hamilton
Panda symbol © 1986 WWF
® WWF registered trademark owner

For a full list of publications please contact:
Earthscan Publications Ltd
120 Pentonville Road
London, N1 9JN, UK
Tel: +44 (0)20 7278 0433
Fax: +44 (0)20 7278 1142
Email: earthinfo@earthscan.co.uk
http://www.earthscan.co.uk

22883 Quicksilver Drive, Sterling, VA 20166–2012, USA

Earthscan is an editorially independent subsidiary of Kogan Page Ltd and publishes in
association with WWF-UK and the International Institute for Environment and
Development

This book is printed on elemental chlorine-free paper

WWF

The World Wide Fund for Nature (WWF), founded in 1961, is the world's largest private nature conservation organization. It consists of 29 national organizations and associates, and works in more than 100 countries. The coordinating headquarters are in Gland, Switzerland. The WWF mission is to conserve biodiversity, to ensure that the use of renewable natural resources is sustainable and to promote actions to reduce pollution and wasteful consumption.

UNESCO

The United Nations Educational, Scientific, and Cultural Organization is the only UN agency with a mandate spanning the fields of science (including social sciences), education, culture and communication. UNESCO has over 40 years of experience in testing interdisciplinary approaches to solving environment and development problems, in programs such as that on Man and the Biosphere (MAB). An international network of biosphere reserves provides sites for conservation of biological diversity, long-term ecological research, and testing and demonstrating approaches to the sustainable use of natural resources.

The Royal Botanic Gardens, Kew

The Royal Botanic Gardens, Kew has 150 professional staff and associated researchers and works with partners in over 42 countries. Research focuses on taxonomy, preparation of floras, economic botany, plant biochemistry and many other specialized fields. The Royal Botanic Gardens has one of the largest herbaria in the world and an excellent botanic library.

Darwin Initiative for the Survival of Species

At the Earth Summit in June 1992, the Prime Minister of the United Kingdom announced the Darwin Initiative as a demonstration of the UK's commitment to the aims of the Biodiversity Convention. The Initiative will build on Britain's scientific, educational and commercial strengths in the field of biodiversity to assist in the conservation of the world's biodiversity and natural habitats, particularly in those countries rich in biodiversity but poor in resources.

DISCLAIMER
While the organizations concerned with the production of this manual firmly believe that its subject is of great importance for conservation, they are not responsible for the detailed opinions expressed nor for the accuracy or style of the text.

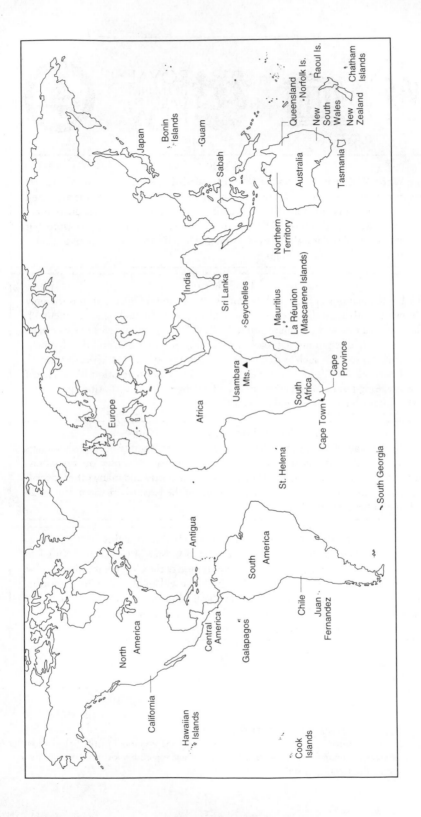

Map 1 The world, showing some of the places and regions mentioned in this book.

Contents

The 'People and Plants' Initiative

This manual is one of a series, forming a contribution to the People and Plants Initiative of the World Wide Fund for Nature (WWF), the United Nation Educational, Scientific, and Cultural Organization (UNESCO) and the Royal Botanic Gardens, Kew (UK). The Initiative has received financial support from the Darwin Initiative for the Survival of Species (Department of the Environment, UK) and the Tropical Forestry Program (US Department of Agriculture). The main objective of the People and Plants Initiative is to build up the capacity for work with local communities on botanical aspects of conservation, especially in countries with tropical forests. The principal intention in the manual series is to provide information which will assist botanists and others to undertake such practical conservation work. Other components of the People and Plants Initiative include demonstration projects in Bolivia, Kenya, Mozambique, Malaysia, Mexico, and Uganda, as well as support for workshops and publication of working papers.

Our aim in producing the present manual is to draw attention to the growing problem of invasive plant species – plants introduced by people to new areas in which they then have become established and spread into natural or seminatural ecosystems. Invasive plants are already a very serious threat to the conservation of biodiversity in many parts of the world, for example on some oceanic islands, in some areas of Mediterranean-type ecosystems, such as the fynbos of South Africa, and in some wetlands. Certain types of ecosystem, like continental tropical forest, are commonly regarded as typically resistant to plant invaders, but this is not true of all tropical forests and the present-day low levels of plant invaders in most tropical forests may, at least in part, be due to history as much as ecology.

We know little of the factors which lead to biological invasions, making it difficult to predict which species will become invasive and where invasion will occur. It does however seem certain that the threat of invasions is growing, as more and more species of plants are moved around the world, planted in gardens or used in agriculture or forestry. Often very little thought is given to the risks of plant invasion, for example by those promoting widespread use of fast-growing leguminous trees in agroforestry schemes in the tropics.

A number of groups of people can contribute to the control of invasive plants, including legislators and customs agents (to prevent initial introductions), scientists (for instance, to devise much needed effective and environmentally friendly methods of control) and land managers (to put control measures into effect). The subject of invasive plants is not so obviously central to the basic theme of the People and Plants Initiative as some of the other titles in the manual series, but nevertheless there certainly are occasions when local communities play a role in the control of invasive plants, as with clearance of invasive *Rhododendron* in woodlands and *Hippophae* on sand-dunes in Britain and Ireland and clearance of *Leucaena* and *Flacourtia* by local conservation groups on Ile aux Aigrettes, Mauritius.

Alan Hamilton
Plants Conservation Officer
WWF International

Panel of advisers

Pierre Binggeli
c/o School of Biological and Chemical Science
University of Ulster
Coleraine
Co. Londonderry BT52 1SA
United Kingdom

David Given
PO Box 84
Lincoln University
Canterbury
New Zealand

Vernon Heywood
School of Plant Sciences
University of Reading
Reading RG6 2AS
United Kingdom

Ian Macdonald
Southern African Nature Foundation
456 Stellenbosch 7600
Republic of South Africa

Clifford Smith
Botany Department
University of Hawaii at Manoa
3190 Maile Way
Honolulu HI 06822
United States of America

Charles Stirton
Deputy Director
Royal Botanic Gardens
Kew, Richmond
Surrey TW9 3AB
United Kingdom

Preface

Cases could be given of introduced plants which have become common throughout whole islands in a period of less than ten years. Several of the plants now most numerous over the wide plains of La Plata, clothing square leagues of surface almost to the exclusion of all other plants, have been introduced from Europe; and there are plants which now range in India, as I hear from Dr Falconer, from Cape Comorin to the Himalaya, which have been imported from America since its discovery. In such cases, and endless instances could be given, no one supposes that the fertility of these animals and plants has been suddenly and temporarily increased in any sensible degree. The obvious explanation is that the conditions of life have been very favourable, and that there has consequently been less destruction of the old and young, and that nearly all the young have been enabled to breed. In such cases the geometrical ratio of increase, the result of which never fails to be surprising, simply explains the extraordinarily rapid increase and wide diffusion of naturalised productions in their new homes.

The Origin of Species: Charles Darwin, 1859

This book is intended as a review of the problem of invasive plants worldwide. Invasion by animals or other organisms is of similar importance, but this study is confined to plant invasions. Its aim is to address the following needs:

1. To increase public awareness of the threat of invasive plants to natural and seminatural ecosystems. Increased awareness will help prevent the translocation of invasive species to new areas. Numerous instances of invasion are given to indicate the nature of the problem.

2. To alert research and governmental organizations to the threat to biodiversity posed by invasive plants, in order to focus and strengthen research and management strategies.

3. To give practical information and advice to managers, conservationists and researchers on how to deal with invasive plants. The use of case-studies of important invasive species is designed to illustrate the wide variety of invasions and control methods, and to make available the results of studies in one region

to managers working in another. The book discusses the importance of recording, evaluation of invasive potential and development of appropriate control strategies.

This work approaches the subject in the context of conservation and concentrates on plant invasion as a threat to wild biodiversity. The definition of invasive plant used here (see section 1.1) reflects this conservation bias and deliberately avoids discussion of agricultural weeds. Our intention is to attempt to change current thinking on plant invaders: from obscure problem to major hazard to biodiversity. The book is intended to be as free from jargon as possible to reach a wide constituency, including amateur naturalists, land managers and decision-makers at all levels, for instance those who can tackle issues such as legislation and prevention. The case-studies of specific invaders are intended to give evidence of the scale and diversity of invasion.

Special mention must be made here of the important contribution of the SCOPE Program. In 1982, SCOPE (Scientific Committee on Problems of the Environment), a subsidiary body of the International Council of Scientific Unions, initiated a project on the 'Ecology of Biological Invasions'. This project has resulted in a number of symposia and associated publications [145, 192, 213, 252, 285]. The main questions that SCOPE has attempted to answer are [6]:

1. What factors determine whether a species will become an invader or not?
2. What site properties determine whether a species will become an invader or not?
3. How should management systems be developed to best advantage, given the knowledge gained from attempting to answer questions 1 and 2?

In studying biological invasions SCOPE has examined a variety of organisms including plants, mammals, microorganisms, insects and fish. There seems to be no consistent use of the term 'invasive plant' in the SCOPE program. Some authors deal with species invading agricultural habitats and threatening crop production, others with adventives and comparatively few consider those that invade natural or seminatural habitats. Many of the authors lump all these categories under the term 'invasive', and this should be borne in mind in interpreting the ideas and conclusions generated by the SCOPE program. Many of the ideas emerging from the SCOPE meetings are discussed in Chapters 1 and 2.

Quentin C.B. Cronk
Janice L. Fuller

Acknowledgements

We wish to acknowledge the many people who generously gave their help in various stages of the compilation of data for this book, and provided valuable information or comments relating to invasive plants, especially the following: P. Adam, P. Binggeli, T. Goodland, A. Hamilton, C.E. Hughes, W. Joenje, D.J. MacQueen, C.H. Stirton, B.T. Styles, C.J. West, T.C. Whitmore, P.A. Williams.

The following contributed comments on the list of invasive plants in Chapter 5: J. Akeroyd, P. Adam, B.A. Auld, P. Binggeli, M. Crawley, L. Cuddihy, N. de Zoysa, C. den Hartog, M. Diaz, I. Edwards, S.V. Fowler, T. Goodland, R.H. Groves, A. Hamilton, R. Hengeveld, V.H. Heywood, G. Howard, R. Jeffrey, W. Joenje, M.H. Julien, T. Lasseigne, W. Lonsdale, D.H. Lorence, I.A.W. Macdonald, R.N. Mack, J.L. Mayall, E. Medina, P.S. Mitchell, P.S. Motooka, M. Numata, A. Rabinovich, P.S. Ramakrishnan, L. Raulerson, M. Rejmanek, C. Ryall, D. Schroeder, C.W. Smith, J.M.B. Smith, C.H. Stirton, W. Strahm, H. Sukkopp, J. Swarbrick, W.R. Sykes, M.B. Usher, P.M. Wade, J. Waage, C. West, H.L.K. Whitehouse, T.C. Whitmore, S. Wiejusundara, P.A. Williams, G. Williams, M.H. Williamson, R. Wise.

The portraits of invasive plants were drawn by Rosemary Wise.

The authors take full responsibility for any remaining errors, and would be pleased to have corrections drawn to their attention. Finally, we would like to record special thanks to Alan Hamilton of WWF and to the series editor, Martin Walters, for their guidance throughout.

The preparation of this work was assisted by a grant to WWF by the Darwin Initiative, Department of the Environment, UK.

1

The nature of plant
invasion

1.1 What are invasive plants?

One of the main threats to biodiversity in the world is the direct destruction of habitats by people (through inappropriate resource use or pollution). Another serious but underestimated problem is the threat to natural and seminatural habitats by invasion of alien organisms, which potentially is a lasting and pervasive threat [73]. It is a lasting threat because when exploitation or pollution stops, ecosystems often begin to recover. However, when the introduction of alien organisms stops, the existing aliens do not disappear; in contrast they sometimes continue to spread and consolidate, and so may be called a more pervasive threat. Conservationists are becoming increasingly aware of the problem of invasive plants as they observe the native vegetation in many areas of interest succumbing to the 'revolutionary' [365] effect of vigorous aliens. The problem of biological invasions has been recognized by SCOPE (see Preface) as a central problem in the conservation of biological communities. Heywood [166] remarks that 'Invasion of natural communities, in many parts of the world, by introduced plants, especially woody species, constitutes one of the most serious threats to their survival, although it is one that is not fully acknowledged by conservationists'.

We define an invasive plant as:

an alien plant spreading naturally (without the direct assistance of people) in natural or seminatural habitats, to produce a significant change in terms of composition, structure or ecosystem processes.

This definition is intended to draw a clear line between the 'invasive plants' considered here and plants invading highly disturbed man-made or agricultural habitats (ruderals and weeds) [212]. It is necessary to make this distinction not only for practical conservation purposes, but also in order to reach any ecologically meaningful conclusions about the nature of invasion. In the literature this distinction is only rarely made [166, 259]. A difficulty arises when one tries to draw the line between 'natural/seminatural' and 'unnatural' habitats. An agricultural habitat is generally a highly managed system that is extremely artificial, differing from

most natural habitats in terms of competition, nutrient levels, diversity, disturbance and composition. As well as agricultural habitats, there are areas which are
highly disturbed by humans and vegetated by opportunistic species.

Our definition of natural or seminatural habitats, for the purposes of this book,
is as follows:

> *communities of plants and animals with some conservation significance, either
> where direct human disturbance is minimal or where human disturbance serves to
> encourage communities of wild species of interest to conservation.*

Several other definitions of invasive plants have been used. An invasive species
has been described as one that 'enters a territory in which it has never before
occurred regardless of circumstances' [259]. This catch-all description includes
species introduced into a new region, without considering whether they become
established, spread or have any effect on the native organisms. 'Adventive' species
is a better term for this kind of plant. Alternatively, 'invasive species are introduced
species that expand their population (and distributional range) in the new geographical location, without further human intervention' [406]. However, this
definition makes no reference to the impact on the habitat or ecosystem invaded
or to the type of habitat invaded. The definition: 'invasive species are introduced
species that have become pests' [404] merely shifts the question to that of defining
a 'pest'.

A much better definition of an invasive species is as an 'introduced species
which must be capable of establishing self-sustaining populations in areas of
natural or seminatural vegetation (i.e. untransformed ecosystems)' [253]. This
definition distinguishes between invaders of natural habitats and weeds ('ruderals')
of agricultural or highly disturbed habitats, and also between transient plants
('casuals') and well-established plants with self-sustaining populations. However,
this definition does not consider the impact on the native flora and fauna, although
aggressiveness of spread is a feature of importance to conservationists. Sukopp
[382] has proposed the term 'Verdrangung' (pushing out) to distinguish alien plants
which displace native species, significantly altering the habitat or ecosystem, from
plants which are introduced and become naturalized as constituents of the native
plant community ('Einpassung' or fitting in) without modifying it greatly. Similarly, Stirton [377] coined the term 'plant invader' to emphasize their capacity to
spread aggressively and cause rapid, often irreversible, changes in the landscape.

1.2 Plant invasion and conservation

1.2.1 General issues

Invasive plants are undesirable in conservation areas not simply because they are
aliens. There should be no serious objection to the introduction of a plant which
spreads naturally in a way that does not decrease the diversity of the native flora

and fauna, or alter ecosystem processes, although some would disagree with this view. *Impatiens parviflora*, for example, has been introduced to Britain and now occurs naturally in some ancient woodlands but does not pose any threat to the native vegetation. Invasive plants, on the other hand, modify natural and semi-natural habitats, for example, by replacing a diverse system with single species stands, introducing a new life form to the habitat, altering the water or fire regime, changing the nutrient status of the soil and humus, removing a food source or introducing a food source where none existed before, or altering sedimentation processes [253, 291, 321, 417]. Such alterations may have profound effects on the composition of both the flora and fauna of the region and on the landscape as a whole.

Plants which are now considered as invasive may have once appeared to be non-invasive when their populations were small or they were only found in habitats influenced by people. For conservation purposes, in environmentally sensitive areas, all aliens should perhaps be considered as potential threats and therefore monitored carefully. There has been a tendency not to record the spread of alien plants (e.g. *Rhododendron ponticum* in Britain [404]), at least when their populations seemed insignificant. Botanists and ecologists generally prefer to study the native flora and may often disregard the aliens. In many regions the number of introduced species that have had no detrimental effect on the native flora and fauna is far greater than the number of 'invasive species' (in Hawaii, for example, it has been estimated that there are 900 native plant species, 4000 introduced plants, of which 870 species which have naturalized and 91 'invasive plants' present significant management problems [361, 416]). As so few introduced species become 'invasive', it has been argued that there is no need for caution when introducing species to new areas. However, this argument does not take into account that those that do become invasive often have effects far out of proportion to their numbers.

1.2.2 Invasion and succession

There is a blurred distinction between invasion by a native species, as part of a succession, and invasion by an alien species. In some nature reserves, the conservation objective is to protect a species assemblage that may be invaded by native species as part of the natural succession. However, invasion by alien species may alter the native habitat more dramatically, in such a way that all native species are pushed out; in extreme cases, species may become extinct. An example of a single species attaining complete dominance is *Psidium cattleianum* in Mauritius and Hawaii. However, as many invasions are relatively recent, it is too early to say what the 'final' stage of their succession will be, particularly for long-lived invaders whose stands have not yet started to degenerate. In New Zealand, the invaders *Cytisus scoparium* (broom) and *Sambucus nigra* (elder) may come to dominate disturbed sites, but in other parts of New Zealand they behave only as early successional species, which are in turn invaded by the native *Melicytus ramiflorus* (mahoe). Broom and elder can therefore be desirable invasives in the re-establishment of native forest [442, 443]. Another example of the same is *Rosa rubiginosa* (sweet-briar) which is an efficient and readily bird-dispersed exotic colonizer of forest degraded by cattle-ranching in Argentina. It aids the recovery of the forest by acting as a thorny protective nurse for the regeneration of native trees such as *Lomatia hirsuta* [100]. However, the *Rosa* invasion lowers species richness [94]. Change is a feature of all ecosystems and what is at issue is not change itself but the rate and direction of change, both of which may be dramatically altered by invasion.

1.2.3 The threats

The examples of invasive species in Chapter 5, although not exhaustive or entirely representative of the global situation, do give an idea of the magnitude of the problem of alien plants spreading into and disrupting native plant communities and ecosystems. This account differs from many previous studies in that it is restricted to plants invading natural and seminatural habitats and having a significant impact on the native organisms. The threat posed by invasive plants to natural ecosystems is illustrated in the following selected examples:

1. *Replacement of diverse systems with single species stands of aliens* In Mauritius and Hawaii, *Psidium cattleianum* has spread to such an extent that it dominates large tracts of wet evergreen forest [239, 361] and has replaced much of the native vegetation with foreign but vigorously reproducing vegetation. Another oceanic island example is *Miconia calvescens* which is now estimated to cover 25% of Tahiti, primarily invading upland cloud forest. In the British Isles, *Rhododendron ponticum* has invaded a wide range of habitats [90]. In suitable conditions, it forms dense, impenetrable stands that prevent regeneration of the native species and removes a habitat for birds and other animals. *Acacia* species have spread over large areas of lowland and montane fynbos in South Africa, often forming stands with few other species present, leading to a reduction in biodiversity [377]. *Salvinia molesta* is an aquatic waterweed which has spread to dominate many freshwater systems in tropical and subtropical regions [279, 391]. The dense, floating mats formed can spread to cover the whole waterbody under sheltered conditions. These mats reduce light and oxygen levels, resulting in the displacement of the native animals and plants.

2. *Invasion that poses a direct threat to the native fauna* Invasion by *Lantana camara*, forming dense impenetrable stands in the Galápagos, threatens to remove the breeding site of an endangered bird, the dark-rumped petrel (*Pterodroma phaeopygia*) [91]. *Casuarina equisetifolia* has spread to such an extent on coastal areas in Florida (as well as other areas) that it is interfering with nesting sea-turtles (*Caretta*

Figures 1.1 & 1.2 Ecosystem effects of invasion. These photographs show the difference after tropical cyclone floods have cleared all the water hyacinth, *Eichhornia crassipes*, from the Enseleni River in Natal (South Africa). This species, originally from South America, can now be found smothering aquatic ecosystems throughout the tropics and subtropics on every continent. (Photos: I.A.W. Macdonald)

caretta) and American crocodiles (*Crocodylus acutus*)[21, 253]. However, while some animals decline in response to invasive plants other members of the native fauna may benefit. For example, there has been considerable range extension of the pied barbet (*Lybius leucomelas*) in South Africa by increased provision of nesting sites and fruit in introduced *Acacia* thicket [244].

3. *Alteration of soil chemistry* *Myrica faya* enriches the nutrient status of young volcanic soils in Hawaii by fixing nitrogen in its root nodules. This may have serious long-term consequences for this naturally nutrient-poor ecosystem, and may yet help ('facilitate') the invasion of other alien species which otherwise would have been unable to invade due to the low nutrient levels [293, 414, 417]. *Mesembryanthemum crystallinum* accumulates large quantities of salt, which is released after it dies. In this way it salinizes invaded areas and may prevent the native vegetation from establishing [204, 418].

4. *Alteration of geomorphological processes* *Spartina anglica* has invaded estuarine mud flats in many areas, including several localities in New Zealand, and as a result has altered sedimentation processes. Invasion by *Casuarina equisetifolia* in some areas is contributing to dune erosion. *Ammophila arenaria* is an aggressive invader in many areas where it was introduced for dune stabilization [253], and has significantly altered the dunes in places. In New Zealand it is said to be increasing the instability of some dune systems [445].

5. *Invasion leading to plant extinction* There are few documented examples of invasion leading to extinction of another species as invasives are usually just one of a number of contributory factors. However, on oceanic islands some extinctions can be attributed almost entirely to plant invasion. An example is the extinct endemic genus *Astiria* of Mauritius, represented by the single species *Astiria rosea* (Sterculiaceae). The last known site for this species is now a dense thicket of exotics and this is the most likely cause of its extinction. Many species are invading areas with endemic, rare or endangered species, and might contribute to their extinction. The spread of *Acacia saligna* in South Africa is directly threatening several species listed as endangered by IUCN [241]; *Passiflora mollissima* is seriously threatening Hawaiian rainforests, home to many endemic species [222]; *Rhododendron* is threatening the survival of rare Atlantic bryophytes in woodlands in the west of Ireland [199]; in Mauritius, *Ligustrum robustum* has invaded wet evergreen forests with many endemic species [239, 240]; *Lantana* invasion threatens several rare composite species in the Galápagos [91]; the invasion of *Pennisetum setaceum* in Hawaii is threatening several species listed as endangered by the US Wildlife Service [422]; *Ageratina adenophorum* is threatening the survival of two endemic shrubs, *Acomis acoma* and *Euphrasia bella*, in New South Wales, Australia [119].

6

6. *Alteration of fire regime* Invasive plants can alter both fire frequency and intensity. Fire frequency is a function of both the frequency of dry periods, ignition events and the flammability of the vegetation which determines the success rate of the ignition events. Many fire-adapted species have adaptations, such as the production of volatile oil or standing dead matter, to increase the frequency of successful ignition, and thus fire is important in their competitive relations with other plants. In Florida, the introduction of *Melaleuca quinquenervia*, which is almost perfectly adapted to fire, has increased the frequency of fires, damaging the native vegetation [115, 296]. Dense infestations of *Hakea* species in South Africa have increased the intensity of fires due to their rapid accumulation of large quantities of inflammable matter [301–303]. Like *Melaleuca*, and many other fire-adapted species such as *Pinus radiata*, species of *Hakea* have seeds with delayed dispersal ('serotiny') and fire promotes their release. By encouraging regeneration and the release of seed by fire-adapted invasives, regular burning in previously non-inflammable vegetation can have dramatic effects on species composition. In this way, fire-adapted bunchgrasses (*Schizachyrium*) in Hawaii are preventing regeneration of native species that are not adapted to regular burning [361].

7. *Alteration of hydrology* *Andropogon virginicus* now dominates areas in Hawaii which otherwise would have supported tropical rainforest vegetation. Its seasonal pattern of growth and formation of dense mats of dead vegetation are increasing water run-off in the area and leading to accelerated erosion [291]. Conversely, taller growing alien plants can invade an open native vegetation and cause a reduction in run-off. *Hakea sericea*, by producing a larger and denser canopy than the native fynbos shrubs, substantially increases evapotranspiration, and thus decreases the amount of water draining out of the area and available to people [303].

These examples show the greater variety of plant invasion in natural, as opposed to agricultural or highly disturbed ecosystems. This is a reflection of the variety of natural ecosystems and invaders. This variety is expressed in the taxonomy, morphology, biology and the ecology of the invading species, as well as in the habitats invaded and the effects (short and long term) on the native animals and plants.

1.3 Where is invasion happening?

Information on the geographical distribution of the problem of plant invasion is difficult to evaluate. In some areas, such as Hawaii, South Africa and Australia, there is an acute awareness of invasive plants, which have been recorded in detail. However, in parts of several large regions, such as South America, north and central Asia and India, there are few, if any, records of the spread of alien plants. This may be due to a lack of resources, local awareness or active recorders, rather than a lack of actual cases. It is therefore difficult to compare numbers of invasive

Figure 1.3 shows the dense invasive colonization of logged land in the East Usambara Mountains, Tanzania by *Maesopsis eminii* (not native to the region). Selective logging has created highly suitable conditions for the spread of this and other invasive species, including *Clidemia hirta* and *Lantana camara*. (Photo: Alan Hamilton)

plants between regions. The regions that contain most species from the sample of invasives in Chapter 5 are Australasia, Africa (mainly South Africa) and the Pacific islands (Oceania).

1.3.1 Invasion on oceanic islands

Islands are often reported to be more susceptible to invasion than continental ecosystems [413]. This susceptibility is illustrated by the high numbers of invasive species found on oceanic islands in the sample of invasive species in Chapter 5. We suggest the following explanations for the greater susceptibility of oceanic islands to invasion.

1. *Species poverty* This is usually attributed to their remoteness from continental sources of animals and plants, making them relatively species-poor. This poverty precludes vigorous competition between species as there is less chance of two species requiring identical or very similar conditions [113, 236, 361]. The lack of competition is demonstrated by the phenomenon, characteristic of oceanic islands, of 'adaptive radiation' or the evolution of plants into new habitats and life-forms in the absence of competition from existing plants in these life-forms.

Figure 1.4 shows the tall canopy of a mature individual of *Maesopsis eminii*, which had seeded into a natural gap in the Amani-Sigi Forest Reserve, East Usambara Mountains. *Maesopsis* is able to invade even apparently undisturbed forest and it is estimated that, unless it is controlled, it will come to form a substantial proportion of the canopy over the next century, seriously threatening the survival of the many endemic species in this forest. (Photo: Alan Hamilton)

By this reasoning alien plants are more likely to establish and spread on oceanic islands than in regions with a rich flora.

2. *Evolution in isolation* The native flora and fauna of remote islands have evolved in isolation, often without adaptation to high levels of competition, grazing and trampling by mammalian herbivores or to regular burning. The absence of mammals (with the exception of bats) is a characteristic of oceanic islands, and oceanic island plants seldom have the typical grazing adaptations, shown, for instance, by Mediterranean plants, of spines, thorns, pungent leaf chemicals, dense thicket-forming growth habit and vigorous resprouting from dormant buds on trunks and shoots. In the presence of grazing or browsing animals, adapted aliens will have a

competitive advantage over natives. For example, the introduction of goats to St Helena, shortly after the island's discovery in 1502, led to the destruction of many endemic species not adapted to grazing by vertebrates, such as the St Helena Ebony [84]. In contrast, the successful alien plants in St Helena, such as *Nicotiana glauca*, are often grazing resistant. In Hawaii, *Sophora chrysophylla* is one example of a native, highly palatable or 'goat ice cream' plant. In some Hawaiian communities, release from grazing produces an increase of native cover, indicating that differences in grazing tolerance are primary. However, in other communities an increase of alien cover follows goat eradication, indicating a greater importance of differences in competitive ability between natives and aliens [379].

3. *Early colonization*   Islands were the first European colonies and they were settled to protect trade routes at a time when climate, disease and indigenous populations made permanent European settlement on continents difficult. Islands that lie in the trade routes have borne the brunt of this colonial activity, particularly those in the Atlantic and Indian Oceans. They were often the first landfalls of explorers and have been subject to disturbance by Europeans for far longer than many continental regions (St Helena was discovered in 1502 and alien plants and animals were introduced immediately, although the island was not finally settled until 1659). They also have a long history of intentionally introduced crops and ornamental plants. However, the situation is different in the Pacific. Although the Hawaiian Islands were settled by Polynesians in around AD 1000, regular contact with European vessels dates from the start of the sandalwood trade (1815) and the first visits by whalers (1819). It was only after the 'Great Mahele' of 1848 that non-Polynesians were allowed to own land.

4. *Small scale*   Their small geographical size means that history is 'concentrated' in a small area and no physical features are large enough to prevent exploitation, disturbance and introduction throughout the island. Often the effect of the small scale can be seen in the relatively high population densities. For example, Mauritius has a population of roughly 530 people per km^2 whereas India, a country with which Mauritius is culturally and historically linked, has only about 240 people per km^2. Islands are small in relation to dispersal distances, so introduced plants can spread quite rapidly throughout an island, giving a worse impression of invasion than an apparently localized invasion on a continent that in fact covers a larger area. Finally, distances between different communities are often small on islands relative to dispersal distances and consequently an introduction can more easily disperse to the best habitat. For instance, in St Helena the zonation between semidesert and cloud forest occurs in 3–4 km and some 600 m altitude, whereas on continents greater distances often separate such divergent communities.

5. *Crossroads of intercontinental trade*   Often oceanic islands were colonized to promote trade routes, and therefore they have been at the crossroads of intercontinental trade and used quite deliberately to transfer living material for propagation ('germplasm') between continents. Islands were often key staging posts for trade and plant transport (the earliest British colonial botanical garden in the tropics was at St Vincent in the Caribbean, established for just this purpose). Often, too, they have had an eventful history. Mauritius changed hands between the Dutch (1598), French (1715) and British (1810) at various points in its history, increasing its chance of receiving plants from different parts of the tropics. The garden at Pamplemousses, to which many introductions came, was established by Governor Labourdonnais as early as 1735. This deluge of disturbance and alien plants goes some way towards explaining the apparent susceptibility of islands to invasion, at least in the case of Atlantic, Caribbean and Indian Ocean islands.

6. *Exaggeration of ecological release*   Alien species come to islands free from their natural array of pests and diseases, thus having an advantage over the native vegetation. This is particularly noticeable on islands, which usually have a species-poor fauna and therefore few generalist insect or other plant herbivores to prey on the alien species. If generalist plant-feeders are introduced, the alien species are more likely than native plants to be adapted to resist them.

1.3.2 Climatic patterns of invasion

Taking the sample of 70 invasive species in Chapters 4 and 5 for which climatic data are given, 18 are invaders of the cool temperate zone, 50 of the warm temperate zone, 47 of the subtropical zone and 16 of the tropical zone (see beginning of Chapter 5 for a definition of these zones). The striking preponderance of the warm temperate and subtropical zones may reflect a sample bias, with South Africa, Australia and Hawaii, where invasive plants have been the focus of intensive studies, weighing the balance in favor of these climate zones. More information is needed for other areas, especially South America and East Asia, to assess the significance of the climatic and geographic distribution of invasives. However, Australia, New Zealand, South Africa, the Mascarene Islands and Oceania (Pacific Islands), which are all regions that include warm temperate and subtropical climate zones, do genuinely seem to have significantly higher numbers of invasive species than other areas.

Few invasions seem to occur in areas with extreme climatic or environmental conditions, such as those which are extremely dry (desert, thorn steppe) or cold (polar regions), and it has been suggested that non-extreme ('mesic') habitats are more susceptible to invasion [324]. Certainly Antarctica is free of invasive species [405], although as continental Antarctica has only two indigenous species of vascular plants the absence of invaders is hardly surprising. The main invasive threat in Antarctica comes from fungi, protozoans and bacteria. However, *Poa annua* is a serious invader on the subantarctic island of South Georgia [226] and aliens have had an impact on the subantarctic Campbell Island [271].

The cool temperate zone appears to have a low number of invasive species relative to the warm temperate zone. Three reasons may be suggested:

1. Some cool temperate regions, such as northern and central Europe, have long been influenced by people and much of the natural vegetation has been destroyed and replaced with vigorous invasion-resistant secondary types of vegetation. Where this vegetation is invaded, it is usually by Northern Hemisphere species, such as *Rhododendron ponticum*. Although Europe has a long list of Northern Hemisphere aliens associated with its disturbed secondary vegetation, it may be that these weedy communities are too vigorous for most Southern Hemisphere species to join, except as casuals. The difference is that there are few areas of natural vegetation left and therefore, under our definition of invasive plant, only a few species qualify.

2. Most regions of the world were affected in one way or another by the climatic changes associated with the ice age cycles of the last 1.6 M yr (the Quaternary). Much of the cool temperate regions was glaciated during the ice ages, and repeated disturbance by glaciation may have encouraged the native flora to adopt characteristics associated with invasive species, making the vegetation inherently resistant to other invasive plants. At the end of the last ice age in northern Europe it is known that a diverse flora, which included many weeds and vigorous herbs, such as *Plantago major* and *Urtica dioica*, grew around the ice sheet, on soils disturbed by frost heave [40, 434]. Furthermore, the trees of formerly glaciated cool temperate regions underwent repeated long-distance migrations from refugia at the end of each cold stage. Most native trees of cool temperate regions therefore have many characteristics of invasive species. The rate of distribution change ('migration') has differed from species to species, but in some cases has been extremely rapid [35].

3. Climatic extremes in cool temperate regions may limit the spread of vigorous invaders. Marked seasonality reduces the length of the growing season and consequently may reduce the fecundity and the potential rates of increase of invasives. Environmental extremes such as frost increase density-independent mortality, while suboptimal growing conditions, for instance when temperatures are low, reduce growth and the aggressive competitiveness of invaders.

Species tend to invade, or grow well, in regions of the same, or similar, climate [23, 144], a characteristic which agriculturalists and foresters use in computerized climatic matching systems to predict the potential ranges of organisms [42, 384]. However, some species are apparently able to invade a wide range of climate zones or habitats outside their native limits. Examples are: *Lantana camara*, which is invading tropical, subtropical and warm temperate habitats; *Pueraria lobata*, which is native to cool temperate regions, but is invading both warm temperate and subtropical areas; and *Ailanthus altissima*, which is native in subtropical and warm temperate China, but is invading areas ranging from cool temperate to tropical. However, the climate zones used for analysis (cool temperate, warm temperate, subtropical and tropical) are broad categories, and it is possible that a closer examination of seasonality and extremes may be more useful in predicting invasion.

1.3.3 Invasions in particular biomes

1. *Tropical forest* Invasive species in large areas of the tropics are under-recorded, but undisturbed tropical rainforest does seem, at least in the Old World, to be fairly resistant to invasion [440]. However, there are some exceptions, such as *Pittosporum undulatum* and *Maesopsis eminii*(see Chapters 4 and 5). Large, intact areas of continental tropical forest, such as central Amazonia, are comparatively isolated and have not been exposed to the same numbers of aliens as more populated and long-colonized areas, and this may contribute to the apparent lack of invasive plants in most continental tropical rainforests. Secondary rainforest and island rainforest does appear to be prone to invasion as seen by the high numbers of alien species in Hawaii [359], Mauritius [239, 240] and Australia [119]. One study, of a sample of tropical nature reserves (Hawaii – Maui, the Galápagos and Australia – Kakadu National Park), against a similar study of Britain [446], suggested that no tropical ecosystems are free from invasive species and that the proportion of introduced plants that have become invasive is far higher in the tropics than in temperate regions [406]. However, nature reserves may not be fully representative of natural vegetation and some nature reserves are significantly disturbed by visitor pressure. A different picture might be gained from a wider survey.

2. *Mediterranean-climate shrublands and grasslands* In areas with a Mediterranean climate, the reduction of woodland cover, a common phenomenon in these regions, has apparently favored invasion; in turn, these invasions have often affected the native ecosystem by altering the natural fire regime. In California, it appears that accelerated soil erosion may be caused by plant invasion, which in the long term may seriously destabilize the native ecosystem [250]. In some Mediterranean-type ecosystems the native flora has been almost entirely displaced, but in others a large decline in native species diversity does not appear to have resulted. In California, Chile and many Australian habitats, the alien flora is mostly composed of annual herbs [300], although annual herbs have not displaced the native bunchgrasses in very similar vegetation in western Guatemala. This may be due to the less severe dry season and the presence of sheep rather than cattle as grazers [411]. In contrast, the South African fynbos vegetation has been invaded mainly by trees and shrubs. This diversity of situations involving invasive

plants illustrates the problem of understanding why certain species become invaders [216].

3. *Arid lands* Plant invasions in tropical savannas and dry woodlands are less frequent in the drier parts of these vegetation types. Here, fire and herbivory by large animals, both accentuated by drought, appear to limit invasion. In moister areas, particularly where the savannas appear to be man-made, shrubs and scramblers such as *Lantana camara*, *Chromolaena odorata*, *Mikania scandens* and *Parthenium hysterophorus* can be a serious problem [248]. Areas with more extreme aridity (deserts and semideserts) have not been invaded to a great extent by plants, except along perennial or intermittent water courses [237].

4. *Wetlands* Wetlands have been strongly invaded in many parts of the world and five of the 17 case studies in Chapter 4 are aquatic or wetland species. There are three main types of wetland invader: floating aquatics, submerged aquatics (e.g. *Myriophyllum aquaticum* and *Lagarosiphon major*) and plants of seasonally-flooded low-lying areas (e.g. *Mimosa pigra*, *Sesbania punicea* and *Melaleuca quinquenervia*). Floods and flowing water are efficient seed dispersal agents for invasives and most species have water dispersed propagules, which may be either vegetative fragments, fruits or seeds. Mineral nutrients brought down as silt during floods, provide growing conditions favorable to the growth of vigorous invasives. Many aquatic species (e.g. *Salvinia molesta*, *Eichhornia crassipes* and *Pistia stratiotes*) are unusual in that they have invaded a large number of regions. This may be due to freshwater habitats being so frequent worldwide and to easy accidental transport by boat traffic. Many of the invasive aquatic species have broad environmental tolerances, which also contribute to their success.

2

How invasion occurs

2.1 Process of invasion

2.1.1 Stages of invasion

There are several stages in the process of invasion. These may conveniently be divided into the following: introduction, naturalization, facilitation, spread, interaction with other animals and plants, and stabilization.

1. *Introduction* The introduction of invasive plants involves translocation of living material by people from one region to another, either accidentally or deliberately.

2. *Naturalization* Once introduced, a plant to be considered invasive, must become established beyond the site of initial introduction to form large self-sustaining populations in natural or seminatural vegetation. While the population remains small, the plant is at risk genetically and ecologically and may be unable to increase. This stage is known as naturalization and its success depends on the species being planted or otherwise introduced sufficiently close to natural vegetation for 'escape' to occur, and also on certain biological features of the plant (e.g. breeding system, successful reproduction) and on the environment (climate, seasonality, soil conditions).

3. *Facilitation* A naturalized plant may remain a rarity unless it is 'facilitated' in some way in order to spread, for example by the introduction of a suitable dispersal agent or pollinator, provision of disturbance in the ecosystem or lack of pests and diseases. Genetic adaptation to the new environment by the selection of the fittest individuals ('microevolutionary adaptation') is a form of facilitation. Another type of facilitation neglected by scientists is the 'fostering' of the plant in the wild by people, for instance *Psidium cattleianum* in Mauritius, where the collection of fruits for Guava wine makes contemplation of the introduction of biological control for this species difficult or impossible. In some estates in Britain *Rhododendron ponticum* has, in the past, been protected from clearance during standard forestry procedures by virtue of its attractive flowers, which have also encouraged people

15

to spread the plant (in some cases by scattering the seed at beauty spots!). Features of invasive plants which promote fostering, such as attractive flowers, edible fruit or nectar for honey, are important adaptations for invasion which can hinder control by promoting management conflicts (Chapter 3).

4. *Spread* If the spread of an alien plant has been facilitated, the rate of its spread depends on the intrinsic growth and reproduction rates of the plant as well as the nature of the invaded habitat including the presence of suitable places ('safe sites' [154]) for reproduction. Efficiency of seed dispersal is an important determinant of rate of spread and knowledge of both average and maximum dispersal distances is important for understanding population expansion. A successful invader often has adaptations for short- and long-distance dispersal, the short-distance bulking up existing populations and the long-distance establishing new foci for further spread, remote from the original site of invasion.

It is often observed that spread may be delayed and that an introduced plant initially occurs at low numbers in its new environment and later suddenly undergoes a population explosion [284]. This poorly understood phenomenon may occur for one or more of the following reasons: the population is actually expanding exponentially, but this is not noticed when numbers are very low; the plant was under-recorded when at low population levels due to its alien status; the population was unable to increase until facilitated in some way, for example through the arrival of a pollinator or the disturbance of habitat; genetic changes allow adaptation to new habitat (this may take a very long time); or the species spreads to an optimal habitat, the first habitat colonized being suboptimal. Once spread starts and if conditions remain suitable, the population of the alien species may increase to such levels that the native animals and plants are endangered and a control program is desirable.

5. *Interaction with animals and other plants* Sooner or later (as when originally planted), the alien species will encounter plants and animals already present in the area. The outcome of this interaction will determine whether the alien will be a 'fitting in' invasive or a 'pushing out' invasive (Chapter 1) with respect to the native animals and plants, and therefore whether it will have a significant effect on ecosystem processes, composition and structure. In some cases competition may restrict the alien species to disturbed sites on which the native vegetation has been or is unable to survive due to extreme environmental conditions.

6. *Stabilization* Some invasions appear to stabilize as single or near single species stands (e.g. *Psidium cattleianum* and *Rhododendron ponticum* – see the case studies in Chapter 4). However, it is often uncertain whether this stabilization is actually illusory. Many invasions are relatively recent and it is possible that the populations

Figure 2.1 shows the wild ginger, *Hedychium gardnerianum*, from India invading a wet gully in Madeira. (Photo: Quentin Cronk)

Figure 2.2 Here on the Indian Ocean island of Réunion *Hedychium gardnerianum* totally dominates the understorey of a stand of native rainforest. (Photo: I.A.W. Macdonald)

Figure 2.3 Seedlings of sycamore, *Acer pseudoplatanus*, growing vigorously alongside the rare endemic orchid, *Dactylorhiza foliosa*, in Madeira. Base-rich sites suitable for this orchid are ideal for sycamore seedlings, whose presence will, in turn, alter the ecosystem. (Photo: Quentin Cronk)

will eventually undergo senescence. It may be more appropriate to regard single species dominance of communities by invasives as analogous to a successional stage. An alternative possibility is that these massive infestations represent an 'ecological overshoot', as seems to have happened in the case of the nineteenth-century invasion of the waterweed *Elodea canadensis* in Britain, which rapidly became a major waterway nuisance before subsiding to its present relatively infrequent level. A similar example is provided by the invasion of *Lagarosiphon major* in Lake Rotorua, New Zealand which, from the massive weed-banks at the height of the invasion in 1958, has now subsided to an innocuous level (Chapter 4).

2.1.2 Modelling invasion

A 'model' is a simplified description of a process or system, sometimes given in mathematical terms, which aids understanding and may even allow predictions to be made given specified initial conditions. Most models of plant invasion do not distinguish between natural or seminatural habitats and disturbed or people-modified habitats [446]. Defining the characteristics and factors for the 'typical plant invasion' is difficult considering the ecological variety of plant invaders and natural habitats. Many models of invasion deal with disease epidemics [283] and there appears to have been little success in modelling plant invasion, particularly of relatively undisturbed natural habitats. Models of community dynamics often

18

assume that the principal barriers to invasion include [83]: (1) competition with established native species; (2) losses caused by generalist natural enemies (including disease); (3) lack of necessary coadapted animals (mutualists) to pollinate, disperse or otherwise help ('facilitate') the invader; and (4) deleterious low density effects operating on the invader itself. Environmental factors, such as climate, particularly seasonality of climate, fire regime, natural disturbance (such as hurricanes, grazing and trampling by native herbivores and flooding) and soil chemistry are rarely considered. However, analysis of the locations of apparently suitable climatic conditions, based on the climatic tolerances of a species in its home range ('homocline analysis'), is potentially a useful method for predicting the future distribution of an invasive plant. Models attempting to simulate invasion (usually for predictive purposes) often break down the process of invasion into stages: arrival, establishment and spread [283, 446], which can be further elaborated. However, even very simple models are useful in generating hypotheses, for instance of the relative effects of altering certain parameters, which can be tested in the field. For example, on the basis of one simple model, the rate of spread appears to differ widely from exponential to linear, depending on changes in simple population parameters, particularly dispersal pattern [15].

2.2 Historical aspects of plant translocation

2.2.1 Beginnings

From the start of agriculture, whenever people have moved, plants have moved too, both through the deliberate spread of domesticated crops and the accidental associated spread of weeds and ruderals [191]. Crop plants (particularly cereals) and associated arable weeds were introduced to Britain from SW Asia and S. Europe by Neolithic cultures some 6000 years ago [133]. Another example is the Japanese honeysuckle, Lonicera japonica. This species is native to E. Asia and is a serious problem in the US, where it flourishes as an agricultural weed in fields, thickets and bordering woodland, from Florida and Texas to New York State and Massachusetts. However, it is only since the seventeenth century and especially more recently (with the increase in ease of long-distance transport) that there has been large scale intercontinental changes in plant distributions. The activities of people have introduced a new order of magnitude into distances of dispersal [154].

2.2.2 Colonialism

The expansion of the European colonial powers (notably Britain, France, Germany, the Netherlands, Portugal and Spain) increased dramatically the transport of living material. One major aim was to discover and exploit new economic crops for the empires [166]. In particular, it was the opening up of the tropics and the discovery of the New World that led to a great wave of plant exchange or, as it has been called, 'ecological imperialism' [87]. The European colonization of Australia, for example, has been described as an 'apocalyptic' event for Australian ecosystems. In the tropics of Asia and Australasia, and on islands, the effects have been magnified by the extent and duration of the colonial period. In tropical Africa the impact on native ecosystems, although significant, has been less severe as, in the main, these countries were not colonized by European powers until the late nineteenth century during the 'scramble for Africa'. Most botanic gardens in tropical Africa date from the late nineteenth or early twentieth centuries, whereas, in contrast, the Calcutta Botanic Garden in India was established in 1787 and the Royal Botanic Garden at Peradeniya, Sri Lanka in 1821. In Latin America, the early withdrawal of Portugal and Spain and the minor involvement of Britain (by far the most active power in plant transport) has meant that the vegetation has suffered very much less than elsewhere in the tropics. The introduction and planting of useful or potentially useful crops and other plants was usually a characteristic and essential part of colonialism, although the dates and purposes of introduction may differ widely. In South Africa, for instance, *Pinus pinaster* was introduced (possibly by French Huguenots in 1688) as a timber tree for the largely treeless Western Cape and was certainly being grown in the Dutch East India Company's Garden in Cape Town around 1690; *Acacia cyclops* and *A. saligna* were both probably introduced to Baron von Ludwig's private garden in the 1830s and were used to plant the Cape Flats from *c.* 1847 onwards; in contrast, *Nasella trichotoma* was probably introduced from Argentina during the second South African War (1899–1902) in the 138 000 tons of fodder for horses imported by the British army [353, 431].

Islands that lie in the trade routes have borne the brunt of this colonial activity. They were often the first landfall for explorers and have been subject to disturbance far longer than most continental regions (St Helena was discovered in 1502 and alien plants and animals were introduced immediately). Islands were often key staging posts for trade and plant transport (the earliest British colonial botanical garden in the tropics was at St Vincent in the Caribbean, established for just this purpose). Often, too, they had an eventful history. Mauritius changed hands between Dutch (1598), French (1715) and British (1810) at various points in its history, and the garden at Pamplemousses, to which many introductions came, was established by Governor Labourdonnais as early as 1735. This deluge of disturbance and alien plants goes some way towards explaining the apparent susceptibility of islands to invasion, at least in the case of Atlantic, Caribbean and Indian Ocean islands.

2.2.3 Botanic gardens

Although many European botanic gardens founded from the sixteenth century onwards were responsible for a considerable amount of plant introduction (for medicinal, ornamental and amenity uses, as well as for scientific study), it was the

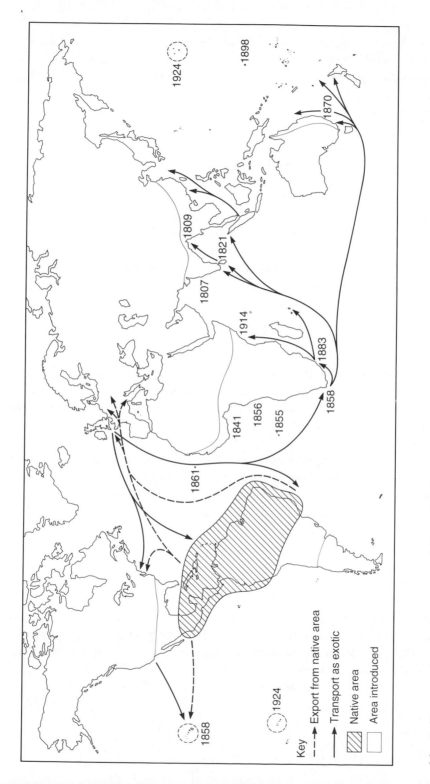

Map 2 Transport of *Lantana camara* around the world. This species has become a major pest in many areas. (After Stirton (1978))

Key
- - -→ Export from native area
———→ Transport as exotic
◲ Native area
☐ Area introduced

tropical botanic gardens that served as the main staging posts or centres of exchange [165]. The Royal Botanic Gardens, Kew, as a colonial institution, introduced Pará rubber, *Hevea brasiliensis*, to the Singapore Botanic Garden (which had been founded in 1859) from Brazil [56]; rubber later significantly altered the Malayan economy, landscape and ecosystems. Although it is a well-known example of plant introduction, *Hevea* is not invasive, but other similar introductions arranged by Kew for economic reasons have invaded important habitats. Examples include *Cinchona succirubra* and *Phormium tenax*, introduced for quinine and fiber production respectively and now established in the endemic-rich tree fern thicket on the central ridge of St Helena [86]. Britain was responsible for a considerable amount of plant introduction as a result of its policy of forming 'networks' of botanic gardens which exchanged vast quantities of living material under the direction of Kew. 'Over-introduction' is a common feature of these activities. Baron von Ludwig set out to introduce useful and ornamental exotic plants to his garden in South Africa, and with the help of his botanical contacts worldwide managed to introduce 1600 species [377].

2.2.4 This century

Modern agriculture and forestry have taken many crops, fruitplants and trees to new regions, and often they have escaped from cultivation and spread into the native vegetation. Examples include *Passiflora mollissima*, *Psidium cattleianum*, *Pennisetum clandestinum*, *Pinus radiata* and *Acacia melanoxylon*. Ever since the seventeenth century, enthusiastic gardeners have, in increasing quantities, introduced exotic species to countries for their ornamental value. Examples are *Pittosporum undulatum*, *Passiflora mollissima* (both an ornamental and a fruit crop), *Sesbania punicea*, *Acacia longifolia*, *Eichhornia crassipes* and *Rhododendron ponticum*. Many species have been introduced to areas for other qualities such as binding sand dunes (*Ammophila arenaria*, *Acacia saligna* in South Africa and Libya, *Casuarina equisetifolia*), erosion control (*Pueraria lobata*), game cover (*Rhododendron ponticum*), aquarium plants (*Crassula helmsii*, *Myriophyllum aquaticum*) and stabilizing mud-flats (*Spartina anglica*). Reforestation and agroforestry projects in developing countries often use fast-growing, alien 'weedy' trees or shrubs instead of suitable native species. These projects have often backfired because the plants have invaded the native vegetation [184]. This century has seen the rise of tourism, which is proving a considerable force for translocating ornamental plants, as well as seeds and spores unintentionally on shoes or clothing. Some countries have recognized this route for the introduction of undesirable weeds and pests and have taken measures to try and prevent it. This is discussed further in Chapter 3.

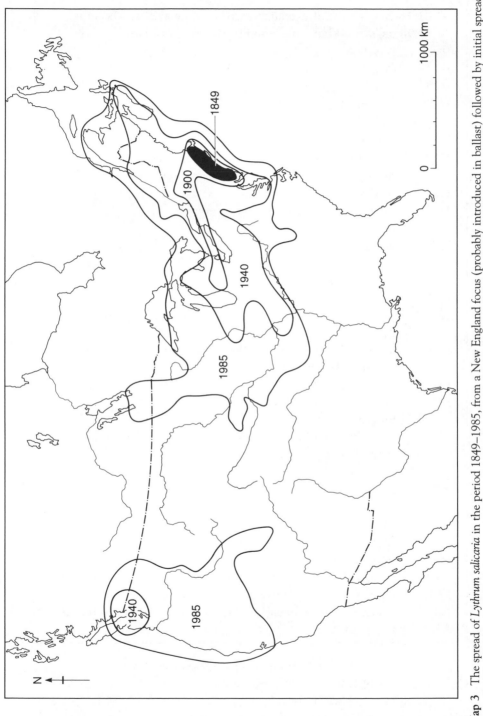

Map 3 The spread of *Lythrum salicaria* in the period 1849–1985, from a New England focus (probably introduced in ballast) followed by initial spread along the Erie Canal. A western focus was subsequently established, probably by long distance dispersal. (After Thompson (1987))

BOX 2.1 Dates of establishment of some selected botanic gardens, which have been major conduits of plant transfer

1543	Pisa, Italy
1621	Oxford, England
1652	founding of the Dutch East India Company's Garden at Cape Town by Van Riebeck to grow grain and vegetables for the new colony
1735	Pamplemousses, Ile de France (Mauritius)
1759	Royal Gardens at Kew, England becomes a botanic garden with the appointment of W. Aiton as Superintendent
1764	St Vincent, Caribbean
1770	Pierre Poivre introduces cloves, nutmeg and pepper to Pamplemousses
1774	Jamaica Botanic Garden
1787	Calcutta Botanical Garden, India established by the English East India Company
1796	Penang, Malaysia
1808	site prepared for the Real Horto, later the Jardim Botanico, Rio de Janeiro, Brazil
1816	inauguration of the Sydney Botanic Garden, Australia, on the Governor's Farm site
1817	Bogor, Java
1821	Peradeniya, Sri Lanka
1822	Singapore (closed 1846)
1841	role of the Royal Botanic Gardens, Kew expands with the appointment of Sir William Hooker as Director
1845	Royal Botanic Garden, Melbourne
1848	refounding of the Cape Town Botanic Gardens (now the Public Gardens), South Africa
1859	Missouri Botanical Garden, USA established by Henry Shaw
1859	Singapore Botanic Garden refounded
1863	Botanic Garden, Christchurch, New Zealand
1892	Botanical Garden of Buenos Aires, Argentina
1898	Entebbe Botanical Garden, Uganda
1913	South African National Botanic Garden at Kirstenbosch near Cape Town

2.3 Characteristics of invasive species

Can we predict which species will invade? Attempts have been made to describe the characteristics of the 'ideal weed' of agricultural habitats [22]. To define an 'ideal invasive plant' of diverse natural habitats is more problematic, but several authors have suggested factors and plant characteristics that appear to be associated with invasion [23, 144, 320]. However, the properties of the habitat seem to be as important in determining invasion as the properties of the invasive plant [306, 330]. Invasive plants are not confined to any particular growth form, although the most successful species in natural or seminatural habitats tend to be trees [122] and by far the majority are perennials (Chapter 5). In New Zealand, for example, over 50% of the invasives in protected natural areas are trees or shrubs over 3m high [395]. The following features seem to be important in characteristics of invasive species.

2.3.1 Seed dispersal mechanism

The 'ideal weed' [23] has adaptations for both long-distance and short-distance dispersal. The most commonly found mechanism of seed dispersal among invasive species of conservation importance appears to be by birds. Over half the woody invaders of New Zealand have bird-dispersed fleshy fruits [443] and this mechanism allows for both short- and long-distance transport of the seeds. Seed dispersal by animals appears to be the most effective method for the widest variety of species [371]. Fruit collected by birds or mammals may be eaten where it is found and the seed ejected, or it may be transported externally or in the crop or gut (for up to 100 hours [319]). Efficient dispersal of seeds by wind works best in open habitats and is thus suited to a more restricted range of habitats. Long-distance dispersal by wind is erratic and seeds need to be light, thus limiting the nutrient reserves they contain. In contrast, animal-dispersed seeds may be large, with additional nutrients to sustain the growing seedling in shade, which may be critical in determining the success of an alien species. The advantage of long- distance dispersal for an invasive species is the potential to establish new points ('foci') of invasion. Each new colony increases the size of the expanding margin of the invasion more than mere expansion of the original colony. This increases the rate of spread and makes control more difficult [284]. Examples of successful invasive species dispersed by birds are:

1. In Australia, many of the indigenous *Acacia* species are associated with ant dispersal, others with bird dispersal or both ant and bird dispersal. In South Africa, where several Australian *Acacia* species have become invasive, it is the species with bird-dispersed seeds (*Acacia cyclops*, A. *melanoxylon*, A. *saligna* [47, 48, 282]) that are the most successful. *Acacia pycnantha* is ant-dispersed and has not spread far in South Africa. The bird-dispersed species (except A. *saligna* which is also dispersed by ants and mammals [47]) have swollen, bright red funicles to attract birds. Exceptions to the association between bird dispersal and success are A. *longifolia* and A. *mearnsii* which are both highly invasive, particularly along watercourses and river valleys. Both are water-dispersed, though A. *longifolia* attracts some bird dispersal which is important in establishing new points of infestation.

2. The dispersal of the large fleshy fruits of *Passiflora mollissima* by birds and feral pigs [222] has confounded all attempts to control it. Many isolated infestations, some in inaccessible areas, have presumably been established originally by long-distance bird dispersal, while local infestation from these foci is promoted by pigs.

3. *Lantana camara* is a ubiquitous tropical weed with bird-dispersed seeds. In Australia it invades in sclerophyllous habitats which have few native bird-dispersed species. *Lantana*'s success is helped by the lack of competition for dispersal agents. In St Helena it is dispersed widely and effectively by introduced mynah birds (*Acridotheres tristis*).

4. *Pittosporum undulatum* produces sticky seeds which are transported both in the gut of birds and by adhering externally. It is successfully invading undisturbed tropical rainforest [136].

2.3.2 Breeding system

For the 'ideal weed' the most suitable breeding system for colonizing new areas is 'self-compatible, but not obligatorily self-pollinated or apomictic' [22]. Self-compatibility allows seed set at low population levels, in the absence of suitable pollinators. Obligate self-pollination, on the other hand, could lead to inbreeding and associated lack of variation and vigour in the population.

This rule does not appear to hold for invasive plants of natural habitats. Taking the plants for which information on breeding system is given in this book, 13% are dioecious and 11% monoecious (and the rest hermaphrodite). This is a similar level of dioecy to that found in the native flora of New Zealand (dioecy 12–13%), which is a flora usually considered to have a high level of dioecy, higher than those of many other places such as the British Isles (dioecy 3%) [30]. A rather high percentage of invasive plants thus appears to be dioecious or monoecious – two mechanisms which usually promote cross-pollination and therefore outbreeding. However, many of the successful dioecious invasive plants have either developed ways of overcoming the disadvantages of dioecy or have been introduced in large numbers and, as such, had no problems in setting seed initially. Several dioecious invaders have effective means of vegetative reproduction. This is particularly relevant for the aquatic species, such as *Lagarosiphon major*, *Myriophyllum aquaticum* and *Hydrilla verticillata*, which reproduce predominantly by vegetative means and are effectively dispersed by water. *Dioscorea bulbifera*, a woody climber, has also spread vegetatively from the botanic gardens in Singapore, where it was introduced, into neighboring rainforest, but its spread has been limited (only 4 km) due to lack of efficient dispersal. *Casuarina equisetifolia*, a dioecious tree and a serious invader, has been widely planted for dune stabilization [21], thus overcoming initial problems of adequate seed set.

Monoecy is associated with similar problems as dioecy. Some monoecious invasive species are self-compatible, allowing them to produce seed when they are

Figure 2.4 A small clump of water hyacinth, *Eichhornia crassipes* (originally from S. America) dispersing down the River Nile (Africa). This species is adapted to dispersing downstream as mat-fragments. (Doug Sheil)

isolated or at low population levels. An example is *Pinus radiata*, in which outbreeding is favored by the way the cones are distributed on the trees, but, in the absence of neighboring individuals of the same species, self-pollination may occur. This ensures seed set in all situations without promoting inbreeding and associated problems [25].

The majority of invasive species are, of course, hermaphrodite, but information on compatibility is unknown for many invasive species. Obligate self-fertilization is a rare condition in plants generally [325], although some opportunistic annuals show a high degree of self-fertilization. Most plants are outbreeders with some capacity for self-fertilization and this seems true of invasive plants. Species with a greater frequency of self-fertilization may be at an advantage when colonizing a new site. However, many successful hermaphrodite invasive species have strong outbreeding mechanisms. Invasive species have often been introduced intentionally in large numbers for horticultural or agricultural purposes, e.g. *Casuarina equisetifolia, Rhododendron ponticum, Ammophila arenaria, Pinus radiata* and *Passiflora mollissima*. They may not, therefore, be disadvantaged by strong outbreeding mechanisms, although it is possible that, if they start from a single location, many small foci may not be successful in establishing viable populations, possibly limiting the rate of spread.

The following examples illustrate the main patterns:

1. *Acacia* spp., invasive in South Africa, are apparently 'obligate outbreeders' [274]. Several of these species, e.g. *Acacia saligna*, have become widespread in South Africa and pose enormous control problems due to the extent of infestation. Their extensive spread has been aided by planting for dune stabilization and timber, but it is mainly due to copious seed production (despite lack of self-fertilization) and efficient dispersal by birds.

2. *Passiflora mollissima* is a self-compatible woody climber which takes advantage of both self-fertilization and cross-fertilization. This characteristic, along with its adaptation for long-distance dispersal, has allowed it to spread into isolated areas, away from the main focus of invasion, where it is invading evergreen rainforest.

3. *Eichhornia crassipes* is also self-compatible, although it mainly reproduces vegetatively. This allows isolated individuals to form new infestations rapidly from seed. *Eichhornia crassipes* shows remnants of a self-incompatibility mechanism known as 'tristyly', which has broken down [27]. Tristylous plants have flowers of one of three lengths, which must be pollinated by a plant with styles of a different length.

4. *Pennisetum clandestinum*, a grass which is causing problems in Hawaii, can reproduce sexually or asexually ('facultative apomixis'). This may help rapid spread in new areas. Partial apomixis allows for some outbreeding and keeps variation in the population. Facultative apomixis 'appears the ideal' breeding system for an invasive species [23].

5. *Ageratina adenophora* is an obligate apomict, producing seed without fertilization ('agamospermy'). It cannot produce seed by sexual means because of its irregular (triploid) number of chromosomes. Apomixis has been suggested to be characteristic of invasive species [144], but, more accurately, it is a characteristic of weediness. *Ageratina* grows best in grasslands and agricultural habitats and is not always successful at invading intact natural or seminatural habitats. However, many habitats of conservation importance are also disturbed and in Australia *Ageratina* threatens the survival of two endemic shrubs (*Acomis acoma* and *Euphrasia bella*) [119]. *Chromolaena odorata* is also an apomictic species and, like *Ageratina*, a member of the Compositae. It is an extremely serious weed in disturbed places, but is not always successful in natural habitats as it is intolerant of shade. However, it regenerates well after burning and has become the most successful invader of savannas in South Africa.

2.3.3 Seed ecology

Longevity of seed is an advantage for weeds [22] and there is some evidence that many invasive species have seeds that can remain dormant for some time, as in *Mimosa pigra*, *Acacia melanoxylon*, *Acacia longifolia*, *Passiflora mollissima*, *Ulex europaeus* and *Acacia saligna*. It is a feature which often frustrates efforts at control. Several invasives that are successful in frequently burnt habitats have serotinous seeds (i.e. with delayed dispersal). Typically, such species have seeds which are only released after fire, as in *Hakea suaveolens*, *H. sericea*, *Melaleuca quinquenervia* and *Pinus radiata*.

Many invasive species, even those that grow tall when mature, reach reproductive maturity relatively early (e.g. *Mimosa pigra*, *Clematis vitalba*, *Melaleuca quinquenervia* and *Acacia saligna*), as well as having copious seed production. Those species which are successful in invading forested habitats often display characters of both the early successional (high seed production, rapid growth) and late successional species (high competitive ability, shade-tolerance – ability to persist under the canopy of a dominant species). *Rhododendron ponticum*, *Psidium cattleianum* and *Ligustrum robustum* are good examples of shrubs combining weediness with high competitive ability.

2.4 Taxonomic patterns of invasion

2.4.1 The taxonomic distribution of weediness

The taxonomic distribution of weediness is very different from the taxonomic distribution of invasiveness. Heywood [166] used *A Geographical Atlas of World Weeds* [177], including both introduced and native weeds, to show that the families containing the most weeds are the Compositae and the Gramineae, a conclusion similar to that of Groves who predicted that most 'invasive' species (i.e. weeds) will belong to families such as the Compositae, Cruciferae or Amaranthaceae [144]. The Compositae are viewed as one of the most advanced families in evolutionary terms, containing a high number of the widespread 'weedy' species, with features ensuring both survival under adverse conditions and a high reproductive rate. This family has many herbs and shrubs with relatively few tree species. Other important families are the Leguminosae (subfamily Papilionoideae), Euphorbiaceae, Labiatae, Cruciferae, Convolvulaceae, Cyperaceae, Solanaceae, Umbelliferae, Rosaceae, Scrophulariaceae, Polygonaceae and Malvaceae. Thus, weediness seems to occur very selectively amongst the angiosperms. The ratio of weed species between monocotyledons and dicotyledons is 16% : 84% (as opposed to a global ratio of 28% : 72%). The smaller than expected number of invaders among the monocotyledons may be partly explained by the almost total absence of weeds in the Orchidaceae (only a few species, such as *Arundina graminifolia* in Hawaii, are weedy), the largest monocotyledon family with about 20 000 species. The Pinaceae and the Cupressaceae are the weedy families in the gymnosperms.

2.4.2 The taxonomic distribution of invasiveness

Invasive species follow different patterns of taxonomic distribution and are found in a wider range of families than those in which weeds of cultivation occur. Data for agricultural weeds cannot therefore be used to draw taxonomic conclusions about invasive plants. Many of the conclusions on weeds above are quite different from those of an analysis of the list of invasives in this book. The sample of 80 *World's Worst Weeds* [178] are distributed among 28 families. However, a random sample of 80 of the invasive species treated in this book are distributed among 40 families. Weeds are therefore found in a smaller number of families than invasive plants, probably reflecting a greater variety of natural as opposed to weedy, habitats. The Leguminosae appear have have the highest number of invasive species and include serious invaders such as: *Acacia* spp., *Mimosa pigra*, *Sesbania punicea* and *Leucaena leucocephala*. The nitrogen-fixing ability of leguminous species may help them to invade nutrient-poor habitats. Many of the leguminous invasive species are rapidly-growing shrubs or trees, with copious production of seeds which often have a high ability to remain dormant and which are efficiently dispersed by birds or water. The majority of the invasive legumes are in the subfamily Mimosoideae, whereas most of the weedy legumes are in the Papilionoideae. In the protected areas of New Zealand the commonest family for invasives is the Leguminosae (14%) and the only other significant families are the Compositae, Rosaceae, Pinaceae and Gramineae (8% each); 27 other families are represented [395].

Examination of the plant list in Chapter 5 reveals that, within the dicotyledons, plants with predominantly unjoined (free) petals (such as the Leguminosae) are often the worst invaders of natural or seminatural habitats. These species often have characters such as bird or mammal dispersal, high seed production and the tree habit, all of which are associated with highly invasive species [122]. In contrast, more specialized plants with joined petals (such as the Compositae) tend to be more weedy, invading highly disturbed habitats, and are often associated with characters such as wind dispersal and the herbaceous habit.

2.5 Predicting invasion

2.5.1 The ecological theory of invasion

Can the invasiveness of a plant, or the susceptibility of a habitat to invasion, be predicted from theory? Two types of hypothesis can be recognized, general theories of invasion, which have little predictive value, and hypotheses relating to specific ecological situations [194] which may give more reliable predictions of invasion in certain more specified instances. Examples of these two types of hypothesis (which may not be mutually exclusive) are given below:

1. *Absence of predators hypothesis* Invasion occurs in the absence of a species' natural pests and diseases, which are usually not introduced along with the invasive plant. *Pinus radiata*, *Myrica faya* and *Clidemia hirta* have been reported to grow and reproduce more vigorously in the absence of specialist pests and diseases [170, 276, 435]. In addition, some species are unpalatable to many generalist herbivores (e.g. *Sesbania punicea* and *Rhododendron ponticum*). Predator-free invasives may have an advantage over the native flora, but predators do not always limit the growth of a plant. In cases where a major contributor to death is crowding of plants (density dependent mortality), pests may have little effect on the plant population [175].

2. *Greater reproductive potential hypothesis* Rapid invasion is made possible by the greater reproductive potential of the invading species than those in the community being invaded. Many invasive plants produce prodigious quantities of seed, which are often retained in the soil as seed-banks. Such seed-banks may be much larger than those of native species [180, 233].

3. *Poorly adapted native species hypothesis* Invasions occur when the native species are not 'well adapted', and when invasive species are more tolerant of suboptimal levels of resources, thus having a competitive advantage. In only a few cases has this been studied experimentally in native and alien species. However, in South Africa different patterns of resource utilization between the native *Protea repens* and the invasive *Acacia saligna* seem to account, at least in part, for the invasiveness of the Australian *Acacia* [451].

4. *Chemical change hypothesis* Plant invasions occur after the chemical characteristics of a habitat have changed, for instance by fertilizer or sewage pollution (eutrophication). This is commonly used as an explanation of aquatic plant invasions, by species better able to take advantage of a superabundant nutrient supply.

5. *Balance of nature hypothesis* Elton, in his classic work on biological invasions [113], suggested that higher 'complexity' of a community leads to greater stability. The more complex a community, the more resistant it is to invasion. Complexity is defined as the total number of interactions between all organisms in the community. However, this assumes that ecosystems are in 'balance', for which there is little evidence, rather than constantly reacting to spatial and temporal environmental variation (the individualistic hypothesis) [163, 164].

6. *Empty-niche hypothesis* The presence of an 'empty niche' allows invasion, as has been argued for the invasion of *Pinus luchuensis* in the Bonin Islands [355]. Invasions of this type should be of the 'fitting in' (Einpassung) rather than 'pushing out' (Verdrängung) type. If immigration and evolution fill all a community's

31

niches, then that community is said to be 'species-saturated' and so immune to invasion. However, there is little evidence for this [449].

7. *Disturbance produced gaps hypothesis* Disturbance is commonly supposed to be important or even essential for invasion by plants, especially where disturbance results in reduced competition [169, 217, 321]. Increased disturbance, for instance due to greater fire frequency [54], may increase the invasibility of a habitat by lowering competition for suitable establishment sites and then, once an alien plant is established, by reducing competition with the native flora. However, there are some examples of alien plants invading relatively undisturbed vegetation such as *Pittosporum undulatum* in Jamaica, *Pinus radiata* in Australia and *Maesopsis eminii* in the Usambara Mountains, Tanzania. However, most invasions do seem to be dependent on the scale and type of disturbance, together with the numbers and timing of invasive propagules deposited in the community per year. Pines, for instance, tend to invade disturbed habitats at all latitudes, particularly grasslands which are often maintained by disturbance such as grazing or burning [327].

The average proportion of bare ground has even been suggested as a workable predictor of the invasibility of ecosystems [83], reflecting the frequency and intensity of soil surface disturbance. However, the amount of bare ground in a community is only one measure of disturbance. Although disturbance is usually defined as the removal of plant biomass [142], other activities, such as alteration of soil nutrient levels or water regime, are often referred to as disturbance (in a broad sense) and may be more subtle and difficult to measure. The concept of 'safe sites' [154] has been applied to invasion [194]. Invasions are said to occur at a rate determined by the intrinsic population growth rate of the invader and the availability of 'safe sites', free of specific hazards such as competition or shade – as in a forest gap. The corollary of this view is that invasions take place under conditions of zero environmental resistance (through safe sites) and the rate and occurrence of invasion can theoretically be predicted from the intrinsic properties of the organism and the habitat. This contrasts with hypotheses of invasion that emphasize the competitive or reproductive superiority of the invader.

2.5.2 Examples of characters associated with invaders in particular habitats

In considering theoretical aspects of invasion in general it is helpful to classify invasive species into the following four main 'ecological groups' with associated collections of characters ('syndromes'), with respect to the habitats they invade. Note, however, that there are many exceptions; the following are merely some of the more common types.

1. *Aquatic habitats* Syndrome: aquatic invaders are generally tolerant of a wide variety of aquatic conditions, have very effective means of vegetative reproduction, grow rapidly, have a free-floating habit, are perennial and herbaceous. They

are often dioecious, but are capable of vigorous asexual reproduction if one sex is not present. Where reproduction is sexual, seeds are efficiently dispersed by water. Examples: *Crassula helmsii*, *Eichhornia crassipes*, *Hydrilla verticillata*, *Lagarosiphon major*, *Myriophyllum aquaticum* and *Salvinia molesta*.

2. *Forest and open woodland habitats* Syndrome: the most 'important' invasive species (those having the most serious impact on natural or seminatural habitats) appear often to be shrubs or small trees, with high seed production, bird-dispersed seeds, rapid rates of growth, early reproductive maturity and which are shade-tolerant. Examples: *Acacia melanoxylon*, *Myrica faya*, *Clidemia hirta*, *Passiflora mollissima* (climber), *Pittosporum undulatum*, *Psidium cattleianum*, *P. guajava*. Exceptions include *Pinus radiata*, which invades undisturbed *Eucalyptus* woodland, and *Rhododendron ponticum*, which invades woodland and other habitats: both have wind-dispersed seeds.

3. *Open habitats* Syndrome: generally herbaceous (perennial herbs or small shrubs), have high seed production, early reproductive maturity, wind-dispersed seeds, often vegetative means of reproduction and rapid rates of growth. They are most commonly dicotyledons from those families characterized by joined petals (these are families that have many weedy members, like the Compositae) or, more rarely, monocotyledons. Examples: *Ageratina adenophorum*, *Erica lusitanica*, *Eupatorium odoratum*, *Mikania micrantha*, *Nassella trichtoma*, *Nicotiana glauca*.

4. *Fire vulnerable habitats* Syndrome: these are fire-adapted invasive species which often promote increases in the frequency of burning or its intensity by producing burnable growth, such as leaves and stems which may contain flammable oils. These are often grasses or shrubs, with vigorous vegetative reproduction (grasses) or high seed production (shrubs or small trees). The seeds usually have mechanisms to survive fire and to delay dispersal (serotiny) or germination, until stimulated by fire. The seeds are usually numerous, light and wind-dispersed. Other characteristics include vigorous resprouting after disturbance, rapid rate of growth and early reproductive maturity. Examples: *Andropogon virginicus*, *Pennisetum setaceum* (grasses), *Hakea sericea*, *Melaleuca quinquenervia*, *Pinus radiata* (shrubs/trees).

2.5.3 Practical prediction

These ecological groups and syndromes of characters are of course extremes, but they represent a series in which there is an increasing amount of disturbance in the ecosystem (disturbance being defined as removal of biomass, whether this is natural or human-induced). The combinations of characters mentioned above may be pointers to invasive potential. Indeed, in attempting to predict invasion, the attributes of the habitat and the species should be considered together. Are the ecological requirements of the species provided by the habitat? An examination of the invader in its native habitat should consider the following: the position of the species in succession, e.g. pioneer or late successional species; its environmental requirements – water or fire regime, nutrients, natural disturbance regime (e.g. frequent hurricanes, wind throw, flooding); its interactions with other animals and plants such as pests and diseases and competitive ability. Dominance or rarity in its native habitat is not necessarily a good predictor on its own, as species apparently of modest vigour have become invasive when introduced elsewhere.

It may not be possible to develop general models or theories which will successfully predict invasion for all species and in all habitats. However, studies restricted to particular species and specific habitats can achieve a high degree of success. As discussed in the section on dispersal, *Acacia* species with a high reproductive output and bird-dispersed seeds should come under immediate suspicion in suitable habitats. Pioneering work on the mountain fynbos has created a flow chart solution for assessing species risk, although it may be easier to predict species that are of low risk rather than to identify the major invasives of the future [330]. An example of ease of prediction within a single genus is provided by *Pinus*. The most invasive pines conform to a remarkably uniform syndrome of characters: early reproductive maturity, fire-adapted serotiny and small seeds with relatively large wings. Extreme caution should be exercised with any pine with this combination of characters. These empirical data on pine invasion have been used to predict risk species in the Australian genus *Banksia* which has analogous ecological behavior to *Pinus*. On this basis, several taxa, such as *B. burdettii*, *B. hookeriana* and *B. leptophylla*, appear to be high risk species if introduced to habitats at risk from invasive pines. There are complicating factors however, such as the susceptibility of *B. burdettii* and *B. hookeriana* to infection by the root-infecting pathogenic fungus *Phytophthora cinnamoni*, which may limit invasiveness [331].

Studies that consider the biological and ecological characteristics of the alien species, and the attributes of both the native habitat and the habitat to which it will be or is introduced, may in time come to achieve a high degree of predictive success. However, the huge volume of species introductions (many accidental and unrecorded) to so many places precludes the possibility of detailed studies for all aliens. Nevertheless, in environmentally sensitive areas the stakes are high enough to investigate thoroughly those species which pose potential threats.

3

Action against invasive
plants

The main categories of action to be taken concerning invasive plants are the following: education and awareness, legislation, prevention of introduction, information, and control. All are essential for effective measures against invasives.

3.1 Education and awareness

The movement of plants by people from one region to another ('plant translocation') is as old as agriculture and is a characteristic feature of human behavior. Not only have colonists carried with them plants as a means of livelihood and accidentally as weeds, but colonists commonly have a desire to 'transport landscapes', as shown by the Europeanization of the landscape of New Zealand by the mass introduction of homely plants. Furthermore, there is a tendency to believe that 'the grass is greener on the other side of the fence' and that the importation of new plants will improve the beauty or utility of a place more readily than proper or improved exploitation of the native flora. In reality, it may lead to devastating landscape change if introduced species become intractable. General awareness of the problem is essential. This involves awareness of the following: (a) the difference between native and alien (exotic) flora; (b) the importance of native plants over and above alien plants (a pride in uniqueness [360]); (c) that alien plants can, in some instances, threaten native ones; (d) that apparently harmless activities, such as gardening or forestry, can result in the naturalization of plants.

Education is essential in order to minimize accidental introductions of species. Education should foster awareness of the potential threat that alien species pose to natural ecosystems and awareness that plant introductions should be accompanied by assessment of their potential to spread and cause damage. Those who are mainly responsible for the introduction of alien plants (such as agriculturalists, horticulturalists, foresters and tourists) need to be made aware of the dangers. Ideally, environmental studies should be a required element in schools, adult education should be conducted through the mass media and tourist education should be introduced by means of visitor literature. Tourist education can also take the form of information video-films for showing on aeroplanes prior to landing [360]. The general public contribute to the spread of weeds, but they could equally well act as watchdogs against the problem if properly informed [187].

Environmental education receives little or no attention in many countries. In 1989, New Zealand, with a population of 3.3 million, had only 30 full-time specialists in environmental education assisting classroom teachers and Hawaii had an even lower ratio of three such professionals at State level for a population of 1.2 million [128]. However, curriculum requirements are changing and, in New Zealand, the environmental component taught by general teachers is increasing.

Staff members who work in nature reserves also need training and this applies to both managers and operations staff. Managers have to allocate resources, often from dwindling budgets, to competing worthy management needs; they must be fully aware of the importance of stemming plant invasions before they get out of hand. Invasive plant control is often the management task most likely to become impossible or costly if neglected, and is best done before the plants become a problem. Operations staff should be aware of the importance and purpose of what are often painstaking and tedious control exercises. They should also be aware of the potential effect of their activities on plant invasion, for instance allowing the introduction of plants by poor equipment and vehicle hygiene, and creating sites for invasion by disturbing native vegetation.

Educational booklets are important, and these should be colorful and easy to use, such as the booklet *Making Your Garden Bush-Friendly*, aimed at informing Sydney suburban gardeners about the dangers to the bush from dumping garden waste in the forest and from seeds washed into the forest by stormwater drains [270]. *The Banana Poka Caper* introduces *Passiflora mollissima* in Hawaii as 'public enemy number 1' with its 'gang' (dispersal agents) [370]. However, it should always be remembered that active involvement with projects in the field is by far the most vivid educational experience.

In several countries conservation groups organize events where laypeople volunteer to work in nature reserves removing problem plant invaders, such as *Rhododendron ponticum* in Ireland. These activities serve to raise awareness about conservation and the problem of invasive plants, as well as achieving some control of invaders in reserves, and are usually thoroughly enjoyed by the participants.

3.2 Legislation

Importation and spread of invasive plants can be prevented by either voluntary restraint or legislation, building on educational awareness. Databases or weed-lists may alert those involved to risk species, based on experience in other regions. The IUCN position statement on translocations [189] advises the adoption of legislation to curtail introductions; it proposes that deliberate introductions should be subject to a permit system. Governments should be aware of international agreements relevant to translocation. These include: the ICES Revised Code of Practice to Reduce the Risks from Introduction of Marine Species (1982); ASEAN Agreement on the Conservation of Nature and Natural Resources; and the Protocol for Protected Areas and Wild Fauna and Flora in Eastern African Region. Special care should be taken to prevent invasive species spreading across international boundaries: the Stockholm Declaration on the Human Environment (Principle 210) enjoins states to 'ensure that activities within their jurisdiction or control do not cause damage to the environment of other states'. Similarly, Article 196.1 of the convention on the Law of the Sea requires states to 'take all measures necessary to prevent, reduce or control . . . the intentional or accidental introduction of species, alien or new, to a particular part of the marine environment which may cause significant and harmful changes thereto'. There are binding obligations (section 11.2.b) in the Council of Europe's Berne Convention on the Conservation of European Wildlife and Natural Habitats calling for action to 'strictly control the introduction of non-native species' [294].

Laws at the level of individual countries are required too. Most import control legislation, such as the Australian Federal Quarantine Act of 1908, controls weed entry by restricting the importation of certain weeds. However, an alternative approach is to prohibit all non-native plants unless the importer can show that the plant will not become weedy: 'guilty until proven innocent'. Unfortunately, plants are more likely to be placed on the schedules after they have become serious problems, not before. Most plant quarantine legislation is anyway aimed at agricultural pests and is rarely implemented seriously in the case of 'environmental weeds' (invasive plants). In the United States the importation of plants is controlled under the Plant Quarantine Act of 1912 and importations need United States Department of Agriculture (USDA) approval, although again this is mainly aimed at agricultural pests.

In cases where invaders are distributed by the horticultural trade, such as *Lythrum salicaria* in North America [392], these laws could be effective at shutting down movement of invasive wild-type horticultural stock. Enforcement should be visible, both for the deterrent effect and to increase public awareness of the problem. Airlines should distribute, and require passengers to fill out, the necessary declaration forms that are required by most countries for living plant material. In Hawaii for instance the import of plants from other states of the US is controlled under the Hawaii Revised Statutes (HRS) and regulated under Department of Agriculture Administrative Rules (DOAAR). If plants are introduced and do become invasive, an 'introducer pays principle' has been suggested [360], whereby the introducer is liable for the costs of clearance operations. Although these measures are excessive for countries with little or no invasive plant problem, in highly invaded subtropical countries (for instance) they may be not only acceptable (especially in conjunction with public education programs) but also essential.

Transport of seed is regulated usually by separate legislation, such as the United States Federal Seed Act of (1939) 1980. However, the ease of seed transport by mail and the difficulty of extensive inspection of mail make this legislation rather ineffective.

Laws requiring the clearance of invasives may be enshrined in protected areas legislation. In New Zealand the National Parks Act 1980 requires that 'native plants and animals of the parks shall as far as possible be preserved and the introduced plants and animals shall as far as possible be exterminated' – an onerous task given that there are so many introduced species [445]. This act is now seldom used to exterminate species and some species, such as Russell lupins (*Lupinus* hybrids), are tolerated in the parks because of their tourist value. Many countries have legislation allowing certain plants to be given 'noxious weed status'. This empowers the state, often in the form of a local weed board, to force landowners to control weeds on their land. Although this can be useful, it can also be a mixed blessing for reserve managers faced with bills for spraying plants which may not even be those prioritized by the manager for control in the reserve. Noxious weed status is usually conferred on plants which already exist as large infestations, calling its utility into question. In the USA only weeds in their invasive phase are treated as noxious and, once completely established, they are no longer listed, which again limits the usefulness of this legal device to conservationists. However, declaring a plant a noxious weed does draw it to the attention of the public [187].

3.3 Preventing introduction and spread

Introduction may be defined as 'the intentional or accidental dispersal by human agency of a living organism outside its historically known native range' [189]. The overwhelming majority of invasive plants have been introduced deliberately and the largest number of these can be traced to gardeners. Some 42% of South African aliens were originally introduced as ornamentals [184] and some 50% of the naturalized plants of Victoria, Australia are readily available in nurseries. In Hawaii, botanic gardens and private gardeners have both contributed, as have agricultural stations [360]. Agriculture and forestry follow as the next most significant sources. Usually little thought is given to the impact these alien species may have on native animals and plants or their ecosystems. Very large numbers of plants have been translocated in this way, but most introduced species do not naturalize and most of those that do naturalize do not become important invasives. However, if plants are translocated in sufficiently large numbers, serious invasives are likely to arise sooner or later.

Foresters continue to introduce rapid-growing woody legumes into many developing countries for reforestation and 30 of these species are known to have become major pests [184]. The following agencies have programs for the systematic exploration, documentation and collection of tropical tree genetic resources for distribution: ACIAR/CSIRO in Australia, CAMCORE/North Carolina State University (USA), the Oxford Forestry Institute and International Plant Genetic Resources Institute (IPGRI) (Italy). These programs are in response to very serious problems of environmental degradation, poverty and fuelwood shortage. However, native alternatives are not usually properly investigated and unwise introductions have been made. A rational approach to introductions is needed [184,189] and the national administration concerned should take the lead. Firstly, governments should formulate national policies on translocation, prevention and control of invasives, based on adequate scientific consultation. Regional development plans that may increase landscape invasibility should take invasives into account. Secondly, pre-existing governmental structures for agriculture and conservation should be used to control introductions, collect information on introductions and conduct scientific research. Government sponsored landscaping (for instance in Hawaii [361]) should use species known not to naturalize. Here it is best to err on the side of caution as the situation can change with the introduction of new seed dispersers or pollinators. *Citharexylum spinosum* has been used extensively as an innocuous landscaping tree in Hawaii, but since the escape of the red-whiskered bulbul (*Pycnonotus jocosus*) on Oahu it has spread and is rapidly becoming a problem.

3.3.1 Planned beneficial introduction

For planned beneficial introductions, the following procedures could be adopted to ensure safe introductions.

1. *Assessment phase* In this phase, basic biology and potential invasive hazard should be examined. The simplest indicator of invasive potential is a thorough review of the literature to see if the species has become invasive elsewhere, while bearing in mind that many invasions have not been adequately reported. The assessment should be carried out in the light of the ecology of the relevant natural habitats, the likelihood of the plant hybridizing with native species to produce new aggressive species or biotypes [1] and prospects for eventual control. Characters, such as breeding system, dispersal mechanism, growth rate, seed production and life cycle, may indicate invasive potential. Habitat information may also be assessed. At the very least this should include assessment of climate and frequency of fire in both the native habitat of the plant and the proposed area of introduction.

2. *Experimental trial* If initially carried out on a small scale this permits complete eradication if there is cause for concern. It is important to ensure that the same genotype is tested as the one eventually introduced.

3. *Extensive introduction* This should be carried out preferably only in areas with little conservation or economic value, for example areas highly disturbed by human activity and away from natural vegetation. Suitable sites might be those resulting from reclamation work in areas denuded of native vegetation by mismanagement, overpopulation, pollution or erosion. Any such introductions should be monitored carefully.

4. *Recording of information* This needs to be in a readily available form, such as a database of invasive plants or potential problems. Records of the introduction and any trials should be kept and made public.

5. *Agreement of liability* It should be clearly agreed at the outset if organizations introducing plants are required to bear the cost of control, should control become necessary.

3.3.2 Accidental introductions

Accidental introductions are much more difficult to foresee and control. However, particular care should be taken with islands and other isolated habitats, for instance by insisting that visitors observe strict hygiene – removing seeds or fruits from shoes, clothing and tents (mud on shoes and trouser turn-ups are traditional routes for plant introduction). The contamination of agricultural seed and other materials should also be controlled. Military bases on islands present particular difficulties, as the large amount of freight transported is uncheckable due to military secrecy [360]. The effect of major engineering projects transporting vast quantities of material and creating disturbed sites potentially suitable for invasion should also be considered [4]. At sensitive sites vigilant surveillance should be maintained as much as possible. In 1984 a scientist visiting Gough Island was able to pull out the South African weed *Senecio burchellii* which had become established around the magnetometer hut, probably introduced with construction materials [420].

The prevention of introductions must be built on existing educational awareness and legislation. These have been discussed above, but explanatory leaflets, in-flight videos shown on passenger aircraft, increasing public awareness of legislation (often people don't know that the relevant laws exist) are obvious suggestions. Introductions can come from unlikely sources: in 1983 some 800 athletes agreed to have the soles of their running shoes scrubbed by volunteers before a marathon run through the Volcanoes National Park in Hawaii. From the washings, 16 species of plants germinated, including one serious invader – *Melinis minutiflora* (although this plant was present in parts of the Park already) [167]. It is not just important to lobby the public, but politicians may be lobbied for vigilant enforcement of legislation. Likewise horticultural firms, garden societies, forestry organizations, developers and tourist operators may be more influential than individual members of the public, and thus may be more suitable targets for lobbying.

Most ecosystems would probably be less invasible if they were not subject to some form of disturbance by people, and habitats should be managed to minimize disturbance and optimize resistance to invasion. Where invasive species are dependent on alien animals for seed dispersal (e.g. *Passiflora mollissima*, dispersed by feral pigs in Hawaii) as much care should be taken concerning the introduction of the animal as with the plant. Containment of an invasion is an important prevention measure. For instance, *Mimosa pigra* has the potential to spread very widely in northern Australia outside its present invasive range. Even though it is expensive, the patrolling of Arnhem Land by the Northern Lands Council to identify incipient invasions has been recognized as a priority. Similarly, careful hygiene should be observed where an invasive has the potential to spread. In the Kakadu National Park vehicles are inspected for propagules of *Salvinia*, an ecologically damaging invader [187].

3.4 Information and recording

The species accounts which follow in Chapter 4 give some indication of the research and information needs of a program to prevent or control invasion. Useful information for the prevention and control of plant invasion is categorized below.

3.4.1 Information about invasive species

Databases and weed lists published in various countries give information on which species are likely to become invasive (see also Chapter 5 and Appendix 2). Knowledge of risk species and patterns of invasion is the basis on which rational policies of import control and reserve surveillance can be built. A single database, global in scope, maintained by international collaboration would be ideal, although expensive, but no such database exists. A more practical solution would be a network of local databases capable of exchanging information in a coordinated way.

3.4.2 Taxonomy and biogeography

Correct identification of the species is essential, but further taxonomic study may be needed (e.g. if the species is thought to be a hybrid). The importance of taxonomic work is evident from the case of the *Lantana camara* complex, in which there are numerous biotypes differing in invasiveness, and from the examples of *Salvinia molesta* and the *Euphorbia esula/waldsteinii* (*virgata*) complex, in which biological control proved difficult or impossible in the absence of detailed taxonomic studies [157, 196]. Taxonomic studies will often reveal biotypes that are non-invasive or even sterile, which may be safely used in the horticultural trade.

3.4.3 Pattern and rate of spread

Accurate recording of alien species is necessary, particularly their patterns of spread, from the original sites of introduction into seminatural or natural vegetation. Many species are introduced accidentally, and prediction of potential to invade is often not possible or very precise. For these reasons, accurate recording of alien species and their rates of spread when they first appear are important pieces of information for attempts to evaluate population dynamics and invasive potential. Valuable information about invasive behavior can be gained from historical studies, for instance using old herbarium specimens and other evidence. The

41

number of plant species invading native bushland in Australia has been estimated at 'thousands' [187] and in this case a uniform geographical database has been suggested for analysis and planning. Information for such a geographical database can come from printed records, herbarium specimens, aerial photos, questionnaires, remote sensing and field survey.

3.4.4 Impact assessment

When an alien species is spreading, its likely impact should be assessed. Information should be collected to evaluate its likely further spread and likely effects on native organisms and ecosystem processes. This impact assessment is important in deciding which species should be given priority for control, as ecosystem effects have important consequences for conservation and control [51, 141, 429]. Impact assessment is also an important stage in the cost/benefit analysis involved in planning control measures, particularly biological control.

3.4.5 Ecological information on plant invaders: growth, reproduction and survival in relation to the environment

Biological and ecological characteristics such as the following, in both native and introduced habitats, should be noted to aid the prediction of spread and control:

1. Seed dispersal mechanism – adaptations for both short- and long-distance dispersal.
2. Seed ecology – high or low seed production; continuous or seasonal; longevity of seeds; dormancy mechanisms.
3. Breeding system – adaptations for self-fertilization and cross-fertilization; ability to reproduce vegetatively.
4. Rate of growth under favorable conditions.
5. Ability to resprout after cutting.
6. Requirements for germination and establishment.
7. Environmental factors – tolerance of frost, fire and shade; nutrient and water requirements, etc.
8. Susceptibility to pests and disease – generalist or specialist pests.
9. Comparative ecology of the invasive species with that of those species, native or alien, which are most likely to replace it after control measures have been taken [429]. There is no point in eradicating an invader to have it replaced by a worse one.

It is important to establish the native range of an alien, along with the biological and environmental characteristics of its natural habitat. This information invariably gives useful insights into the biology and ecology of the plant, and thus into its invasive potential.

3.4.6 Information on control: the effects of herbicides and potential for biological control

The information detailed above will help managers of nature reserves evaluate the threat posed by an invasive species and to draw up a suitable control program, if it is necessary. However, whatever control method is chosen further information is required in implementing it. If it is decided that chemical control is a necessary option, special care is needed. Plant responses to chemicals differ widely, and it may be necessary to conduct trials of different chemicals at different application rates to different parts of the plant, and at different times of year, to optimize effectiveness and minimize cost. With physical control too, the plant and ecosystem responses vary according to method of cutting and time of the year. This sort of information is helpful to maximize cost-effectiveness. Biological control requires detailed taxonomic and ecological information about the plant and biological control species, both in the native and invaded range, together with information about all other species in the ecosystem that may be affected. Nevertheless, biological control may offer the best possibility for many species in terms of minimizing the impact on the native flora and fauna.

3.5 Planning a control program

As a last resort, where prevention has failed, there are four main options for control (although they are often used in combination). These are: **physical, chemical, biological,** and **environment management** control. Control measures should have careful **planning** – strategic and tactical decisions must be made at the outset when the **coordination of control methods (integrated pest management (IPM))** must be considered. This section considers the issues involved in planning. As Coblentz [73] has suggested: 'Programs to eradicate exotic organisms provide an opportunity to combine good science and good conservation into functioning conservation biology'.

3.5.1 Prioritizing species

The choice of species for control priority should take into account that prevention is the best method of control and that early intervention is desirable. Control should therefore be aimed at newcomer invaders as well as established ones. Here, delays can be critical as most successful invaders reproduce readily – Salvinia (an extreme case) can double its population in 10 days. Unfortunately, funding is much easier to obtain if an invasion is already very serious. On the other hand, ecological research and research on biological control have high capital outlay and work on widespread invaders can maximize the return from research input. For instance, research on the biological control of Salvinia has been applied all over the tropics, with transfer of technology between regions at comparatively low cost. Although widespread invaders are often very difficult to eradicate, such methods can reduce their impact.

Box 3.1 Control and conservation

Almost any program of control of invasive plants raises conservation questions which are impossible to resolve fully. If the use of pesticides is contemplated, then attention should be given to the possible effects on non-targeted organisms both at the site of application and more distantly. If biological control is envisaged, then consideration must be given to possible adverse effects on the native fauna and flora of organisms introduced as control agents.

Most human action has some environmentally damaging consequences. In the case of invasive species it is up to managers and their scientific advisers to evaluate which control measures, if any, are most appropriate in particular cases. There is also a need to be acquainted with relevant laws and regulations and to take all recommended safety precautions. The intention of this manual is not to make decisions for managers; but to provide information which will assist them in this task.

Decisions on whether and how to control invasive species can bring into sharp focus the difficulties of making wise environmental decisions. WWF insists that invasive plants sometimes represent serious threats to the conservation of biodiversity, and that their control is often highly desirable and in some cases urgent. On the other hand, it is also WWF policy to advocate reduction in herbicide use. As an ideal, WWF advocates integrated pest control measures (in which a systems model is used to to optimize control by different measures, while seeking to minimize ecosystem disturbance). However, WWF is also fully aware that this ideal has hardly been applied in practice to the control of invasive plants, and may be considered very theoretical by a manager faced with controlling a serious invasion on a minimal budget.

WWF advocates the precautionary principle in attempts to engineer the environment. Ecosystems are full of non-linear relationships and feedback loops, making it impossible to predict fully the consequences of human activities. It thus makes sense to take a careful step-wise experimentally-based (or adaptive management) approach in tackling plant invasions, reviewing progress and assessing side-effects on a continuing basis.

Further information on some known adverse environmental effects of some major pesticides is given in Appendix 1.

The most important criterion must be conservation impact and, where invaders are threatening other species with extinction, their eradication should always take precedence. Invasions in areas which are poorly known scientifically should also take precedence because there is a possibility that undescribed species may be threatened. Control should, however, be seen as the 'art of the possible' and no control measures, except perhaps containment, should be taken against species whose control is inherently impossible. Species with a realistic control potential should therefore be prioritized, particularly where there is a possibility of total eradication. Similarly, control measures should start with those species whose biology is well known so that the causal mechanisms of the invasion can be addressed, not just the symptoms. When the ecology and biology of a species are well known, there is a better chance of preventing re-infestation based on informed habitat management.

Careful consideration of the invaders on a case by case basis is often revealing, as has been done for the Kruger National Park in South Africa [247]. This reserve of some 19 400 km^2 of tropical and subtropical savanna is relatively little affected by invasive plants. The native flora is well adapted to regular fires and heavy grazing by large hoofed mammals, which keeps many alien plants at bay. However, it has 113 invasive plants [249], of which seven have serious ecological impacts. A long-term strategy of control has succeeded in eliminating 10 non-native plants from the park and control is feasible for another 14. The other plants are either 'out-of-control' (and thus control is too expensive to contemplate), not serious enough in their ecological impacts to merit control or regularly renewed from outside the park (so control would be pointless).

3.5.2 Prioritizing areas

In some situations a geographically planned approach will be more suitable than a species based one, especially where a variety of invaders are threatening localized reserves. In Hawaii, success has been achieved by concentrating control on small areas with high conservation value – special ecological areas (SEAs) [400]. In all planning a clear statement of what the control is intended to achieve is important; usually this is the protection of the most pristine and biologically important reserve areas. More generally, the aim of control should be to further wider conservation aims, usually those of the government or regional organization concerned or that of the World Conservation Strategy 'to conserve species diversity, genetic diversity and the ecological processes that sustain them' [187]. In the early stages of invasion a containment strategy may be adopted: early detection of the invasion followed by complete local eradication is used to contain spread, perhaps leaving the core-area of the invasion for later attention. Continuous monitoring is required, especially of non-reserve areas around key reserves. If an invasion is contained, it is not only very much easier to deal with but total eradication remains a possibility. Some nature reserves are intrinsically more invasible than others and this should be considered not only in reserve design, but also in planning control strategies. Reserves that are less likely to be re-invaded should be given priority. In a survey of 95 New Zealand reserves, the most invasible were found to be small, narrow (high boundary to area ratio) disturbed remnants with fertile soil close to towns, with road or railway lines nearby [394]. Similarly, ecosystems which have been severely damaged by invasive plants, such that rehabilitation with native plants is unlikely, should not command high priority.

3.5.3 Choosing control methods

Indiscriminate herbicidal or mechanical clearance is counter-productive in nature reserves, because this is likely to have adverse effects on the ecosystem as a whole and may endanger diversity and rare species. Instead, a control program of 'spot' herbicide use (minimum herbicide use, carefully targeted), careful physical removal or biological control must be tailored to the particular demands of the ecosystem. Systems of invasive plant control have occasionally been devised for particular vegetation types, such as the 'Bradley method' for Australian bushland near Mosman [50]. However, sometimes even the total destruction of all vegetation in a small area can be justified if this is the only means to save the reserve in the long term, as has been the case with *Pereskia aculeata* in coastal for   est reserves of Natal, South Africa.

What is apparently the cheapest control in the short term is not always cost-effective in the long term. In agricultural systems, cost-benefit models, together with knowledge of patterns of weed spread, have been used to optimize cost-effectiveness [18, 19, 412]. In the case of *Nasella* in the Australian Tablelands, the control measure cheapest for the government (containment herbicide spraying of light infestations) does not give the greatest public economic benefit in the long term, mainly due to lost revenues ('opportunity costs') from highly degraded pastures. The expensive option of wholesale *Nasella* eradication and pasture rehabilitation makes economic sense in the long term [16, 20]. These analyses are difficult to apply to nature conservation because of the difficulty of quantifying the 'opportunity costs', not only of possible lost revenues from tourism and recreation caused by invasive plants, but also the intrinsic aesthetic, scientific and cultural 'costs' of landscape degradation by invasion. These may, however, be roughly quantified as the costs the state or the public are prepared to bear out of pride and concern for natural ecosystems (a function of environmental education).

Similarly, biological control may appear to be an unattractive option because of the very high outlay costs, typically requiring government support. The development costs of chemical control are typically less and borne entirely by the chemical industry and passed on to users. On the face of it, chemical methods of control may appear to be financially attractive, but may involve ongoing and repeated costs, so that in the long run biological control may thus be more cost-effective [396]. However, there is usually a problem in raising the required initial investment.

3.5.4 Setting up a voluntary action group

Informal groups ('hack groups') to work on their own or alongside reserve management teams have been formed very successfully in Australia and South Africa [299, 377]. Such groups are well advised to establish clear aims before starting, based on a careful assessment of the site. An action plan with a tightly defined, manageable objective is a good spur. Liaison with local authorities and local conservation organizations will prevent duplication of work. Provision of tools and instruction in plant identification must precede action and any special skills of group members should be used to the full. Safety and first-aid equipment should also be provided and appropriate safety procedures established. Written and photographic records of work done are valuable. Not only can 'before and after' comparisons be made, but good records can provide useful research data and help in the planning of further work. This information might include lists of invasive plants and natives, perhaps backed by a collection of pressed plants for reference. Identification problems should be solvable with the help of an herbarium or museum if adequate field-guides are not available.

3.5.5 Coordinating control measures

Integration of the various control and prevention measures is possible on two levels. Firstly, the different control, regulatory, research and conservation management bodies, both statutory and voluntary, should work in harmony. Secondly the control and management techniques used against invasives should operate in concert. Different control techniques used together can often strikingly reinforce each other. In one example, biological control of *Chondrilla juncea* by rust fungus gave 55% control and control by improved pasture competition gave 35%. However, the two used together gave 95% control [146]. Many approaches may be needed. Research to identify critical points in the life cycle will be ineffective unless this is translated into management action. Effective communication is important. Recently, attention has focused on the concept of 'Integrated Pest Management' (IPM) as a formalized, concerted, many-sided control strategy [44, 348]. A systems model is used to optimize control by natural processes, application of herbicides, biological control and other measures, while seeking to minimize ecosystem disturbance. Where adequate research data exist to support it, this approach holds out great promise.

3.6 Physical control

This form of control includes hand-pulling (for annual herbs and tree seedlings), cutting and slashing (for lianes, tree saplings and trees), digging/levering (with mattock or crowbar, for plants regenerating from underground parts, or tree seedlings/saplings which will regenerate from cut shoots) or mowing/discing (for herbaceous plants) [270, 299]. It may be very effective for controlling some species,

Figure 3.1 Physical control by hand-weeding, Mondrain, Mauritius. In this species-rich ecosystem chemical control cannot be used, so careful removal must be carried out by hand. The invasive privet, *Ligustrum robustum*, is a serious problem on the island, preventing regeneration of native species. It has now been removed from this plot, which is fenced to keep out introduced pigs and deer. (Photo: Alan Hamilton)

Figure 3.2 The boundary between a weeded and an unweeded plot at Mondrain, Mauritius. In the unweeded plot the mortality of native tree seedlings is much higher. No biological control system has been devised for *Ligustrum robustum*. (Photo: Quentin Cronk)

for example pine trees, which do not resprout or regenerate from underground shoots. However, many species do resprout after cutting and are only killed if chemicals are applied to the cut surface. Physical control of shrubs or trees is very labor intensive, especially if they cover a large area. Other forms of physical control, such as burning, which grades into environment management control (below), may be effective but can only be used where such techniques do not damage the native flora or fauna. Some aquatic weeds may be removed by hand or using large mechanical harvesters and the organic matter used as compost for neighboring agricultural land. This method is reasonably effective and produces a useful by-product for local farmers. However, aquatic weeds are never eradicated completely, and physical disturbance and removal may in fact encourage their spread. Thus, while for some species physical control is adequate and effective it does not work for many others, including most of the more serious invasive species, in which physical control is frustrated by features such as resprouting after cutting, a long-lived seed-bank, regeneration from fragments and copiously produced, efficiently dispersed seeds which re-infest from neighbouring areas. However, the tedious and painstaking work involved is often worthwhile in isolated ecosystems, such as small islets, where complete eradication is possible. Here extreme caution must be taken to prevent accidental re-infestation, or introduction of new species by the weeding parties. A supply of tents and bedding should preferably be left on the islet, to reduce the need for rigorous cleaning on each visit.

3.6.1 The situation in Mauritius

One of the most interesting and important studies of physical control comes from Strahm's work on the WWF project on rare plants in Mauritius [381]. This island is so badly invaded that only a very small part of the natural vegetation can realistically be preserved. Lowland vegetation has entirely disappeared except on two off-shore islands on which physical clearance projects have been initiated. These islands are Round Island (where rabbits were finally completely eradicated in 1986) and Ile aux Aigrettes. Much more upland vegetation remains, but almost all is badly invaded. As a holding measure the Mauritius Forestry Service, in association with WWF, is weeding eight small plots, covering a total area of 3 ha. As these are of great scientific importance, often as the last examples of particular vegetation types, and are rich in endemic species growing amongst the aliens, special care has to be taken with the weeding, which is consequently slow and painstaking work. In 1990 the Forestry Service in Mauritius spent 1969 work-days weeding the 3 ha of plots at a cost of Rs 275 730. Initially, at two sites (Macabé and Brise Fer) some plants of the main invasive species, *Psidium cattleianum*, were left to provide partial shade. Without this, the weedy herb *Laurentia* invades, but now the last *Psidium* plants have been weeded out. Hasty eradication of invasives can have deleterious ecosystem effects, the lesson being that, with severe infestation, clearance should proceed with caution [436].

There is evidence that repeated weeding of plots on Mauritius eventually results in a reduction in the effort needed to maintain invasive-free plots. In the case of the 5 ha reserve of Mondrain [380], the first year of intensive weeding (1989) required 594 work-days (although some weeding had been carried out previously), while in 1990 only 460 work-days were needed, representing a considerable decrease [381]. This suggests that given regular weeding the 'maintenance load' will eventually diminish, even in the most intractably invaded areas. However, the main invasive species at Mondrain, *Ligustrum robustum* var. *walkeri*, is very widespread and abundant on Mauritius and is bird-dispersed, so re-infestation will constantly occur and there are no prospects of total eradication.

The effect on regeneration of indigenous trees after weeding has been studied in a 1.3 ha plot at Brise Fer. The response is quite dramatic. In comparison with an adjacent control (unweeded) plot, over a four-year period there was more seedling recruitment (4×), better seedling survival (3×) and higher seedling growth rates (6×) [381].

On the off-shore islands of Mauritius, the invasive plant covering the largest area on Ile aux Aigrettes is *Flacourtia indica*, which became established after widespread military disturbance on the island during the Second World War. Unfortunately the fairly large stumps left after cutting resprout well, so that they have to be treated with 10% Tordon, which usually prevents regeneration. On Round Island the problem is quite different. The introduced rabbit had previously kept both the native and the introduced vegetation under severe check. However, after total eradication of rabbits by repeated capture methods in 1986 (with the purpose of allowing regeneration of the native vegetation), the introduced small weedy shrubs *Desmanthus virgatus* and *Desmodium incanum* expanded, requiring hand pulling. Fortunately, these species were only present as localized populations which can be eradicated, with the eventual aim of total elimination from the island. In this instance the ideal weeding party consists of six volunteer weeders, with the turnover kept down to two novice weeders per trip. There are a number of reasons why experienced weeders are at a premium: there is less chance of them pulling out important plants, and items of natural history interest will be 'old hat', so they will spend less time on what have been dubbed 'snake breaks' [381].

3.7 Chemical control

There are several problems with the use of chemicals in areas of conservation importance. Herbicides may reduce the numbers of an invasive species, but, unless repeatedly applied, they will not limit its spread or prevent re-invasion. Many herbicides are unspecific and may damage the non-target flora and fauna. Many are also very persistent and may accumulate in soil or leaf tissue. Herbicides are expensive and an unwelcome large recurrent cost in the budgets of reserve managers (although physical control may be more expensive). When infestations are large, the herbicides have to be mixed and transported in bulk, which is not easy in difficult terrain. If the species are fairly tolerant of herbicides, as are many woody invaders, and regenerate fast, the herbicides will have to be applied almost continually. However, herbicides are often the only option available to managers and are a front-line defence.

3.7.1 Methods of application

There are many different methods of application [270, 290]. Adequate protective gear should be worn when working with all herbicides. **Careful compliance with the latest directions on safety and use is essential.** Appendix 2 gives notes on some herbicides commonly referred to in the literature about invasive plants.

1. Woody species

Frilling (notching or 'hack and squirt'). In this method the base of the stem is notched with an axe or a machete at about 10 cm intervals all round, into a frill of bark slivers, behind which the herbicide (usually 2,4-D or glyphosate) is applied to the moist sapwood. Care must be taken not to bark the tree completely, as this will prevent transport of herbicide within the plant. The herbicide may be applied with a brush or squirted from a plastic bottle. Each stem of a multistemmed plant must be treated, as translocation is not very efficient between major portions of the tree.

Stem injection. A drill ('brace and bit') is generally used to penetrate below the bark (although not into the heartwood). An injection gun is then used to deliver a 2 ml herbicide dose into each hole. This herbicide is then taken up by the sapwood and translocated around the tree. Again, if the plants are multistemmed, each stem must be injected.

Side branch reservoir application. Herbicide is applied from reservoirs on lateral shoots. This is a technique that has been developed for the control of *Myrica faya* in the Volcanoes National Park in Hawaii [124]. A lower side branch is cut near the main stem and a length of surgical tubing is stretched over the cut end to form a small reservoir into which 1–3 ml of undiluted 'roundup' (glyphosate) is inserted; this is absorbed in 30–40 minutes. The technique is often easier than stem-injection and translocation around the plant may be more efficient. It is a potentially useful method when stem injection or frilling is time-consuming or costly because plants have multiple stems, or the main stems are too small to drill or made inaccessible by lateral branches.

Basal bark application. Herbicide may be painted or sprayed onto the bark at the base of trees. An oil-based formulation is used (often of 2,4-D), using a light oil (e.g. diesel) capable of penetrating the waterproof bark of the tree and being translocated (mainly upwards). The bark should be treated all round and as close to the soil as possible [290].

Cut stump application. If cut stumps are likely to sprout, they should be treated (usually with undiluted glyphosate or a 2,4-D formulation) within 30 seconds of being cut, when translocation from the damaged sapwood is still occurring.

2. *Vines*

Painting of stem bunches. Treatment of vines is often difficult as (with the exception of some large woody vines (lianes)) there may be no obvious main stem. Bunches of stems may be gathered up, cut and the cut ends painted with herbicide.

Stem scraping. Vines with aerial tubers need special care since, when the plants are cut, the tubers may fall from the dead stems and regenerate massively on the forest floor below. In such cases the plants should be left intact, with herbicide applied to a scrape on the side of the vine stem, allowing translocation from the exposed sapwood throughout the plant.

3. *Herbaceous species*

Foliar spray. This is the only economically feasible method for large scale application. It can be used at any scale from knapsack sprayers to aircraft. Application techniques can affect efficacy of application greatly, and modern electrostatic spraying techniques can reduce the volumes of herbicide needed and go some way to preventing inaccurate delivery of herbicides and drift [168]. Foliar herbicides should be sprayed on still, cool, dry days during the growing season. However, woody species are almost never killed by a single application (rapid defoliation is not necessarily an indication of kill). It is very important that the optimum timing, dose and choice of herbicide are determined before use. An alternative to foliar spraying is the use of a 'weed wand', which allows more accurate application to small plants by touching them with a wick.

Soil application. This is usually in the form of picloram granules scattered around the plant. Application by broadcasting the pellets is easy and avoids the need to transport bulky oil- or water-based preparations. Many plants are highly susceptible, even when other herbicides have proved ineffective. However, the persistence and mobility of picloram in the soil are serious problems and this method should not be used in watershed areas. It is not normally used in conservation work.

3.7.2 Choice of treatment

Plants vary greatly in their susceptibility to different herbicides, methods of application, formulations (carriers or surfactants), concentrations and times of application. Often very extensive trials are needed to work out the optimum treatment. This information is usually readily available for agricultural weeds but not for plants invasive of natural ecosystems. However, some work has been carried out. In Hawaii a trial of different herbicides on a range of introduced plants suggested (for instance) that the optimum control methods for *Hedychium gardnerianum*, *Rubus argutus* and *Tibouchina urvilleana* differed widely. The chosen methods were: broadcast picloram pellets (Tordon 10K), although problems with persistence were evident (*Hedychium*), 2% foliar spray of roundup in water (*Rubus*) and 20% Garlon 4 in diesel oil on cut stumps (*Tibouchina*) [344].

Different countries have their own regulations for the use of herbicides. In particular it is difficult to find herbicides that are safe to spray near water [304, 305]. Early control of *Lythrum salicaria* in the USA used Dicamba with modest success, but in 1982 a new formulation of glyphosate (Rodeo-EPA) with a new surfactant Ortho X-77 was approved for spraying over water, which aided control significantly. However, spray efficacy in this case is much greater if the herbicide is sprayed in the late flowering season (August). Not only is the kill rate better, but there is less re-infestation with *Lythrum* seedlings [392]. Glyphosate is a particularly useful herbicide, as it is inactivated almost at once in soil and is not thought to have any residual effects in terrestrial ecosystems [368].

The Kruger National Park in South Africa is an example of a natural area where herbicides have been used extensively [247]. In fact the chemical control measures are said to take up a large part of the reserve budget (58 000 Rand in 1983 for the control of *Lantana* and *Salvinia*). Very extensive whole plant spraying of *Lantana* and *Opuntia* has been carried out, initially using 2,4,5-T (which was discontinued after concern about dioxin contamination emerged), now with glyphosate. On the whole this program has been successful and *Opuntia* has been effectively eradicated from the park. However, some concern has been expressed about effects on non-target species. Likewise *Salvinia* appears to have been eradicated by aerial spraying of clarason, but re-infestation by this water-borne plant is almost certain to occur eventually. Control has been least successful where circumstances promote regular re-infestation. *Eichhornia* is not controlled as it is abundant and uncontrolled in headwaters outside the park; *Melia*, which responds to ringbarking, spreads along the Crocodile River and complete control is impossible as it is not controlled on the south bank. In the case of *Xanthium*, the infestation is so massive that no attempts at control could possibly be realistic, although some cosmetic control is possible by mowing road verges. These examples highlight the weaknesses of chemical control and the need for integrated approaches.

3.8 Biological control (biocontrol)

This method uses natural enemies to regulate the numbers of invasive plants. When successful, the utilization of natural enemies is an inexpensive, non-hazardous means of reducing pest populations and maintaining them, often permanently, well below economic or conservation injury levels. The critical aspect of biological control of plants is the selection of organisms that are highly host-specific and will not themselves become pests on other plant species. Fortunately many invertebrates are highly host specific, but to ensure that host switching will not occur requires lengthy trials of the potential biological control agent with the plants it may encounter in the habitat to which it is introduced, as well as with the intended host. In the past, there have been notable disasters where organisms were introduced to control weeds with little regard to non-target organisms, but now extensive codes of practice and legislation are in place to set out required

Figure 3.3   The long-leaved wattle, *Acacia longifolia*, native to Australia, is highly invasive in moist sites in the Mediterranean-type climate zone of the southern Cape Province. (Photo: I.A.W. Macdonald)

Figure 3.4   The gall-wasp, *Trichilogaster acaciae-longifoliae*, was introduced deliberately from Australia in the mid 1980s, reducing the reproductive success of the wattle almost to nil. This has enabled managers of invaded nature reserves to concentrate on clearing out established stands without having to worry about further spread of this species. Biological control is less labour-intensive than physical control but the initial cost of development is often higher. (Photo: I.A.W. Macdonald)

procedures for testing and quarantine. Nevertheless, procedures can break down. For exaple, agriculturalists in Florida have introduced *Cactoblastis* near to sites for native *Opuntia* species, with the result that one species has been very badly affected. Despite these very real concerns about mistakes, there have been many well-regulated successes in regard to the use of biological control for weed species and, increasingly, biological control is being used for invasive species too.

3.8.1 Advantages

Properly conceived biological control is highly host-specific, with little or no ecosystem damage. However, there is still considerable resistance to biological control use, resulting from examples of disastrous ecosystem effects after some early introductions. Macdonald compared attitudes of North American and South African reserve managers to biological control and found the latter more sympathetic to it [246]. This he attributed to the fact that South African problems were more intractable. As more plant invaders get 'out-of-control' he predicted that biological control will grow in importance. For some invasives there is no alternative method. Biocontrol also has the advantage of permanence and, despite high initial development costs, may be the cheapest in the long term.

3.8.2 Disadvantages

Damage of native plants by biological control agents is a considerable worry but seems rarely to happen. This is partly because biological control organisms are now thoroughly screened against an extensive range of native plants. However, even when native plants are attacked to a degree in the laboratory this is rarely carried over into the wild, probably due to competitive exclusion by more closely adapted native insects [196]. Certainly there are cases of one biological control organism displacing another, such as the moth, *Cactoblastis cactorum*, replacing the previously effective coreid (squash bug) *Chelinidea vittiger*.

One problem with biological control is the high failure rate, with some 60–75% of control attempts proving ineffective [196]. This may be due to failure to establish, to the established population densities being too low or to ineffective control even after successful establishment. A biological control agent must still be able to survive, even after it has brought the invasive plant down to a low level. However, the rate of success is likely to increase with better procedures for selecting control agents, based on better understanding of the ecological mechanisms behind population regulation [341, 419] and more accurate taxonomy at the species and biotype level (the better to match invasive plant and control organism). The taxonomic problems inherent in the biological control of *Salvinia molesta* and the *Euphorbia esula/virgata* complex have already been mentioned. Looking for control organisms in inappropriate biotypes, because of misidentification, can be an expensive mistake.

Another problem with biological control is that its development is slow and expensive. Programs for a single plant may take 5–10 years from conception to release and the cost can be in excess of £500 000 (US$ 815 000). A Canadian study in 1979 estimated biological control costs of plants by insect-agents at $1.2–1.5 million per species [155]. Once released, the beneficial effect can be further delayed by the length of time taken for the biological control agent to build up its numbers [263]. However, perhaps the most important problem is due to often sharply conflicting interests surrounding biological control [5]. These conflicts may be economic (the invasive plant may be a honey source), ecological (in places, invasive plants may bind the soil and prevent erosion) and aesthetic (invasives can sometimes be very attractive and can be stoutly defended by local people). Grasses are used as food and fodder crops throughout the world and any proposed biological control measure for a grass species would immediately provoke suspicion, and hence conflict. A conflict arises too when the native and non-native range of a species lie close together. There is thus a conflict over the possible introduction of the South African noctuid, *Conservula cinisigna*, to control *Pteridium aquilinum* in the UK where it has become a weed of pastures [225], since this introduction would also affect the perfectly natural populations of *Pteridium* which are characteristic of certain woods and heaths.

3.8.3 Cost-benefit analysis

Biological control of *Lythrum salicaria* in North America is highly promising, as it is attacked by 120 species of plant-feeding insect in Europe. A cost-benefit analysis has been carried out, which estimates costs of *Lythrum* control at $1.7 million per year (mainly the cost of lost honey production after *Lythrum* eradication, since the direct annual cost of the biological control program is only $100 000) [392]. The benefit is estimated at $45.9 million per year (which includes increased land values, wild hay, muskrat fur, duck hunting and wildlife tourism values). The cost benefit ratio is therefore 1 : 27, amply sufficient to justify a biological control program on economic grounds alone. Such exercises may be valuable in helping to commit resources, but may be a hindrance in natural ecosystems where the main benefit may be the prevention of the extinction of rare endemic species. Economic valuation of endemic species is difficult, although not impossible to compute in financial terms. Often the scientific and heritage value of endemic species may be much greater than their wildlife tourism or natural product value.

3.8.4 Biocontrol procedure

The procedure for classical biological control follows a number of steps.

1. Find region of origin of invasive plants. This will involve taxonomic and biogeographical research.
2. Examine the ecology of the target plant in its native area and identify candidate

biological control agents (such as invertebrates (principally insects) and diseases).

3. Organize with host country and program country arrangements and authorization for collecting and shipping candidates.

4. Construct certified quarantine facilities in program country for testing and screening candidates, with no danger of accidental release.

5. Determine biology of candidate biological control agents and methods for raising them in large numbers.

6. Evaluate candidates. Which ones are most likely to achieve control? Up to 20 candidates may have to be evaluated.

7. Test host specificity of likely candidates. This involves the intensive study of candidates over one to two years. It may involve investigating the feeding habits of up to 10 candidates on some 100 test species of plants.

8. Approve agent for release. Results of specificity testing are reviewed by expert panels of scientists, agriculturalists and government officers.

9. Release agent. A carefully planned release program should be conducted, with timing and locations planned to maximize impact and establishment.

10. Monitor the agent's populations for 5–10 years to determine the impact on the invasive plant or the reasons for failure, as well as effects on non-target species.

3.8.5 Prospects for biological control

In Hawaii, biological control of most of the introduced weeds is the long term goal of conservation managers. At present only 21 Hawaiian weeds are controlled biologically, following 70 insect introductions with a 50% success rate [263]. Biocontrol of invasive plants of natural areas poses special problems not applying to weeds. For instance, the insect quarantine facilities at Honolulu are at sea-level, whereas the invasive Passiflora mollissima will only grow at the altitude of the montane forests; an insect quarantine facility therefore had to be built in the comparative isolation of the Volcanoes National Park. This problem was solved by sealing and caulking the joints of a greenhouse to make it insect proof and then ventilating it with insect-proof fans. Entry is through two darkened anterooms with light traps and fully sealing doors, only one of which is open at any one time [125]. Taking the facilities to the reserve may be better than taking the reserve to the facilities, although prevention of escapes becomes doubly important. There is much scope for research and new developments, not only in classical biological control but also in other biological control fields. These include augmentative biological control (in which repeated releases of a non-persistent agent supplement other control [156]) and mycoherbicides (inundative biological control), in which a fungus is used in the same way as a herbicide [19, 159].

Mycoherbicides are a particularly promising development, although so far success has been achieved against only a small number of plant species. In some cases, common fungi have been used, such as *Colletotrichum gloeosporoides* and *Fusarium solani*, with specificity achieved by using a host-specific type ('forma *specialis*') [49]. Rust fungi have also been used for highly specific biological control [427]. Good control of *Morrenia odorata* (introduced from South America to the Florida citrus groves) has been obtained using *Phytophthora citrophthora* [334], by means of a fungal suspension which is stable for up to six months and is manufactured commercially [201]. After the initial kill there is some residual control from increased levels of pathogen in the soil. Similarly, *Eichhornea crassipes* has been successfully treated with the fungus *Cercospora rodmannii* used in conjunction with arthropod biological control for a reinforced (synergistic) effect [64, 67]. There are prospects of important further developments in this field.

3.9 Environment management control

Measures to reduce disturbance are measures that affect the whole ecosystem and are not just targeted at the invasives. However, this sort of 'environment management' is important in reducing invasion. Reduction of disturbance complements other control measures. Gap size is often crucial. In the Cape Forests of South Africa, natural gaps are usually very small, caused by single standing dead trees. Artificial gaps larger than 0.1 ha led to a deteriorated microclimate, dry soil and the establishment of herbaceous species, and there is no regeneration of native trees [126]. In these circumstances, as in disturbance at the forest fringe by fynbos fires, the invasive *Acacia melanoxylon* can invade.

The prevention of disturbance may require the resolution of conflicts. In Hawaii, introduced goats and pigs are major causes of disturbance but in some areas the State maintains populations of these animals for hunting [361]. Another conflict is the planting of alien grasses to 'improve' native rangeland [187]. Even if these grasses do not prove to be invasive, the disturbance of planting may allow other invasions. The control of invasives, particularly when these form large single species stands, is in itself a form of disturbance and some attention should be paid to the effect of clearance, in particular to its timing with regard to the regeneration of other species. In Australia, the clearance of invasive *Tradescantia* has been found to be followed only by massive regeneration of *Ligustrum*, another invader [378]. In these situations, it may be necessary to sow or plant non-invasive temporary replacement species. In the USA, removal of *Lythrum salicaria* from wetlands which experience lowering of the water-table in summer, merely results in massive germination of *Lythrum salicaria* seeds on the exposed mud. To pre-empt this, the non-invasive replacement species, *Echinochloa frumentacea* (a grass), has been sown [392]. This species is more favorable to waterfowl than *Lythrum salicaria*. Ideally, replacement species should gradually yield to a more diverse range of species (preferably native). Other management techniques include the maintenance of grazing pressure above the optimal level for invasives (where the native vegetation is adapted to grazing or browsing by hoofed mammals), maintaining the frequency of fires and adjusting water regimes, for instance by the judicious control of sluices in wetlands, so that the ecosystem remains resistant to invasives. Such techniques usually require a close knowledge of the ecology of invaders.

3.10 Prospects for the future

Species introductions will continue to take place, either accidentally or intentionally. As most do not cause any significant problems in relation to conservation there is no cause for concern for the majority – although the pressure of accelerating environmental and climatic change may increase the instability of natural ecosystems and allow more species, which are not at present a problem, to invade. Kangaroo Island near Adelaide, Australia has gained over 200 alien plants at a rate of one to two per year and the rate appears to be accelerating [205]. However, the relatively small invasive fraction poses huge conservation problems, with the risk of diverse natural vegetation being replaced by monocultures of aliens. Dominance is the opposite of diversity, and in many parts of the world there is no hope of conserving native biodiversity unless we can improve our ability to regulate ecosystems for diversity, as opposed to dominance imposed by plant invaders [85]. Invasion may lead to species extinction, either due to direct replacement by aliens or the indirect effects of alien species on the ecosystem. The problem is one worthy of further research and resources for practical management as it poses a very serious threat to the conservation of biodiversity, perhaps second only to that of direct habitat destruction.

Foresters, gardeners and agriculturalists should accept their responsibility as principal agents in species introductions and be cautious when introducing species. A global database network listing the invasive species worldwide, and relevant ecological details, would be an extremely useful source of information when deciding whether or not a species should be introduced. In the absence of a worldwide database of invasive plants, species that are a serious problem in one area may be unwittingly introduced to another by those unaware of the potential threat. For example, *Passiflora mollissima*, one of the most serious invasive plants of the Hawaiian forests, was noticed recently spreading in native forest in South Africa [245]. Fortunately, the forestry board in South Africa was quickly alerted to the danger. It had apparently been introduced by an enthusiastic gardener and was being sold in plant nurseries. This is a good example of how conservationists need to be vigilant about threatening species as well as about threatened species.

4

Case studies of some important invasive species

IMPORTANT NOTE

These accounts show measures of control which have been tried. This information should be considered not so much as recommendations, but rather it is to be used in the making of informed decisions.

4.1 Introduction

The following case studies are intended to show the range of invasive species, covering different habitats, life forms and plant families, to demonstrate the importance of the phenomenon of invasion, causes of invasive behavior and the range of control strategies which have been employed to combat these species. The species below do not include all the 'worst' invaders but are chosen as examples of particular types. The system of climatic zones used is that of Holdridge, which is based on mean annual temperature and rainfall (see Table 5.1, p. 129). Although crude, its use does give some indication of the climates of regions of natural occurrence and introduced range of invasive species. The 'invasive categories' are as follows:

0	Not weedy or invasive
1	Minor weed of highly disturbed or cultivated land (man-made artificial landscapes)
1.5	Serious or widespread weeds of 1
2	Weeds of pastures managed for livestock, forestry plantations or artificial waterways
2.5	Serious or widespread weeds of 2
3	Invading seminatural or natural habitats (some conservation interest)
3.5	Serious or widespread invaders of 3
4	Invading important natural or seminatural habitats (i.e. species-rich vegetation, nature reserves, areas containing rare or endemic species)
4.5	Serious or widespread invaders of 4
5	Invasion threatening other species of plants or animals with extinction

As Table 4.1 illustrates, the examples include a range of serious invaders with a variety of life forms. Choice of species is also conditioned partly by the available information; only well-studied species are included.

Table 4.1 Some examples of serious invaders and their characteristic life forms and habitats

Species name	Life form	Invasive category	Habitat invaded
Acacia saligna	tree	5	Open
Andropogon virginicus	herb	3.5	Fire-prone
Clematis vitalba	climber	4.5	Forest
Clidemia hirta	shrub	3.5	Forest
Hakea sericea	tree	5	Fire-prone
Lagarosiphon major	herb	4	Aquatic
Lantana camara	shrub	4.5	Open (dry)
Melaleuca quinquenervia	tree	4.5	Fire-prone (wetland)
Mimosa pigra	shrub	4.5	Open (wetland)
Myrica faya	tree	4.5	Forest (open)
Passiflora mollissima	climber	5	Forest
Pinus radiata	tree	4	Forest (open)
Pittosporum undulatum	tree	5	Forest
Psidium cattleianum	shrub	5	Forest
Rhododendron ponticum	shrub	4	Forest
Salvinia molesta	herb	4.5	Aquatic

4.2 Species accounts

Acacia saligna (Labill.) Wendl. {*Acacia cyanophylla* Lindl.} (Leguminosae)

Port Jackson willow (South Africa); golden wreath wattle, blue-leaved wattle, orange wattle (Australia)

Description and Distribution

Habit Dense shrub or small tree, 2–6 m tall (in South Africa reaches 9 m [47]); bark smooth, gray to red-brown becoming dark gray and fissured with age.

Phyllodes (flattened leaf-like stalks) variable, linear to lanceolate, 8–25 × 0.4–2 cm (often much larger towards the base of the plant), straight or sickle-shaped, often pendulous, hairless, green to glaucous, midrib conspicuous. Solitary gland situated on upper margin of phyllode, oblong to circular, 1–2 mm diameter.

Figure 4.1 *Acacia saligna*

Inflorescence racemose (occasionally reduced to a single flower head), usually axillary but sometimes terminal; heads stalked, globular, 5–10 mm in diameter, with 25–55(–78) flowers.

Flowers bright yellow, calyx ½–⅓ length of corolla, shortly 5-lobed; petals 5, (1.5–) 2–3 mm long, joined for ⅔–¾ their length.

Fruit a legume, linear, (3) 8–12 × 0.4–0.6 cm, slightly contracted between seeds, surface slightly undulate.

Seed oblong (4) 5–6 × (2.5) 3–3.5 mm, dark brown to black, shiny, hard and long-lived. A large seed-bank develops under the mature trees [47, 265].

Invasive category 5.

Region of origin Australasia – southwest Australia [265].

Native climate subtrop. arid. *Acacia saligna* is commonly found on sandy soil in areas with yearly rainfall greater than 380 mm [47] and a dry period during the summer months (3–7 months) with low to high humidity during the remainder of the year. In more arid areas, Acacia saligna is restricted to creeks and rivers.

Regions where introduced Acacia saligna has been extensively cultivated outside its native range, both for its horticultural value and as a source of tannin. It has become naturalized or invasive in the following areas: Africa – South Africa (invasive) [127, 180, 265]; North America – California (naturalized) [143].

Climate where invading wmtemp. dry, wmtemp. moist. In South Africa Acacia saligna is confined mainly to the coastal plain in areas with yearly rainfall of more than 250 mm. The climate is similar to that in its native range with a dry period in the summer lasting for three to five months but fairly humid for the rest of the year.

Acacia saligna is included here as an example of one of the worst woody invaders, a plant that has run amuck in a threatened biome, rich in endemic plant species. In its native Australia it grows best in the deep sands and loams associated with water courses. Where *Acacia saligna* occurs on the coastal dune system, it often forms dense thickets in the hollows between the sandhills [265]. From Australia, *Acacia saligna* was introduced to the Cape in about 1833 and planted to bind drifting sand dunes. From there it has spread to mountain fynbos, lowland fynbos, eastern Cape forest, southern forest, succulent karoo, grassveld and to the southern margins of the karoo[47]. The spread of *Acacia saligna* is threatening several species cited as threatened by IUCN [241], such as *Restio acockii, Chondropetalum acockii, Serruria ciliata, Leucadendron verticillatum* and *Gladiolus aureus*. In areas it is replacing native vegetation. It occurs on all substrates where adequate water is available. It is ranked as the most serious alien plant invader in the fynbos biome on the grounds of both the extent of its current infestation and its potential to spread [179].

Acacia saligna is a variable species [265], which matures early and has a relatively fast growth rate [274]. It is tolerant of drought and sprouts readily after cutting or burning, regenerating easily from the large seed-bank that develops under the canopy of mature trees. The seeds germinate rapidly after fire. They have a water impermeable seed-coat so they remain dormant until heat ruptures the lens (a specialized area of the seed-coat in legumes) allowing water uptake and breaking of dormancy [180]. In common with other Acacia species, Acacia saligna produces large numbers of hard dry seeds and one square metre of canopy can produce 10 500 seeds per year. The seedlings are robust and have an extensive root system. The seeds may be bird-dispersed (starlings and doves in South Africa [47]) but most fall directly to the ground [180] and may be transported further by water or people. Despite poor long-distance dispersal, Acacia saligna has become widespread in the west, south and eastern coastal zones of the Cape [127].

The above-ground biomass of dense *Acacia saligna* infestations is much greater than that of uninvaded native vegetation in South Africa [409]. Falling leaves have a higher nitrogen content than those of native species and inputs of nitrogen from the litter are consequently higher, leading to greater levels of nitrogen in the litter and top layer of the soil. The invasion of the coastal lowlands of the Cape by *Acacia saligna* results in an increase in the nitrogen status of the fynbos during the early stages of invasion. This may have important consequences for adjacent native vegetation, possibly leading to changes in species composition and structure [450].

The following ecological characteristics of *Acacia saligna* may be suggested as reasons for its success as an invasive species:

1. widespread planting of *Acacia saligna* for dune stabilization;
2. comparatively rapid growth rate on soils low in nutrients;
3. early reproductive maturity;
4. copious production of seeds that may remain dormant, producing a large seed-bank in the soil;
5. ability to survive fires as seed;
6. ability to sprout after cutting or burning;
7. tolerance of a wide variety of substrates;
8. nitrogen fixation;
9. preadaptation to the Mediterranean climate and nutrient poor soils [450, 451] (this may be said for all the invasive *Acacia* species invading the fynbos);
10. extensive root system, with abundant root nodules and mycorrhizal association (the root systems of invasive *Acacia* spp. have more extensive laterals than those legumes that are native to the Cape [171], and *Acacia saligna* has very rapid depth penetration of the soil by the seedling taproot [451]);
11. higher stature (more than 3 m) than fynbos plants (less than 2 m), allowing it to overtop and shade them.

Control and Management

Physical control Any program to clear *Acacia* scrub manually must always include treatment to kill the seedlings, as large amounts of viable seed remain in the soil even after burning, and also treatment of the cut stumps, since these readily produce new shoots.

Chemical control If trees are cut, the stumps must be painted with herbicide to avoid regrowth [47].

Management program The large seed-bank of *Acacia saligna* is a major obstacle to successful control [179], which is possible only if every individual is removed (it is a prolific seed producer) and the seed-bank is reduced to zero. The optimal program

Figure 4.2 *Andropogon virginicus*

[256] is to clear the mature trees, treat with chemicals to prevent regrowth and burn the site (burning stimulates germination), repeating the burning treatment and applying herbicide once the seeds have germinated (or the young seedlings may be pulled by hand). This may need to be repeated. The aim is to remove all existing and potential seed-producing individuals, which may act as foci for reinvasion; one surviving seed-producer may re-infest the whole area. Follow-up treatment must involve repeated physical control (mattocking) in subsequent years. This treatment is expensive but repeated burning and application of herbicides may damage the native vegetation, which can be slow to recolonize due to lack of propagules of native species. Costs of the first five years of such a program for 1 ha have been estimated to exceed the cost of one person-year of labour [256]. There are some 425 600 ha of densely infested fynbos.

Biological control There are no fully effective biological control measures against *Acacia saligna* yet available, although some are under development. Biological control is the only possible cost-effective method. It may not decrease dramatically the area invaded by *Acacia saligna*, but it could slow the rate of spread and prevent the formation of such dense stands as now occur without causing unacceptable environmental damage.

Andropogon virginicus L. (Gramineae)
Broom sedge

Description and Distribution
Habit Perennial tall bunchgrass with tufted stems, 50–100 cm tall, branches 1–3 at node.

Leaves leaf-sheaths, more or less tuberculate-hirsute on the margins with long usually lax hairs; ligule yellow-brown, membranous, truncate, white-fringed at edge; blades 40 cm long or less, 2–5 mm wide, rough or roughish, hirsute on the upper surface near the base; spathes 3–5 cm long, extending beyond the racemes.

Racemes 2 (–3–4), 2–3 cm long.

Spikelets sessile spikelet 3–4 mm long, twice to half again as long as the internode, the awn straight, 10–15 mm long; pedicellate spikelet wanting or rarely present as a minute scale, pedicel exceeding the sessile spikelet [357].

Flowers either sessile and hermaphrodite, or stalked and staminate, sterile or not developed [374].

Invasive category 3.5.

Region of origin North America – Florida to Texas and Mexico, north to Massachusetts, New York, Ohio, Indiana, Illinois, Missouri, Kansas and Oklahoma; Central America – West Indies and Central America [374]. Occurs in prairies, fallow or abandoned fields, along railroad tracks; rarely in wet open and swampy places. The occurrence of this grass usually indicates an acid soil. *Andropogon virginicus* is found on dry or moist soil [357] and is an occasional weed in waste places [295]. It forms part of the primary succession in abandoned pasture lands, followed by *Pinus taeda* L. and later by southern mixed hardwood forest [134].

Native climate wmtemp. moist, subtrop. moist.

Regions where introduced Oceania – Hawaii (invasive) [291]; Australasia – Australia (invasive).

Climate where invading subtrop. dry, subtrop. moist. In Hawaii there is a summer dry period lasting four to five months with the remainder of the year humid, though in places humidity may be high all year round.

In Hawaii, *Andropogon virginicus* is considered one of the most threatening aliens. It occurs in disturbed grassland and scrub on Oahu from about 50–250 m, on red clay soils in places where the native forest vegetation has been replaced by introduced woody and herbaceous plants. It was introduced to Oahu inadvertently in 1932 and probably to the other Hawaiian islands at about the same time. In Australia, *Andropogon virginicus* has invaded communities which are extremely deficient in nutrients and were thought for this reason to be uninvasible. As *Andropogon virginicus* is highly flammable (due to accumulated standing-dead material), it alters the fire regime in areas where the native flora is not adapted to frequent fires, which has serious consequences for these ecosystems.

Andropogon virginicus rapidly invades burnt or bare areas [359]. It grows vigorously, forming an extremely dense cover with dry shoots which remain standing, together with the active, green shoots. Stands of *Andropogon virginicus* appear yellow throughout the year because of these accumulated dead shoots. They are shed annually during the season of higher rainfall (October to April), at which time the grass goes into partial dormancy, indicated by the drying up of most of the current-year crop of photosynthetic shoots. Only a central core of shoots remains active during the winter rains, so there is little transpiration of excess soil water. This drying up of the shoots mulches the soil, which also prevents direct soil evaporation at a time when rainfall is excessive [291]. The mulch effect lasts all year so there is continual excess water under *Andropogon virginicus* communities (evaporation and transpiration through the grass cover is insufficient) not only during its period of partial dormancy but even during the more productive summer season.

The monthly run-off of water from the areas covered with *Andropogon virginicus* is much greater than would be expected, because water does not penetrate readily into a soil that is already water-saturated. The result in lowland areas is accelerated erosion, as seen in the form of slumps on steep slopes and deeply cut erosion channels in the grassland. In addition to being a poor utilizer of the productive capacity of the rainforest habitat, introduced *Andropogon* is causing damage to the landscape and probably contributing to siltation in the Knaeohe Bay area on Oahu. Reforestation with climatically adapted evergreen species, and fire protection, may be the answer to the problem [291]. Unless a solution can be found, *Andropogon virginicus* may have serious long-term consequences in Hawaii by altering the hydrology and fire regime, with resulting soil erosion. Infestations of *Andropogon* are preventing the natural re-establishment of rainforest vegetation in these areas.

In Australia, *Andropogon virginicus* disrupts native communities, which were once thought to be resistant to invasion due to the low nutrient status of the soil, by increasing the frequency of fires. *Andropogon* is tolerant of very low nutrient levels, but it is outcompeted by other species if nutrients are added to the area in which it occurs [140].

The following ecological characteristics of *Andropogon virginicus* may be suggested as reasons for its success as an invasive species:

1. vigorous growth, producing a continuous, dense cover;
2. production of allelopathic substances [359];
3. well adapted to burning. The dead material provides an excellent fuel, while *Andropogon virginicus* spreads rapidly onto burnt ground.

Control and Management

Biological control Any attempts to control *Andropogon* by introducing a natural pest or disease will probably be resisted by the sugar industry [359].

Chemical control As *Andropogon virginicus* is also a weed of agricultural habitats several chemical control methods have been devised [140]. Effective control can be achieved by application of bromacil, hexazinone, tebuthiuron, bromacil & diuron and buthidazole at 4.5 kg ha^{-1}. Use of these herbicides with addition of fertilizers can accelerate the removal of *Andropogon virginicus* from infested pastures.

Clematis vitalba L. (Ranunculaceae)

Old man's beard, traveller's joy, mile-a-minute, hedge feathers, graybeard (New Zealand), herb aux gueux (France)

Description and Distribution

Habit Deciduous, perennial woody petiole-climber [433] with stems up to 30 m long, 6-angled, strongly ribbed.

Leaves pinnate with usually 3–5 leaflets; leaflets 3–10 cm long, ovate, acute to acuminate, rounded or subcordate at base, coarsely toothed or entire, hairless or slightly pubescent.

Flowers greenish-white, c.2 cm in diameter, in terminal axillary cymes, fragrant, hermaphrodite. Perianth segments obtuse, pubescent. Anthers 1–2 mm. Slightly protogynous. Nectar is secreted from the filaments and the flowers are visited by various bees and flies for both pollen and nectar [71]. Generally thought to be wind-pollinated, but insect pollination has been reported [433].

Achenes in large heads on the pubescent receptacle, scarcely compressed, with long white plumose styles. Copious seed production – it has been estimated that 17 000

Figure 4.3   *Clematis vitalba*

viable seeds are produced for every 0.5 m^2 of *Clematis vitalba* canopy [433, 445]. Seeds dispersed as achenes by wind, water, people and other vertebrates [445].

Invasive category 4.5

Region of origin Europe – south, west and central Europe. Its distribution extends north to the Netherlands, south to the Mediterranean and east to the Caucasus mountains [433].

Native climate Temp. moist. Annual rainfall of less than 800 mm and low summer temperatures found at high altitude appear to be limiting.

Regions where introduced Australasia – New Zealand (invasive), South Australia (naturalized) [433]; Europe – Ireland, Scotland, Poland, Denmark (naturalized) [433]; North America – Oregon, USA (naturalized) [433].

Climate where invading wmtemp. moist–wet (New Zealand).

Clematis vitalba appears to have different ecological behavior in its native and alien ranges. An innocuous climber in Europe, in New Zealand it can have a devastating impact on various ecosystems. In Britain, *Clematis vitalba* is native to Wales and southern England, associated with chalk and limestone, although in central Europe it is found on a wider range of soils from weakly acid to weakly basic [112, 433]. It requires a substrate with moderate to high fertility and medium to good drainage [200]. Low calcium levels in the soil appear to retard the growth of *Clematis vitalba* in Britain [62], but on base-rich soils it is common in hedgerows, thickets and on wood margins [71].

In New Zealand *Clematis vitalba* is invading tall and low forest, scrub and forest margins, shrubland, waste land, willow vegetation along river courses and hedgerows in coastal and lowland areas [428, 445]. *Clematis vitalba* was first recorded as a naturalized plant in New Zealand in the mid-1930s in both southern North Island and northern South Island [318]. *Clematis* invasion has a dramatic impact on the native vegetation. The vine can easily smother native trees over 20 m high, including podocarps [428]. After the native vegetation has been killed by *Clematis vitalba* it gradually collapses, and the *Clematis* then continues to grow in thick layers (which can become metres deep) along the ground, preventing regeneration of native trees [445].

Clematis vitalba can regrow from fragments after cutting and this is an important feature in its spread. Regeneration of fragments is related to age, since older stem sections have better water retention and larger nutrient resources than softer young tissue [200]. *Clematis vitalba* has a high growth rate (young plants and new shoots can grow up to 2 m per year) and it reaches reproductive maturity relatively early if exposed to full sun (it can reproduce sexually after one to three years, and asexually after one year). Vegetative reproduction involves rooting from stem fragments and attached stems. It appears to be tolerant of only moderate shade [112, 200, 433] and requires high light for growth and reproduction. *Clematis vitalba* usually produces many climbing shoots per plant which cover the host, often resulting in its death. It is tolerant of frost partly because it is deciduous. It spreads wherever land is not intensively managed or grazed, especially along river margins [445].

The following ecological characteristics of *Clematis vitalba* may be suggested as reasons for its success as an invasive species:

1. rapid growth rate;
2. early reproductive maturity;
3. ability to spread easily vegetatively and from fragments;
4. rapid recovery from physical damage by resprouting;
5. high seed production and effective wind dispersal of seeds.

Control and Management

Physical control Small seedlings can be pulled, but larger stems have to be cut and removed from the area and the roots grubbed out, otherwise they will resprout [363].

Chemical control A variety of herbicides have been shown to be effective in controlling *Clematis vitalba* [317]. In New Zealand, the application of picloram granules to soil near the base of the plant has shown to be effective. However, the picloram affects the surrounding vegetation and has residual effects in the soil [363]. The method recommended by the Department of Lands and Survey (now the Department of Conservation) in New Zealand is to cut the vines at ground level and waist high and treat both cut ends with 2,4,5-T in diesel [317]. Roundup has also been used, with varying levels of success: when applied at a suitable time of year, it results in a complete kill of the vine, and it does not appear to affect the surrounding bush [363]. Tordon Brushkiller and Garlon 520 applied to vine bases in fall (autumn) have been found to be very effective in killing *Clematis vitalba* [106].

Biological control A survey of insect predators of *Clematis vitalba* in England has produced a list of some possible candidates for biological control in New Zealand. Further research on host specificity will be required before these insects can be considered for introduction to New Zealand as there are several native species of *Clematis*. Possible biological control candidates [62] are: *Horisme vitalbata* (Lepidoptera: Geometridae), which attacks the leaves of *Clematis*; *Melanthia procellata* (Lepidoptera); *Eupithica haworthiata* (Lepidoptera), which damages the flowers; and *Xylocleptes bispinus* (Coleoptera: Scolytidae), which attacks the structural and vascular tissue of the stems.

Prospects The inherent difficulties with physical and chemical control, due to the vigorous resprouting response of *Clematis vitalba* when cut, mean that research into biological control is essential for practical and economic reasons. As the biology and ecology of *Clematis vitalba* have been fairly well studied in its native region (unusual for an invasive plant), it may present a good case study to determine the basis for its different ecological behavior in New Zealand. Fortunately, this species does not appear to have been introduced elsewhere where it might become a pest. It is important that the problems associated with it are made known so that future introductions to potentially 'invasible' areas are prevented.

Figure 4.4 *Clidemia hirta*

Clidemia hirta (L.) D.Don. {*Melastoma hirta* L.} (Melastomataceae)

Koster's curse (Fiji, Hawaii), soap bush (Jamaica)

Description and Distribution

Habit Densely branching shrub rarely more than 1.5 m high in native region [2]; reaches a height of 4 m in Hawaii [435]; all parts densely hairy.

Leaves papery, petiolate, mostly 4–15 cm long, acute or short-acuminate, usually 5-nerved, margins often crenulate and denticulate.

Inflorescence 3–5 cm long, axillary.

Flowers white or pinkish, 8–10 mm.

Fruit a berry, sweet, variously described as red-purple to blackish (Jamaica) or dark blue (Hawaii), containing 100 or more seeds.

Seeds c. 0.5mm in diameter, most likely dispersed by birds. It fruits continuously with prolific seed production [132, 435].

Invasive category 3.5.

Region of origin Central and South America. *Clidemia hirta* has a wide natural range in humid tropical America, extending from southern Mexico to Argentina and including the islands of the West Indies [2, 435].

Native climate trop. dry, trop. moist, usually characterized by very high humidity for most of the year with a dry period of about two months (February–March) prior to the summer months; however, in some areas, the dry period is during the winter, lasting for three months.

Regions where introduced Oceania – Hawaii (invasive [362]), Fiji (invasive/ruderal), Java, Samoa, British Solomon Is, Tonga and Palau [435]; Malagassia – Madagascar (naturalized) [186, 435]; Africa – Tanzania (naturalized) [435]; S., E. and SE Asia – Sri Lanka, India, Singapore (invasive) and Sabah [78, 335, 435].

Climate where invading subtrop. wet–dry. In Oahu, *Clidemia hirta* is widespread in areas that receive more than 1270 mm of rain annually [435] (although in Fiji it apparently occurs in drier habitats). It does not appear to be limited by elevation as it is found from almost sea-level up to the highest ridges at 900 m. It can also be found in areas of annual rainfall in excess of 7600 mm, with no dry season.

Clidemia hirta is an example of a pantropical weed which, in places, has been able to spread out of managed habitats to become a conservation nuisance in native forest. In its native range, *Clidemia hirta*, like many of the other members of its genus, is a plant of secondary succession [435]. In Trinidad and Jamaica it is characteristically found in moist, shaded localities, on the edges of clearings and stream-banks, in ditches, along paths and roadways and in moist pastures and thickets; the altitude range is 30–900 m^2.

It has now become very widespread, being introduced to Fiji from Guyana before 1890 [309] and to Java in the late nineteenth century [435]. By 1934, *Clidemia hirta* had become established in Samoa, British Solomon Islands and Tonga. It was noticed in Hawaii 1941 and Palau in 1971. The routes and methods of its introduction are unknown, but it was probably introduced to most places accidentally. In both Hawaii and Fiji, approximately 30 years elapsed between its first sighting and the time when it was perceived as a serious pest [309].

In Hawaii it is established in a variety of habitats. On Oahu, more than 40 000 ha are infested [398]. It is spreading into undisturbed vegetation such as rainforest, as well as into disturbed vegetation. It can be found under many of the common introduced species such as *Psidium cattleianum*, *Melaleuca quinquenervia* and *Eucalyptus robusta*, as well as with the native *Metrosideros collina* and *Acacia koa* [435]. Under the forest canopy, *Clidemia hirta* may be replacing the native fern *Dicranopteris linearis* as well as other native species. More recently, it has also spread into forests on the islands of Hawaii, Maui, Molokai and Kauai, with the greatest infestations occurring in the Puna and Waiakea forests of Hawaii.

In Fiji it has, in the past, invaded rubber and cocoa plantations, grasslands and forested areas, but is now controlled by an introduced insect in many areas, excluding the native forests and shaded places where the biological control agent (see biological control section) has not been very successful due to intolerance of shade [309, 435]. In Singapore it invades older secondary and primary forests [78].

Clidemia hirta is found in light conditions ranging from full sunlight to 100% canopy cover, demonstrating broad tolerance [435]. Forest fire seems to give *Clidemia* an advantage over the native and non-native flora as several months after burning it has often become the dominant species. *Clidemia* has a rapid growth rate and, where it is established outside its native range, it appears to grow larger, producing more fruit and forming dense, almost impenetrable thickets over such extensive areas that it is evidently able to compete successfully in a greater range of environmental conditions than where it is native. This is probably due to the absence of the burden of native pests and diseases.

The following ecological characteristics of *Clidemia hirta* may be suggested as reasons for its success:

1. tolerance of a wide range of environmental conditions;
2. prolific seed production;
3. rapid growth rate;
4. long-distance dispersal by birds;
5. formation of dense thickets which prevent regeneration of native tree species.

Control and Management

Biological control Biocontrol agents were sought in Trinidad and feeding experiments indicated that a thrips, *Liothrips urichi* (Thysanoptera: Phlaeothripidae), was highly host-specific and would not attack plants of economic importance. The thrips were imported to Fiji in 1930 and field releases were made immediately. Within a few months they multiplied rapidly, spread to other islands and caused a widespread collapse of the *Clidemia hirta* population [435]. The thrips provide excellent control in most areas by reducing the plant's competitive ability [196], the exception being in moist and shady habitats.

Liothrips urichi is a sucking insect which attacks terminal shoots, causing leaf drop and reduced vitality, which results in the smothering of *Clidemia hirta* by other plants [435]. The insect shows a strong preference for sunlight and, although it has been found in deeper shade than in its native range, it has not significantly suppressed *Clidemia hirta* in Fijian forests. *Liothrips* was also introduced to Hawaii in 1953 but was not as successful as in Fiji, possibly due to predation by *Montadoniola moraguesi* (Hemiptera: Anthocoridae) and *Pheidde megacephala* (Hymenoptera: Formicidae) [323] and also because it cannot tolerate the low light levels found under a forest canopy. *Liothrips* provides moderate control in open pastureland but is ineffective in conservation and watershed areas where the greatest problem exists. *Liothrips* was introduced to the Solomon Islands on several occasions but failed to establish [196].

Other organisms are being tested as potential biological control agents in Hawaii [297]. For example, the fungal pathogen *Colletotrichum gloeosporioides* has been isolated from *Clidemia hirta* plants growing in Panama [398]. Tests have shown it to be a highly aggressive pathogen of cultivars from Hawaii. The disease symptoms are severe premature defoliation and tip dieback of the plants. This pathogen shows promise as an agent for biological control and specificity tests are underway. Another organism, a pyralid moth, *Bleparomastix ebulealis* (Lepidoptera: Pyralidae), was introduced to Hawaii from Puerto Rico. It has become established but so far has been ineffective in controlling *Clidemia hirta* [196, 435].

More research into a suitable biological control agent for forest habitats is needed. Physical or chemical control is not a viable option considering the extensive areas covered by *Clidemia hirta*.

Hakea sericea Schrad. {*H. acicularis* R. Br., *H. tenuifolia* (Salisb.) Domin} (Proteaceae)

Syerige hakea, silky wattle (South Africa); needlebush, prickly hakea (New Zealand)

Description and Distribution

Habit An erect single stemmed, much branched shrub or small tree, 2–5 m high. Shoots densely hairy, somewhat angular.

Leaves dark green, simple, terete, 2–6 × 1 cm, hairless except when very young, rigid and spiny.

Flowers few, in axillary clusters, perianth white.

Fruit a woody follicle, 2–3 × 1.4–2.5 cm, mostly very corrugated, with 2 small horns at the beaked apex; purplish-brown changing to gray with age; serotinous.

Seeds 2 per follicle, winged, wind-dispersed [332, 452].

Invasive category 5.

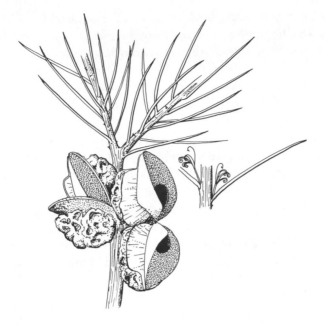

Figure 4.5 *Hakea sericea*

Region of origin Australasia – SE Australia (Victoria, New South Wales and some Bass Strait islands). *Hakea sericea* is found on coastal heath, in open sclerophyll forests on the highlands and on coastal dividing ranges [303].

Native climate wmtemp. moist; usually in areas that are humid all year round with very high rainfall in places.

Regions where introduced Africa – South Africa (invasive). Nearly all the coastal mountain ranges in the western, southern, and southeastern Cape [303]. Its potential range corresponds roughly to the areas of mountain fynbos and to sandstone and granite areas on mountain ranges, with rainfall in winter or throughout the year. Australasia – New Zealand (ruderal). Common to abundant on North Island in north Auckland, the Auckland region, Great Barrier Island, Coromandel Peninsula, Bay of Plenty and the Wellington area; on South Island it is found in Waikakaho valley and is locally common in northwest Nelson [428].

Climate where invading wmtemp. dry–moist; dry in summer with winter rain or else humid all year round.

Hakea sericea is a fire-adapted species, an important factor in its achievement of remarkable dominance in species-rich vegetation of great nature conservation importance in South Africa. It occurs up to 100 km inland in mountain fynbos vegetation and, by forming in places dense impenetrable thickets, threatens the indigenous vegetation. *Hakea sericea* and *Pinus pinaster*, another alien invader, are considered the 'greatest threat to the mountain fynbos vegetation' [303]. It was probably introduced into South Africa in the nineteenth century and has been used to bind sand dunes and also as a hedge plant [303]. In New Zealand it occurs in gumlands and scrub and on open hillsides. It was introduced into New Zealand as a hedge plant but now is rarely used [428].

Hakea sericea is well adapted to survive the periodic fires which are a feature of the fynbos in South Africa. It reaches reproductive maturity relatively early, after about two years, and is strongly outbreeding [109]. Lack of specialized pre-dispersal seed predators and prolific seed production ensure a large seed load (seed production appears to be higher in South Africa than in its native Australia). The winged seed is retained in woody, heat resistant follicles and is released only on death of the parent plant or branch. Standing plants killed by fire liberate seeds within a few days. Germination is equally good on burnt and unburnt substrates [332]. The seeds may then be dispersed by wind over great distances. Infestations of *Hakea sericea* may become so dense that they smother the surrounding vegetation. The invasion of fynbos vegetation by *Hakea sericea* results in a 60% increase in fuel load for the area and the low moisture content of the leaves ensures that they burn vigorously [409] upsetting the natural fire regime and threatening the native flora and fauna [303].

The following ecological characteristics of *Hakea sericea* may be suggested as reasons for its success as an invasive species:

1. serotinous seed dispersal which leads to massive and simultaneous release of canopy-stored seed after fire or felling;
2. winged seeds which aid in long-distance dispersal;
3. formation of dense stands which smother the native vegetation;
4. prolific seed production [333];
5. germination requirements not specific;
6. early reproductive maturity;
7. adaptation to fire.

Control and Management

Biological control Several biological control agents have been introduced to South Africa in the past but have had limited success. *Carposina autologa* (Lepidoptera: Carposinidae) was introduced from Australia in 1972 but did not survive long after introduction [196]. *Cydmaea binotata* (Coleoptera: Curculionidae) was introduced in 1980 but only a few colonies have survived and the damage they caused is probably insignificant. *Erytenna consputa* Pascoe (Coleoptera: Curculionidae), introduced in 1972 with poor results, was reintroduced in 1974 causing significant seed destruction in dry inland localities [208]. Recently [206, 288, 332] *Hakea sericea* has suffered from a gummosis and die-back disease in many areas of the Cape. The symptoms are stem and branch cankers exuding quantities of gum. These cankers may eventually girdle the stem, killing the host plant. Shoot tips of mature plants may also be affected and die back progressively. The growing points of young shoots are attacked, necrosis extending down the stems to kill the whole plant [289]. The origin of this disease is uncertain [206], but the causal organism, a form of the fungus *Colletotrichum gloesporioides* [289], is endemic to South Africa and appears to have a limited host range. The disease has been spread artificially but this has been found to be unnecessary as natural spread is rapid [332]. It is now widespread in the Cape and is causing extensive mortality [196]. It is thought that this fungus combined with the other biological control agent, *Erytenna consputa*, may cause a significant reduction in the extent and spread of *Hakea sericea*.

Physical control Areas invaded by *Hakea sericea* are systematically cleared and then burnt 9–12 months later [206]. This form of control is not very satisfactory considering the expense [332], time taken and need for continual vigilance to maintain an area free of *Hakea sericea*, which is a prolific seed producer. The intense fires produced by burning *Hakea sericea* may damage the native flora and fauna [303, 332].

Lagarosiphon major (Ridl.) Moss {*L. muscoides* Harvey var. *major* Ridl.} (Hydrocharitaceae)

Description and Distribution

Habit Submerged aquatic herb, with elongated, branched, brittle stems, about 3 mm in diameter.

Leaves alternate to subwhorled, *c.* 1.6 cm × 0.2 cm, tapering, stiff, recurved, with short blunt teeth.

Spathes axillary, shortly and bluntly toothed, solitary and unisexual (dioecious). Male spathe is ovate and many flowered (*c.* 50 flowers per spathe); female spathes one-flowered.

Flowers with 6 perianth segments; male: stamens 3, staminoids 3; female: staminoids 3, styles 3, stigmatic surface red.

Invasive category 4.

Region of origin Africa – South Africa. An endemic species found in high mountain freshwater streams and ponds [421].

Figure 4.6 *Lagarosiphon major*

Regions where introduced Europe – Britain (naturalized), Italy (naturalized); Australasia – New Zealand (invasive) [182, 266]; Malagassia – Mascarenes (naturalized).

Lagarosiphon major provides an extraordinary example of a restricted endemic, able to spread explosively when introduced to freshwater lakes and streams in New Zealand, to the extent of coming near to eliminating the indigenous aquatic vegetation in Lake Rotorua [66]. The first report of *Lagarosiphon major* naturalized in New Zealand was in 1950 in the Hutt Valley and, by 1957, it was established in nuisance proportions in Lake Rotorua [182]. *Lagarosiphon major* was introduced to Lake Rotorua with the intention of improving the oxygenation levels. It is thought to have been introduced to Lake Taupo around 1966 by recreational boat traffic. It has since spread to many other freshwater lakes in New Zealand.

Lagarosiphon major has the ability to form tall closed-canopy stands in sheltered freshwater habitats. In Lake Rotorua, New Zealand, it once formed thick, dense mats of weed, up to 0.4 km wide and to depths of 2–3 m, although it has declined since the early 1980s. The greatest height and biomass are produced in sites with fine sediment and steep slopes, and it is not tolerant of exposure to large wind-runs. *Lagarosiphon major* has pushed out *Elodea canadensis*, previously the dominant alien species in Lake Taupo. *Elodea*, which did not form monospecific stands in the oligotrophic waters of Lake Taupo, had been coexisting with the native vegetation rather than replacing it. The barrier to further invasion by *Lagarosiphon major* is likely to be wave action. *Lagarosiphon major* directly displaces the native flora over large areas of the lake littoral zone. It attracts large herbivores such as swans and detritivores such as crayfish, which adversely affect the native flora. As in Rotorua, the native flora of Lake Taupo has been directly replaced or reduced in many areas as a result of its spread [182]. *Lagarosiphon major* is intolerant of low water transparency associated with accelerated eutrophication and declined in abundance in some lakes in New Zealand after they became more eutrophic [74]. In Lake Rotorua the population collapse, associated with turbidity and storms in the early 1980s, has now reduced *Lagarosiphon major* to approximately the same abundance as *Elodea canadensis* (common but not dominant). However, another alien water plant, *Egeria densa*, promises to form similar weed beds to those that used to be formed by *Lagarosiphon major* [432].

Lagarosiphon major is dioecious and in New Zealand spreads entirely by vegetative means (only the female plant has been introduced). Efficient vegetative reproduction and water dispersal allows it to invade New Zealand lakes despite being unable to set seed. Before its decline in Lake Rotorua, *Lagarosiphon major* formed dense growths up to 5 m high reaching to the surface between 2–6 m depth. It now grows sparsely, with growths most commonly around 1 m long, in sheltered sites growing to within 50 cm of the surface [432].

The following ecological characteristics may be suggested as reasons for the success of *Lagarosiphon major*.

1. formation of dense stands which crowd out the native flora;

2. rapid growth rate;

3. vegetative spread.

Control and Management

Biological control There have been proposals to introduce grass carp to control adventive plants such as *Lagarosiphon major*, but it is feared that this will damage the native flora, since an examination of the food preference of the fish shows that some of the native species are highly preferred [182].

Chemical control In places *Lagarosiphon major* has been controlled by spraying with diquat [66].

Prospects Lagarosiphon major has directly displaced native species in New Zealand [66, 182] and therefore the development of some control method is essential. The use of chemicals in a freshwater system is not desirable, as residues may enter the human food chain as well as having deleterious effects on the native flora and fauna. A biological control agent would therefore be the most desirable and economic method, but host specificity of any introduced control organism will be difficult to achieve.

Lantana camara L. {*L.aculeata* L., *L.brittonii* Moldenke, *L.scabrida* Ait.} (Verbenaceae)

White sage, wild sage (Caribbean), tickberry (South Africa)

Description and Distribution

Habit Perennial, erect or (in shady places) straggling, aromatic shrub, 1–2 (–6) m tall. Stems four-angled, often armed with recurved prickles, more or less pubescent.

Leaves opposite, ovate to ovate-lanceolate, with a strong odour when crushed, 2.5–10 cm × 1.75–7.5 cm, margins crenate to dentate, rough above, hairy below.

Inflorescences axillary or terminal in dense corymbs, 2.5 cm in diameter, flowers maturing from the outside of the head inwards.

Flowers yellow or pink on opening, changing to orange or red, rarely blue or purple (in wild type *Lantana camara* the flowers change from yellow to red [218]), corolla a slender tube, shortly but densely pubescent outside, with four unequal lobes. Stamens 4, in 2 pairs, epipetalous.

Fruit a small drupe, globular, dark purple to black, *c.* 6 mm across at maturity.

Seed c. 1.5 mm [364].

Taxonomy Lantana camara is not homogeneous, but consists of a number of forms of mixed hybrid origin [375]. These plants are collectively referred to as the *Lantana*

Figure 4.7 *Lantana camara*

camara complex or *Lantana camara* sensu lato. The most aggressive taxon, *Lantana camara* L. var. *aculeata* (L.) Moldenke [387] is characterized by its vigor, long weak branches and numerous recurved prickles.

Invasive category 4.5.

Region of origin Central and South America. *Lantana camara* L. sensu stricto occurs as a wild plant in dry thickets in the West Indies and widely in the Neotropics [2], but the distribution is complicated by the introduction of non-wild forms in these countries.

Regions where introduced Oceania – Hawaiian Is [359], Society Is, Cook Is, Samoa, Fiji, New Caledonia, New Hebrides, New Britain, New Guinea, Micronesia (e.g. Ponape, Guam [103]), Tonga, Niue and Makatea; Isolated Oceanic islands – Galápagos [91], St Helena; Australasia – Australia (New South Wales) [211, 364],

New Zealand (North Island) [387], Norfolk I. [387]; Africa – South Africa, where infestations are said to cover some 400 000 ha in Natal alone [70, 247, 375]; Malagassia – Madagascar [211]; S. Asia [211] – Indo-China, Indonesia, SE Asia, India; North America – USA [91].

Climate where invading wmtemp.-trop. dry–moist. In South Africa it does not invade very dry regions, such as the Orange Free State, and it is abundant only where the temperature does not frequently drop below 5°C [70]. Generally, however, the complex grows throughout a considerable climatic range.

Lantana camara is probably familiar to anyone who has been in warm-temperate, subtropical or tropical regions. The main adaptation responsible for its rapid spread has been its brightly colored flowers, which have induced gardeners to spread it widely. The early hybridizations, carried out by European gardeners during the eighteenth and nineteenth centuries, probably involved two or more species [375]. The height of popularity of *Lantana camara* in Europe happened to coincide with the expansion of colonial powers into the tropics and many imported varieties escaped from gardens to become serious weeds. Diploid, triploid, tetraploid, pentaploid and hexaploid forms of *Lantana camara* have been reported [375], resulting from auto- and allo-polyploidy [298]. The breeding system is both sexual and asexual [202]; most weedy types appear to be tetraploid.

Lantana camara is mainly a weed of highly disturbed habitats and rather rarely invades natural and seminatural habitats to threaten native flora and fauna. It is included here mainly as an example of a man-made hybrid becoming a serious pest. In South Africa, since its introduction in about 1880, *Lantana camara* has come to invade natural forests, plantations, forest margins, overgrazed or burnt veld, waste ground, orchards, relatively undisturbed rocky hillsides and fields [70, 108, 376]. In Australia, it occurs at the margins of rainforest or in rainforest clearings [364].

In the Galápagos *Lantana camara* is found from the arid zone to the *Scalesia* forest regions [151] and has replaced, on Floreana, *Scalesia penduculata* forest and a dry vegetation of *Croton, Macraea* and *Darwiniothamnus*. Some small populations of rare native plants in these areas are in danger of being eliminated. This is true of two of the three populations of *Lecocarpus pinnatifidus* and of a population of *Scalesia villosa*, both of which are endemic to Floreana Island. The impending spread of *Lantana camara* to the crater area of Cerro Pajas, where the dark-rumped petrel (*Pterodroma phaeopygia*) nests, is of grave concern. The resultant dense thicket of *Lantana camara* will keep the petrels, which nest in burrows, from occupying their breeding site [91], the last remaining nesting colony on the Galápagos. Likewise, rare endemic plant species may also become extinct [91].

In Ponape (Caroline Is) it 'has replaced the native vegetation in many areas and formed closed communities' [387]. In New Caledonia it 'has replaced the native vegetation and infested the coastal districts on both the windward and leeward coasts and penetrated into the mountain passes of the central range. It has transformed the native "niaouli" (*Melaleuca leucadendron*) savannas into impenetrable thickets, colonized both pasture and cultivated land, and transformed previously native forests into impenetrable thickets as well as suffocating both mature trees and seedlings which served to support it' [387]. In Hawaii, *Lantana camara* is found up to 600 m on all islands, principally in dry areas, though it also grows in mesic and wet habitats [359].

Lantana camara is capable of growing on poor soils in full sunlight or semi-shade. It can survive fire by regenerating from basal shoots [359]. *Lantana camara* only occurs at temperatures above 5°C and is susceptible to frost which kills the leaves and stems; it cannot tolerate permanently wet soils [387]. The branches are brittle and easily broken. It can reproduce vegetatively from branch fragments, aiding rapid spread [387]. It has naturalized in a range of habitats, from coastal areas to elevations of over 300 m on both the windward and drier leeward sides of most major Pacific islands.

Lantana camara is unable to compete with taller native forest tree species, although it is commonly found scrambling through the branches of taller vegetation. Once established, it quickly covers open areas forming dense thorny thickets [178]. The leaves and seeds cause photosensitivity and gastrointestinal disorders in sheep and calves [376]. Allelopathic substances are produced by shoots and roots [359]. Hybridity and polyploidy may contribute to its success [298, 356]. *Lantana camara* is apparently adapted to butterfly pollination [28], but in India it appears to be pollinated by thrips [268]. The flowers of *Lantana camara* undergo colour changes triggered by pollination [281]. It is a facultatively apomictic outbreeder [202].

The following ecological characteristics of *Lantana camara* may be suggested as reasons for its success as an invasive species:

1. bird dispersal of the fleshy drupes may result in long-distance dispersal providing new foci for invasion; *Lantana camara* is particularly well dispersed by the mynah bird (*Acridotheres tristis*) which has been widely introduced in the tropics;

2. toxicity to many mammals means that it is not prone to herbivory by large herbivores;

3. ability to reproduce easily by vegetative means;

4. ability to invade a wide range of environments;

5. introduction of alien animals to isolated islands has disturbed the native vegetation and allowed *Lantana camara* to spread, as it thrives on disturbed or mildly eroded soils and is resistant to grazing;

6. production of allelopathic substances increases competitive ability against native species;

7. flowers profusely for much of the year under favorable conditions, setting copious seed.

ROSEWARNE
LEARNING CENTRE

Control and Management

Biological control A large number of insects (at least 33 species [196]) have been tried in many of the countries where there is a serious *Lantana camara* invasion, often because it is an agricultural pest. One insect, *Calcomyza lantanae* Frick (Diptera), was introduced from Trinidad to Australia and South Africa in 1974 and 1982 respectively. It spread rapidly in Australia causing considerable damage initially, but since then has been declining except in low rainfall areas. In South Africa this insect is still expanding its range and its effects are still being evaluated. *Cremastobombycia lantanella* Busk (Lepidoptera) was introduced to Hawaii from Mexico in 1902. It is now on all the Hawaiian islands providing partial control in dry areas. *Teleonemia scrupulosa* Stal (Hemiptera) has been introduced to Australia, Hawaii and Fiji from Mexico or Brazil [196]. In Australia it caused extensive defoliation but appears to be declining. In Hawaii it causes considerable damage and provides control in dry areas. In Fiji it once prevented flower production and seed set over considerable areas but its influence has been adversely affected by wet weather and predation.

Physical control Mechanical eradication can be an effective but labor intensive and expensive method of control. The bushes need to be cleared and the roots grubbed out [376].

Prospects This case study highlights the importance of bibliography, taxonomy and autecology in the control of widespread invasive plants [375]. The need for a taxonomic review of the *Lantana camara* complex cannot be overstated, since the exact type of *Lantana camara* seems to be significant in determining its susceptibility to pests and diseases. Control experience in agricultural ecosystems needs to be applied to *Lantana camara* in natural ecosystems.

Melaleuca quinquenervia (Cav.) Blake {*M.leucadendron* (L.) L., *Metrosideros quinquenervia* Cav.} (Myrtaceae)

Melaleuca, cajeput (Australia), punktree (Florida)

Description and Distribution

Habit Slender upright tree with papery bark reaching 12–25 m in height.

Leaves 70 × 5–18 mm, lanceolate to oblanceolate with 5 longitudinal veins, 3 of which are usually quite prominent.

Flowers white, in cylindrical spikes up to 5 cm long, borne in the axils on the current season's growth with further growth and leaves appearing beyond the flowers; stamens conspicuous.

Figure 4.8 *Melaleuca quinquenervia*

Fruit woody, capsule 3-celled, containing approximately 250 seeds, serotinous.

Seeds minute and unwinged (34 000 seeds per gram); dispersed by wind or water [116, 296].

Invasive category 4.5.

Region of origin Australasia – eastern Australia, Papua New Guinea and New Caledonia [115]. In its native habitat *Melaleuca quinquenervia* forms single species stands which burn regularly [115]. It is a common tree around the margins of lagoons and swamps along the coast northwards from New South Wales to Queensland [116].

Native climate subtrop. moist–wet, trop. dry, ranging from high humidity all year round to seasonally dry for six months of the year.

Regions where introduced North America – Florida [21, 115, 296] (invasive). It occurs in the following major natural areas of southern Florida [296]: (1) the Atlantic coastal ridge and eastern flatlands; (2) the Everglades; (3) the big Cypress swamp; and (4) the western flatlands.

Climate where invading subtrop. moist, characterized by high humidity for about six months of the year (including summer), with the rest of the year wet or dry.

Melaleuca quinquenervia has a unique combination of adaptations to disturbance, fire and flooding which has allowed a dramatic invasion of disturbed wetlands in Florida, where the native species are not adapted to such high levels of disturbance. It was first introduced into Florida in 1906 by a forester [21] and shortly afterwards began to invade wet prairies and marshes. Seeds of *Melaleuca quinquenervia* were scattered from a plane in 1936 with the aim of reforesting the Everglades.

Melaleuca quinquenervia readily invades depressions in drier pine flatwoods [296], wet pine flatwoods, the herbaceous perimeter frequently found around pond cypress swamps, the transition zone between pine forest and cypress swamps and shallow pond cypress swamps that have been burned. *Melaleuca quinquenervia* appears to be displacing native species such as pond cypress, *Taxodium ascendens*, in the zone between pine and cypress forests [115]. When *Melaleuca quinquenervia* invades wet prairies or marsh systems the species diversity decreases by 60–80% [21]. It is capable of invading relatively undisturbed areas, although favored by fire and disturbance. When colonizing new areas it increases rapidly, from 5% to 95% infestation in about 25 years [220].

Several factors, including soil moisture, light, fire, soil type and competition interact to influence seed germination and survival of *Melaleuca quinquenervia*, determining which areas are most susceptible to colonization by this species. Huge numbers of *Melaleuca quinquenervia* seeds are released, usually following a late dry season fire. Initial establishment, although greatly influenced by fire, is ultimately controlled by the water regime [296], that is when and for how long critical moisture requirements are met. Timing of seed release is crucial. Seedlings that germinate either before a site becomes flooded or which germinate immediately after flood water recedes, have the best chance of surviving the next dry season. Successful establishment depends on adequate growth during the wet season to ensure survival during the dry season. Soils that remain moist to saturated, but rarely submerged during the four to six months wet season, are ideal for establishment. Throughout its native range, *Melaleuca quinquenervia* is reported to grow on sandy soils and, in Florida, acid sandy soils appear to be favored for its germination and growth.

Melaleuca quinquenervia is almost perfectly adapted to fire. The thick, spongy bark insulates the cambium and the outer layers are flaky and burn vigorously. This conducts flame into the canopy, igniting the oil-laden foliage. The leaves and branches are killed, but dormant lateral buds on the trunk germinate within weeks. This prolific resprouting greatly increases the surface area of small branches and therefore the tree's reproductive potential. Furthermore, it can flower within weeks after a fire. Each serotinous capsule on a *Melaleuca quinquenervia* tree contains about 250 minute seeds which are released after fire or frost or any event which severs the vascular connections to the fruit. After fire the tree may release millions of seeds, which are dispersed short distances by wind and water [115].

Natural communities into which *Melaleuca quinquenervia* invades, such as pine and cypress forests, are maintained by fire. In some cases, *Melaleuca quinquenervia* appears to pre-empt sites where the native vegetation would normally regenerate following fire. It accomplishes this by producing seed rapidly after fire. Once established it forms a dense canopy, shading out or preventing the establishment of seedlings of other species, resulting in a *Melaleuca*-dominated community maintained by fire. It tolerates a broad range of site conditions, growing in places subject to extended flooding, under conditions of moderate drought and also under conditions of moderate salinity [115]. Under flooded conditions, *Melaleuca quinquenervia* produces a fibrous sheath of 'water roots' that clothe the base of the trunk up to the high water level. An allelopathic influence of this species on pine seedlings has also been demonstrated [296]. *Melaleuca quinquenervia* is intolerant of frost [452] and this may limit its spread northwards in Florida.

The following ecological features of *Melaleuca quinquenervia* may be suggested as reasons for its success as an invasive species:

1. widespread planting and dispersal of seed of *Melaleuca quinquenervia* for reforestation of the Everglades;
2. fire adaptation;
3. prolific seed production;
4. production of allelopathic substances;
5. toleration of extended flooding, moderate drought and some salinity;
6. ability to flower and produce seed soon after fire.

Control and Management

Physical and chemical Melaleuca quinquenervia control is complicated by the fact that death of the aerial portion of the tree results in both seed release and sprouting. Present control efforts use mechanical cutting, followed by application of herbicides [296], and take advantage of present knowledge of its ecology and reproductive biology. Fire and herbicides may be applied at critical stages in its life cycle. For example, treatment of seed trees with herbicide following frost reduces resprouting. A late wet season or early dry season prescribed burn puts the seed on the ground at an unsuitable time.

Prospects Melaleuca quinquenervia is expanding rapidly in southern Florida and threatening to alter the structure and composition of the Everglades. Wetlands are a diminishing habitat worldwide and extra care should be taken in introducing this species to other tropical wetland areas. *Melaleuca quinquenervia* may be considered in the future by foresters for commercial introduction in various parts of the world [43], but should not be introduced without a thorough environmental impact assessment.

Mimosa pigra L. {M. *pellita* Humb. & Bonpl. ex Willd., M. *asperata* sensu Bentham} (Leguminosae)

Giant sensitive plant, zaraz, dormilona

Description and Distribution

Habit Shrub, height to 6 m, stems armed with broad based prickles up to 7 mm long.

Leaves bipinnate, sensitive to touch. Straight, erect or forward pointing, prickle at the junction of each of the 6–14 pairs of pinnae and sometimes with stouter spreading or deflexed prickles between the pairs. Leaflets 20–42 pairs per pinna, linear – oblong, 3–8 (–12.5) mm long, 0.5–1.25 (–2) mm wide, venation nearly parallel with midrib, margins often bearing minute bristles.

Inflorescence of tight, subglobose pendunculate heads 1 cm in diameter, each head containing *c.* 100 flowers, produced 1–2(–3) together in the upper axils.

Flowers mauve or pink, calyx minute, lacinate, 0.75–1 mm long; corolla about 2.25–3 mm long; stamens 8.

Pods clustered, brown, densely bristly all over, breaking transversely into about 21 (14–26) partially dehiscent segments, each containing a seed, the pod sutures persisting as an empty frame.

Seeds light brown to brown or olive green, oblong, light, dispersed by water and floating for an indefinite period [51, 53, 234]. The *Mimosa pigra* group comprises a complex of six tropical American species [26]; *Mimosa pigra* being the conserved name for the widespread weed.

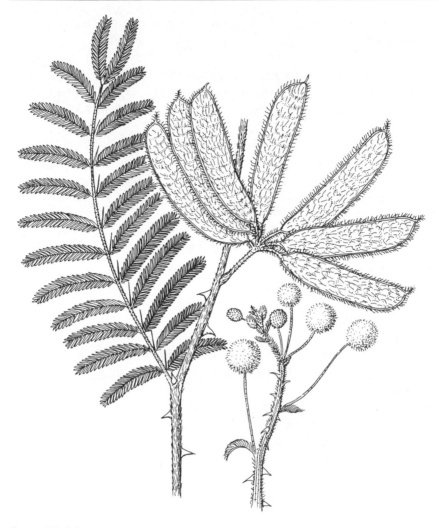

Figure 4.9 *Mimosa pigra*

Invasive Category 4.5.

Region of Origin South and Central America. *Mimosa pigra* is thought to have originated in tropical America and is now widespread in the tropics [234]. Bentham noted in 1875 [37] that is was widely found by early explorers in tropical Africa and the Mascarene Islands, yet was unlikely to represent a relict of some primitive flora as it had not diverged into specifically African varieties and was present in the form most commonly found in America [234]. The early widespread distribution in Africa has not yet been adequately explained, and indeed some people consider *Mimosa pigra* to be native to Africa as well as tropical America [230].

Native climate trop. dry, characterized by a dry period for four months and very high humidity for the rest of the year.

Regions where introduced Australasia – Australia (Northern Territory) (invasive) [51, 232, 234]; S. Asia – Thailand (invasive/ruderal) [234]; Central America – Costa Rica (naturalized) [190]; Africa – Zambia (Kafue flats) (invasive).

Climate where invading trop. dry. *Mimosa pigra* favors a wet/dry tropical climate with a high summer rainfall and relatively pronounced drought during the winter months [234]. Except in permanently wet areas, it is not likely to be a problem in regions with less than 750 mm annual rainfall [272].

Mimosa pigra is a pantropical weed which poses the most serious of all invasive threats to tropical wetlands. Where native, *Mimosa pigra* occurs in cultivated clearings, cocoa plantations, swampland and heavily disturbed land by rivers [229], and when introduced it also favors moist situations such as floodplains and river banks, on soils ranging from cracking clays through sandy soils to coarse siliceous river sand. In northern Australia, *Mimosa pigra* invades sedgeland and grassland in open floodplains particularly where water buffalo (*Bubalus arnee*) or fires have removed the vegetation [234]. It invades the paperbark (*Melaleuca*) swamp forests fringing floodplains, forming a dense understorey and shading out native tree seedlings. *Mimosa pigra* also invades billabongs (seasonally dry river beds), leaving only small remnants of open water at the centre.

Mimosa pigra was introduced to the Darwin Botanic Gardens prior to 1891, probably as a botanical curiosity because of its sensitive leaves [273]. At first it remained at low densities in the Darwin area, occasionally causing a problem, and was noticed upstream from Adelaide River township in 1952. By 1968, it had spread downstream on the Adelaide River to the Marrakai crossing and by 1975 had reached the Arnhem Highway bridge. The population subsequently increased dramatically until by 1981 much of the Adelaide River floodplain was covered by practically single-species stands [234]. It now poses a huge conservation problem in Australia where a largely intact natural landscape is being completely altered [51]. *Mimosa pigra* is invading these fertile wetlands with little human help. It has been estimated that 450 km^2 of floodplain and swamp forest have been covered by dense monospecific stands of this species.

Mimosa pigra thickets contain fewer birds and lizards, less herbaceous vegetation, and fewer tree seedlings than the native vegetation [51]. It is probable that the magpie goose (*Anseranas semipalmata*), which once had a range extending as far south as New South Wales, but now depends on the wetlands of northern Australia for its survival, is endangered by the spread of this invasive plant, since it requires dense stands of native sedges for nesting and food [234]. Kakadu National Park, a World Heritage site in northern Australia, is under serious threat from *Mimosa pigra*. Thousands of visitors come to the park every year to see the abundant bird life of the wetlands, thus the area is important in economic as well as conservation terms. The paperbark forest, which is being invaded by *Mimosa pigra* [51], provides the main rookery sites for the sacred ibis (*Threskiornis aethiopica*), royal spoonbill (*Platalea regia*) and little pied cormorant (*Phalacrocorax melanoleucos*), as well as the main nesting sites for most of the raptors in the area. Large groups of flying-foxes (*Pteropus alecto* and *P. scapulatus*) roost and feed in these forests for much of the year, which is important as these animals are major pollinators and seed dispersers for trees throughout northern Australia.

In Thailand *Mimosa pigra* is considered to be a serious weed, particularly in irrigation systems. It was introduced to Thailand in 1943 as a green manure and cover crop [234]. In Zambia *Mimosa pigra* is invading the wetland area of Kafue flats, which is of considerable conservation importance.

Beneath the impenetrable thickets of *Mimosa pigra* a dense carpet of seedlings emerges at the start of the dry season [232]. There is considerable mortality of seedlings, probably from drought rather than shade or competition from other seedlings. Under ideal conditions plants begin to flower six to eight months after germinating. Although pollinated by bees where native, the prolific seed production observed in isolated plants indicates that it is self-compatible [234]. Seed production is copious, estimated at 9103 seeds per m^2 per year in a typical mature stand [231]. The seed pods are covered with bristles that help them float and assist in dispersal by rivers. *Mimosa pigra* has a rapid growth rate and, under favorable conditions, it can grow at about 1 cm per day [232]. Development from flower bud to seed takes about five weeks [234].

In seasonally moist sites, mature plants survive the dry season (which may last from May to December in the Australian Northern Territory savanna zone) by steadily losing leaves until around August, when 40–50% have fallen [234]. In permanently moist sites, such as river banks, growth and flowering continues almost all year round. *Mimosa pigra* also survives the dry season as seeds buried in the soil [233]. The seed-bank densities at some sites in northern Australia average over 12 000 m^2. Seedlings of *Mimosa pigra* are susceptible to competition from grasses and its success was probably facilitated initially by the overgrazing of floodplains by massive herds of feral water buffalo in the mid to late 1970s. However, *Mimosa pigra* is also capable of invading relatively undisturbed sites [51].

The following ecological characteristics of *Mimosa pigra* may be suggested as reasons for its success as an invasive species:

1. prolific seed production;
2. autogamy, if it occurs, allowing an isolated individual in a new site to reproduce without being dependent on the presence of other plants of the same species for outbreeding and also eliminating any possible reliance on the presence of a suitable pollinator;

3. large seed-bank which makes control difficult and allows the species to survive adverse weather conditions as seed;

4. growth into dense monospecific stands, suppressing the growth of the native vegetation which is not able to survive the low light conditions and reducing intraspecific competition;

5. early age of reproductive maturity in favorable conditions;

6. dispersal by water resulting in long-distance dispersal downstream;

7. rapid growth rate.

Control and Management

Chemical control Mimosa pigra is susceptible to a number of herbicides [234].

Biological control For long-term control, biological methods are probably the most cost-effective considering the extent and ecology of this species. Palatibility to higher animals is low but, in its native range, it is attacked by more than 200 species of insect herbivores and fungal pathogens [234]. The first insects introduced to Australia as controlling agents were the seed-feeding beetles *Acanthoscelides quadridentatus* and *A. puniceus* (Bruchidae) from Mexico. They were released in Australia and Thailand in 1984 and 1985 respectively, but have not attained high population densities and have had little impact on seed production of *Mimosa pigra* [448]. Two stem-boring moths, *Neurostrota gunniella* (Gracillariidae) and *Carmenta mimosa* (Sesiidae), were released in Australia in 1989; of these, *N. gunniella* established readily. The young larvae mine leaf pinnules and the older larvae tunnel in the stems, causing them to die [98]. *Carmenta mimosa* complements the action of *N. gunniella* by tunnelling stems of larger diameter. Other important insects currently being tested for their host specificities in Mexico and Australia are the seed- and flower-feeding weevils *Apion* sp., *Chalcodermus serripes*, *Sibinia fastigiata*, *S. ochreosa*, *S. pervana* and *S. seminicola*.

Two fungal pathogens, *Phloeosporella* sp. (Coelomycetes), and a rust, *Diabole cubensis* (Uredenales), severely debilitate *Mimosa pigra* in Mexico [234]. *Phloeosporella* sp. attack leaves, branches, main stems and seed pods, causing leaf fall and cankers of the stems and leading to ring barking and die-back. *Diabole cubensis* causes chlorosis in stems and leaves resulting in premature leaf fall. Both fungi are attacked by hyperparasitic fungi in their native range and it seems likely that their effects on *Mimosa pigra* could be even more damaging in Australia if they were to be introduced without their natural enemies. These fungi are under investigation in Mexico and Britain. The number of insects which feed on leaves and flowers (generally) in Northern Territory, Australia, compared with Central America (the place of origin of *Mimosa pigra*) is low. It has been suggested that leaf- and flower-feeding insects be sought in Central America as future biological control agents [118]. It is possible too that some control may be assisted by insects native to Australia. Some of these have been found on *Mimosa pigra* and two, *Mictis profana* (Hemiptera: Coreidae) and *Platymopsis humeralis* (Coleptera: Cerambycidae), have been observed to cause considerable damage.

Management and prospects Prevention of overgrazing by water buffalo and other large herbivores may limit the success of *Mimosa pigra*, as it spreads only slowly into undisturbed vegetation. While it is already a serious weed in the wetlands of northern Australia, southeast Asia and parts of Africa, many of which are of great conservation importance, it has the potential to become a serious pest in other areas. Further research into the prospects of biological control is needed, to halt its spread.

Myrica faya Ait. (Myricaceae)

Fire tree, faya (Hawaii)

Figure 4.10 *Myrica faya*

Description and Distribution

Habit Evergreen shrub or small tree, to 4–16 m, with shoots covered with peltate hairs [52].

Leaves oblanceolate, alternate, aromatic, 4–12 cm, smooth, shiny, dark green, cuneate at base, margins somewhat revolute.

Catkins usually branched, borne amongst the leaves of the current year's growth. Dioecious, but sometimes pistillate plants may have a few staminate flowers and vice versa.

Flowers male with four stamens, borne on small catkins near the branch tips; female flowers in threes, accompanied by a bract, grouped in small catkins further back from the branch tip.

Fruits small edible drupes in dense clusters, red to purple when ripe, prolific.

Invasive category 4.5.

Region of origin Oceanic Islands (Macaronesia) – The Azores: mountainous volcanic areas associated with *Erica azorica, Laurus azorica, Picconia azorica* and *Juniperus oxycedrus* [107]; Madeira: an important component of the understorey along with *Erica arborea, Clethra arborea, Ilex perado, I. canariensis* and *Juniperus oxycedrus*; Canary Islands: in forests and degraded forest scrub on the western islands, often associated with *Laurus azorica, Persea indica, Apollonias barbujana* and *Ocotea foetens* [52, 170, 224, 358].

Native climate wmtemp. dry, wmtemp. moist.

Regions where introduced Oceania – Hawaii (invasive) [224, 358, 437, 438].

Climate where invading wmtemp. moist, wmtemp. wet. Within Volcanoes National Park *Myrica faya* occurs at elevations of 666–1210 m, normally only in places with mean annual rainfall greater than 875 mm.

Myrica faya is a remarkable case of an oceanic island endemic being introduced to oceanic islands on the other side of the globe with very similar environmental conditions. However, while it is a valued constituent of protected native forest in Macaronesia, it is a pernicious forest weed in Hawaii. In the Azores *Myrica faya* is a colonist of young volcanic soils and often forms extensive stands on old lava flows [170]. It is locally common in the Canary Islands, particularly the western islands, and in Madeira is abundant in both undisturbed and secondary native forests up to 900 m elevation. *Myrica faya* grows in a type of relict warm temperate rainforest known as 'laurisilva' or laurel forest.

It was introduced to Hawaii in the late 1800s by Portuguese immigrants, presumably as an ornamental. Later, the Hawaiian Sugar Planters Association obtained seeds from a Portuguese farmer in Hawaii for reforestation [437]. *Myrica faya* has been planted in reforestation projects on the islands of Kauai, Oahu and Hawaii, but by 1937 the invasive character of this species had been recognized. It now occurs on nearly all the major Hawaiian islands and covers a total area of approximately 34 365 hectares [437]. Populations are densest in open seasonal montane forest and pastures, but it is also found in the understory of closed *Metrosideros polymorpha* forests, in forest stands damaged by volcanic ash and in open volcanic ash deposits as young as 10–12 years [401, 415]. Although *Myrica faya* often invades disturbed areas, it can compete successfully with the native vegetation in such areas [170]. It seems to be able to adapt to a wide range of habitats with soils ranging from recent thin ash over lava to deep well-developed silty clay loam soil [437]. Dense stands of *Myrica faya* prevent regeneration of native species.

Myrica faya is relatively shade-intolerant and has bird-dispersed seeds. Consequently, it is a ready colonizer of open sites with some perch trees for birds [224]. It forms a symbiotic association with a nitrogen-fixing actinomycete, *Frankia* [414]. No native nitrogen-fixing plants occur in primary rainforest in Hawaii in the early stages of succession, despite the occurrence of *Acacia koa* in the later stages. Invasion by *Myrica faya* is altering primary successional ecosystems in Hawaii by increasing the amount and availability of fixed nitrogen [415, 417]. *Myrica faya* may enhance its own survival, perhaps to the exclusion of native species, by enriching the soil with nitrogen [359]. Young volcanic soils have characteristically low levels of nitrates and the native plants are adapted to survive in these conditions. As susceptibility to invasion in Hawaii is apparently dependent in part on soil fertility, other alien species which have previously been confined to the richer soils may now be able to invade areas where *Myrica faya* has enriched the soil with nitrogen [401], although this has not yet occurred [293].

Myrica faya forms a dense, interlocking canopy with little or no understory due to heavy shading and possibly the production of allelopathic substances. The microhabitat under *Metrosideros collina* appears to favor germination and seedling development of *Myrica faya* [358]. In dry sites it seems to grow poorly, especially when mature.

Low germination rates of *Myrica faya* seeds collected in the field, contrasted with copious seed production and rapid dispersal of the species, has led to the hypothesis that scarification from bird ingestion greatly improves germination rates [437]. Many species of birds are probably involved in the seed dispersal of *Myrica faya*, including the Japanese white-eye (*Zosterops japonica*) from Asia [32], house finches (*Carpodacus mexicanus*) and 'oma'o (*Phaeornis obscurus*), the latter being only an occasional visitor to *Myrica*, though, when it does so, it eats large amounts of fruit [224]. Feral pigs also disperse the seeds.

The following ecological characteristics of *Myrica faya* may be suggested as reasons for its success as an invasive species:

1. prolific seed production;
2. long-distance dispersal of seeds by birds;
3. symbiotic association with nitrogen-fixing organism;
4. possibly production of allelopathic substances which may inhibit potential competitors;
5. formation of a dense canopy under which the native species are unable to regenerate.

Control and Management

Chemical control To date, herbicides have been the main method of control.

Biological control In 1955 an expedition visited the native habitat of *Myrica faya* in the Azores, Maderia and the Canary Islands to study its natural pests and diseases. A number of insects and diseases that appeared initially promising were later rejected either because of lack of host specificity or because they did not thrive in Hawaii. Another more recent search for control agents in the native habitat concluded that pests and diseases are not limiting growth, reproduction and distribution of *Myrica faya* [170]. Research is still underway with several organisms being investigated, including the fungus *Ramularia destructiva*, in the hope of finding a suitable biological control agent.

Management Since feral alien birds and other animals are implicated as dispersal agents for *Myrica faya* seeds, they should be controlled as far as possible to limit further spread.

Prospects Myrica faya may have serious long-term consequences for the nutrient-poor ecosystems in Hawaii in which it is invading. With the failure of biological control, it would be desirable to develop an integrated control program using physical control, herbicides and ecosystem management.

Passiflora mollissima (H B K.) Bailey {*P.tomentosa* Lam., *Murucuju mollissima* Spreng.} (Passifloraceae)

Banana poka (Hawaii), banana passion fruit (Australia and New Zealand), curuba, tintin, tumbo, trompos (South America), granadilla cimarrona (Mexico).

Figure 4.11   *Passiflora mollissima*

Description and Distribution

Habit Woody climber to 20 m or more, shoots densely covered with white or yellowish hairs.

Leaves three-lobed, lobes lanceolate to ovate, minutely glandular-toothed, leathery, lower surface usually densely hairy, upper surface usually hairless; stipules not persistent, somewhat kidney-shaped; petioles channeled, 1–7 cm long, with 4–9 (rarely 0) obscure, sessile to subsessile, glands.

Flowers solitary in leaf axils, pendant; epicalyx of 3 ovate bracts, 3–5 cm long, margins entire; hypanthium tubular, 5–8 × 1cm, dilated at the base, olive green and occasionally red-tinged on outer surface, white within.

Fruit elliptic to ovate, yellow at maturity with a soft downy (rarely hairless) leathery pericarp.

Seeds broadly obovate, dark brown at maturity, 50–200 per fruit; aril fleshy, translucent, orange.

Taxonomy Passiflora mollissima (as now recognized) is a morphologically variable species and may be a hybrid between certain original, less variable species, (such as *P. mollissima* in a restricted taxonomic sense and another, unknown species of *Passiflora*) [221, 222].

Invasive category 5.

Region of origin South America – eastern Cordillera of the Andes of Colombia, southeastern Andean slopes of Peru and western slopes of the Bolivian and Venezuelan Andes [203].

Native climate temp. moist–wet, wmtemp. moist–wet.

Regions where introduced Oceania – Hawaii (invasive), in a variety of habitats including both open and closed forests of *Acacia koa* and *Metrosideros collina*, mixed native species associations and tree fern (*Cibotium*) forests [221–223]; Africa – South Africa (naturalized) [245]; Australasia – New Zealand (naturalized) [428, 445].

Climate where invading Hawaii: temp. moist–wet, wmtemp. moist–wet [222]; South Africa: wmtemp. dry. Knysna Forest, where it is found in South Africa, has a climate which is fairly humid all year round with little in the way of a dry period and no frost.

Passiflora mollissima is at first sight an innocuous gardener's plant, spread for ornament and fruit and apparently modified by hybridization. However, in Hawaii it has become a destroyer of forests. It grows wild in the Andean upper montane forest (known as 'ceja de la montaña') above 2000 m, a forest type composed of evergreen woody vegetation with abundant epiphytic ferns, orchids, mosses and bromeliads, and with a cool, moist, foggy climate [222]. *Passiflora mollissima* is extensively cultivated in the Andean highlands from Venezuela to Bolivia and has been introduced to many subtropical and tropical mountainous areas both as an ornamental and for its fruit. It was first reported in Hawaii in 1921, probably planted in gardens from which it then spread. It is now proliferating in mid to high elevation forests, both disturbed and undisturbed, on the islands of Hawaii and Kauai. The total area covered by a continuous distribution of *Passiflora mollissima* was over 190 km^2 in 1983 [425] and it has successfully invaded areas of diverse climate and vegetation. On the island of Hawaii it can be found from 300 to 2500 m elevation, in habitats ranging from dry lava flows with sparse open scrub to montane rainforests and pastures [222]. Dense curtains of the vine extend to the ground from canopy branches, sometimes causing branches to break and toppling trees during storms. Where the canopy has been opened, dense mats of vines also mantle the understory trees and shrubs and inhibit regeneration of the native trees [292, 351]. Endangered endemic forest birds are affected by the increase of *Passiflora mollissima*, which alters the structure and composition of the forest [425]. On Kauai, the populations are centered in Koke'e and are found in both open and closed *Acacia* forests from 850 to 1300 m elevation.

In South Africa it was only noticed in the wild as recently as 1987; it is available for sale in nurseries [245]. It appears to have naturalized in some forests in South Africa but is not yet widespread. It has been seen in Knysna Forest of the southeast Cape Province as well as in other areas. In New Zealand it occurs mainly in forest plantations, margins and on isolated trees and is sometimes a serious weed [428, 445].

In its native habitat of the moist Andes from 2000 to 3600 m [264], populations of *Passiflora mollissima* are sparse, with only about two to three plants per hectare; its flower and fruits are heavily predated by numerous insects [425]. In Hawaii, it is found at densities far in excess of this. *Passiflora mollissima* grows best in cool regions and can tolerate occasional frosts to −2°C [222], although it occurs in Hawaii under a broad range of environmental conditions and on several types of soils, from ash to weathered basalt [425]. The relatively shade-tolerant seedlings (there is usually a large seedling bank resulting from the continuous and prolific seed rain) grow rapidly in full sun. *Passiflora mollissima* can invade closed forests through gap-phase replacement involving its rapid growth in gaps caused by fallen trees; it forms a dense tangle of vegetation which smothers the undergrowth. Individuals reach reproductive maturity at an early age and mortality is low after establishment: the life span may exceed 20 years [222].

Flowers can be found during all months of the year and fruit is copiously produced. The abundant fruit set observed in Hawaii seems to be due to a mixture of spontaneous self-pollination and pollination by alien insects. The newly opened flowers have exposed stamens, favorable to cross-pollination by insects; if cross-pollination does not occur, each flower later pollinates itself through movement of the stigmas to touch the stamens. Where native, it is thought to be pollinated

Figure 4.12 In Hawaii, the weight of the South America climber banana poka, *Passiflora mollissima*, tears branches from native forest trees which are poorly adapted to climbers. Alien plants often do most damage to native communities where they invade an apparently vacant niche. (Photo: I.A.W. Macdonald)

by hummingbirds and large bees. *Passiflora mollissima* exhibits continuous growth and reproduction, but peak flowering occurs in the dry season in both Hawaii and South America [222]. The seeds are dispersed by frugivorous animals, in Hawaii principally by feral pigs (*Sus scrofa* L.). Birds aid in long-distance dispersal to uninfested areas, providing new foci for invasion. Pigs provide a fertile medium for seedling growth in the early stages of establishment [222] and their rooting activities create an environment with low competition, favorable for *Passiflora*.

The following ecological characteristics of *Passiflora mollissima* may be suggested as reasons for its success as an invasive species:

1. prolific, continuous seed production;
2. effective dispersal by feral pigs in Hawaii; long-range dispersal by birds;

3. facilitation by the 'rooting' activities of pigs, disturbing the soil and providing suitable areas for seedlings to establish and a fertile medium of pig dung in which the seedlings initially grow;

4. ability to tolerate low light levels and exploit gaps;

5. combination of auto- and allogamy;

6. relatively fast growth rates leading to early reproductive maturity.

Control and Management

Physical and chemical control Since the 1970s, several attempts by the State of Hawaii and the National Park Service at control by physical and chemical means have met with little success [425]. The extent and density of infestations make these methods uneconomical as well as ineffective. Long-distance dispersal of *Passiflora mollissima* initiates new populations in isolated or inaccessible areas and provides new foci for invasion. However, one exception is where forests of the endemic *Acacia koa* are being re-established on degraded montane forest land infested by *Passiflora mollissima*. The application of a high dose of glyphosate (6 kg/ha) prior to planting *Acacia* significantly reduced the mortality of *Acacia* by *Passiflora mollissima* after 10 years; in contrast, all *Acacia* trees were killed on untreated plots [350].

Biological control The only realistic hope for control of *Passiflora mollissima* in Hawaii is biological control [425]. *Passiflora mollissima* is attacked by many pests and diseases in its native range [222] but at present only one candidate, a moth, *Cyanotricha necyrina*, has been cleared by officials for release [263]. Studies on the potential of *Fusarium oxysporum* f. sp. *passiflorae* are in progress [361]. High host specificity is needed due to the large commercial passion fruit (*Passiflora edulis* Sims) industry on Hawaii and the potential damage which might be caused to this by more generalist control agents.

Pinus radiata D.Don {*P.insignis* Dougl. ex Loud., *P.californica* H.&A.} (Pinaceae)

Monterey pine

Description and Distribution

Habit Symmetrical tree, flat-topped at maturity, 15–25 m high, branchlets orange to dark red-brown.

Bark dark brown with narrow ridges.

Leaves in threes, deep glossy green, 8–15 cm long, slender.

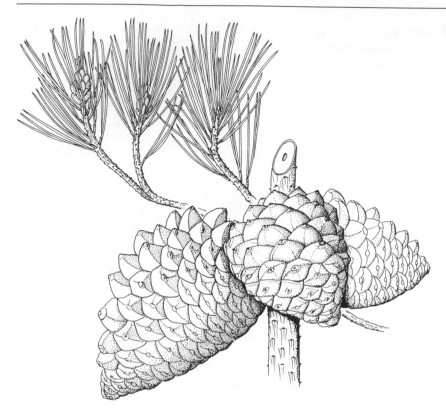

Figure 4.13   *Pinus radiata*

Cones male cones yellow, about 12 mm long; female cones asymmetrical, ovoid, 7–15 cm long, brown, shiny, bluntly pointed, lower scales on outer side thickened, armed with slender prickles that usually wear off, the cones remaining closed and persisting for years.

Seeds winged, dark, rough, 6–7 mm long, wings 12–18 mm long, dispersed by wind [276, 295].

Invasive category 4.

Region of origin North America – California: limited natural range – 4000 ha in three small areas on the Californian coast [59] and few little-known populations in Mexico (var. *binata*).

Native climate wmtemp. dry, characterized by a dry period of three to five months during the summer months and high humidity for the rest of the year.

Regions where introduced Pinus radiata has been introduced to warm temperate regions all over the world and cultivated as a timber crop. In the following regions it has spread from cultivation and is invading natural and seminatural vegetation: Australasia – Australia [68], New Zealand [445]. Africa – South Africa (southwestern Cape Province) [329].

Climate where invading wmtemp. dry (Australia, South Africa), wmtemp. moist–wet (New Zealand). In Australia it occurs in areas with no marked dry season but with maximum humidity during the winter months. In South Africa it occurs in areas characterized by a dry period lasting for two to three months in the summer and very high humidity during the rest of the year.

Pinus radiata has been the subject of an intensive selection program by foresters, who have converted the poor wild form into a straight-trunked, fast-growing tree crop which is highly invasive. In the wild it occurs on dry bluffs and slopes below 1200 m in coastal areas of California [295]. As an exotic Pinus radiata is remarkably successful, having been planted to cover nearly one million hectares of land in different parts of the world [68], which contrasts strongly with its limited natural range estimated to cover only 4000 ha [276]. Pinus radiata has been widely planted in Australia and New Zealand where it now forms the major softwood source [68, 276]. In Australia Pinus radiata is invading an open and relatively undisturbed type of dry sclerophyll Eucalyptus forest. In New Zealand it is reported to be a 'significant problem' in scrub and forest margins, shrubland, sand dunes, open land, and short and tall tussockland [445]; while in South Africa it is a major weed of the mountain fynbos [331]. Pinus radiata has been present in South Africa since 1865 but has only recently (since about 1930) been planted on a large scale [410].

In natural forests invaded by Pinus radiata in Australia, the seedlings of Pinus grow faster than the native Eucalyptus [59, 68], but the rate of Pinus radiata recruitment appears to be slow due to high seedling mortality, apparently caused by drought. The small, light, winged seeds of Pinus radiata allow for easy long-distance dispersal by wind [410]. Pinus radiata is self-compatible (although there is considerable variation in self-fertility) and thus isolated individuals can produce viable seed. Colonization is likely to be accompanied at first by an increase in inbreeding, but outbreeding will tend to be restored as population density increases. This flexible breeding system may help it to cope well with both the colonizing and the sedentary phases [25].

The invasion of fynbos by Pinus radiata is characterized by a rapid but sparse influx of initial colonizers throughout an area. This is followed, in the absence of fire, by slow and erratic establishment of seedlings around these trees, and, with fire, the recruitment of dense daughter stands. Pinus radiata is reported to produce viable seed after seven years in California, after about 10 years in Australia and after 10–12 years in New Zealand. Cones are first produced after six to seven years in South Africa but ripe cones require three to four years to dry out sufficiently to allow opening [329]. Seeds may be held in the cones for five years or longer with no loss of viability. Seeds are released from the cones in hot dry summers in South Africa when the strongest winds blow from the southeast [329].

Fire stimulates simultaneous release of large quantities of seed from the cones and creates favorable conditions for germination and establishment [269, 329]. However, *Pinus radiata* is often killed by serious fires, whereas native *Eucalyptus* species have dormant buds under the bark which resprout after fire. Regeneration of *Pinus radiata* after fire (particularly surface fires in which parent trees survive) results in dense stands which radically alter the structure and composition of natural plant communities [329]. However, as the cones vary from semiserotinous to serotinous, *Pinus radiata* can establish on sites burnt only infrequently. Native animals and birds, as well as rabbits and introduced animals, are known to damage alien pines in Australia, but the rapid growth of *Pinus radiata* soon puts it out of reach of mammalian herbivores. In one study of invasion of *Eucalyptus* forest in Australia, invasion did not begin until 20–21 years after the establishment of local plantations [68], possibly because of the elimination of rabbits by an epidemic of myxomatosis about four years before invasion commenced.

In general, the densest invasions in Australia occur on open dry sites with poor shallow soils. Wet sclerophyll forests in Australia seem to be resistant to invasion. Those dry sclerophyll forests prone to invasion are more open and this feature, coupled with the pendent leaves of some species of *Eucalyptus*, permits ample light through the canopy. Once established, *Pinus radiata* intercepts much more light than *Eucalyptus* [68] and it has been estimated that trees may persist up to 150 years [276].

The following ecological characteristics may be suggested as reasons for the success of *Pinus radiata* as an invasive species:

1. large and widespread planting as a timber crop;
2. vigorous growth when released from the burden of pests and diseases [59];
3. reproductively mature at a young age and prolific seed production;
4. degree of serotiny insuring that regeneration by seed is rapid after fire;
5. small, light, winged seeds easily dispersed long-distances by wind;
6. self-compatibility allowing isolated individuals to produce seed.

Control and Management

Biological control As *Pinus radiata* is such an economically important species and *Pinus* such an important genus, biological control methods have never been sought.

Physical control A combination of cutting followed, a few months later after the seeds have germinated, by fire, may be a method of control in habitats which are naturally adapted to fire.

Prospects Pinus radiata poses a threat to 'Mediterranean' ecosystems worldwide and foresters should be aware of the potential dangers before including it in forestry schemes. There are good prospects for experiments to determine appropriate ecological management regimes in order to minimize invasion.

Pittosporum undulatum Vent. {*Pittosporum phillyraeoides* Haw., non DC.} (Pittosporaceae)

Sweet pittosporum, mock orange, Victorian box, Victorian laurel

Figure 4.14 *Pittosporum undulatum*

Description and Distribution

Habit Slender branched shrub or tree, with smooth gray bark, 5–13 m tall.

Leaves alternate, elliptic-oblong to oblanceolate, 6–16 cm long, entire, green above, paler beneath with undulate margins.

Inflorescence terminal, 4–5 flowered, about 2 cm long, borne on the youngest branches.

Flowers white, fragrant; petals 5, recurved above; stamens 5–11 mm long, sometimes reduced to sterile rudiments; stigma slightly longer or shorter than the stamens. The flowers are usually hermaphrodite, but dimorphic flowers occur in the native area and unisexual individuals have even been found [138].

Fruit a globular dehiscent capsule, 2-valved, yellow to brown [77].

Seeds 12–22 per capsule, sticky, black or red; birds feed on the seeds after the ripe fruits have burst open [328].

Invasive category 5.

Region of origin Australasia – Australia. *Pittosporum undulatum* occurs naturally seawards of the Great Dividing Range from Brisbane to Western Port in Victoria [130], also in Tasmania. It extends inland for about 280 km in New South Wales but only 120 km inland in Victoria, where it reaches altitudes of around 400 m [130].

Native climate subtrop. moist (subtropical rainforest and wet sclerophyll forest of New South Wales), wmtemp. dry (dry sclerophyll forest of E. Victoria). Although found in a wide range of habitats, the climate throughout its range is characterized by the absence of a pronounced dry season [8,130].

Regions where introduced Australasia – Australia (south central Victoria) (invasive) [130], Norfolk I. (invasive) [328], Lord Howe I. (invasive) [314], New Zealand (naturalized) [328]; Central America – Jamaica (invasive) [136]; Africa – South Africa (invasive) [328]; Oceania – Hawaii (ruderal) [158]; Oceanic Islands – Macaronesia (Azores, Pico Island (invasive) [150], Canary Islands (naturalized) [130]), Bermuda (naturalized) [77], St Helena (naturalized).

Climate where invading trop. wet (Jamaica), with mean annual rainfall 2690 mm at 1500 m altitude [147], wettest between August and December [136]. Wmtemp.

dry (South Africa). In Jonkershoek Valley, where it is invading, there is a summer dry period, but otherwise a moist climate. In Australia it is extending westwards into areas with slightly less rainfall than in its native habitat; its spread may perhaps have been encouraged by a reduction in the frequency of fires, following human control.

Pittosporum undulatum is an example of an invasive ornamental spread initially by the network of British colonial botanic gardens. It is found sporadically in subtropical rainforest in New South Wales and in 'tall open' *Eucalyptus* forests [130] (wet sclerophyll forest, height greater than 30 m [366]) and dry sclerophyll forest in Victoria. In Australia it is invading up to 200 km outside its natural range into coastal or subcoastal areas at low elevations covered by relatively undisturbed *Eucalyptus* forest or scrub. Invasion of forests in south and west Australia may be restricted by the very dry summers, although the wet karri (*Eucalyptus diversicolor*) forests in southwest Australia may be prime candidates for invasion when the right vectors are present [130]. It is also invading Norfolk and Lord Howe Islands, which have a continually wet climate.

Pittosporum undulatum is often planted as an ornamental or hedge plant. In Jamaica, it was introduced in 1870 to the Cinchona Botanic Garden and is now invading fairly undisturbed montane sclerophyll rainforest, containing many endemic species [147]. In South Africa it was introduced in 1901 to the Tokai Arboretum [328] and is now invading mountain fynbos with vegetation dominated by *Olea europaea* ssp. *africana*, *Kiggelaria africana*, *Rhus angustifolia* and *Maytenus oleoides*, as well as undisturbed patches of riparian forest [328]. Introduced to Hawaii in 1875, probably as a timber crop, it now occurs in moist to wet regions along roadsides, in forests and as a weed of pasture and rangelands [158]. In the Azores it has spread widely in lowland cloud forest, which contains many endemic species [150].

Pittosporum undulatum flowers when only four or five years old. In Jamaica it flowers and sets fruit earlier in the year than most native trees [136] and the lack of competitors for pollinators may be an advantage. Early emergence may also give seedlings a competitive advantage. The flowers appear to be suited to nonspecialized insect pollinators, as are the flowers of most tree species in the Blue Mountains of Jamaica [136]. Prolific quantities of sticky seeds fall directly below the crown or are eaten by, or adhere to, animals and birds. In Australia and South Africa invading *Pittosporum undulatum* initially tends to be clustered around the base of established trees [129, 328], and seedlings seem to have greater resistance to drought under shade than in the open. It can exploit high light levels but appears to have the capacity to endure shade, and is a successful gap colonizer. It often forms dense growth of tree seedlings in forest gaps, in which it can out-compete native tree species. Seedlings of *Pittosporum undulatum* in Jamaica and Australia seem to emerge after the winter rains [131, 136], which usually last for three months. Seedlings establish more easily on humus rather than on bare soil and appear to prefer sites which are less heavily shaded. The mortality rate of recently germinated seedlings appears to be considerably less in gaps [136]. Throughout the areas of undisturbed forest invaded in Jamaica, all size classes of *Pittosporum undulatum* individuals may be observed.

The shade cast by the low, very dense, canopy of *Pittosporum* dramatically reduces the amount of light that reaches the forest floor. Apical dominance is weak, hence a bushy habit develops and the crown diameter may not be much less than the height, although it is capable of relatively rapid growth. The foliage of *Pittosporum undulatum* contains many oils, resins and saponins which may be allelopathic. When tested in the laboratory, leachates from the foliage significantly inhibited the germination of several species of *Eucalyptus* such as *E. obliqua*, *E. melliodora* and *E. goniocalyx* [130]. However, no such effects, other than those expected from deep shade, have been demonstrated under canopies in the field. Litter production of *Pittosporum undulatum* is high. Soil from beneath *Pittosporum undulatum* clumps is often more fertile than that under native *Eucalyptus* in Australia, the leaf litter containing higher levels of nutrients [130]. The capacity of *Pittosporum undulatum* to withstand fire is not great, as the bark is thin and resinous. If the fire burns through downwards to the mineral soil, the basal buds in the trunk are killed. However, light fires do little permanent damage and saplings (above 2 m high) will sprout vigorously.

The following ecological features of *Pittosporum undulatum* may be suggested as reasons for its success as an invasive species:

1. prolific seed production;
2. bird-dispersal results in long-distance dispersal of seeds, which may become foci of new invasions;
3. toleration of shade and exploitation of gaps;
4. dense canopy shades out ground vegetation and inhibits regeneration of native tree species, thereby reducing competition;
5. not adapted to a specific pollinator;
6. artificial suppression of fire by people in Australia, outside the native region of *Pittosporum undulatum*, and the infrequency of fire in Jamaica;
7. the litter enriches soils which may not favor plants such as sclerophyll shrubs adapted to poor soils [130];
8. the adaptable root system allows it survive in a wide range of soil types [130];
9. early age of reproductive maturity [136].

Control and Management

Physical control Seedlings can easily be hand-pulled but stumps sprout vigorously [328].

Chemical control Application of 2,4,5 T and diesel mixture to stumps cut just above ground level prevents coppicing [328].

Biological control No biological control program has been initiated to date.

Prospects Pittosporum undulatum is unusual as it appears to be invading relatively intact species-rich rainforest vegetation in Jamaica. It may become a serious pest in other areas, for example in South Africa, as it continues to be spread by gardeners. Studies of its ecology are needed to devise appropriate control strategies.

Psidium cattleianum Sabine {*P.littorale* Raddi} (Myrtaceae)
Strawberry, Chinese, purple, or pineapple guava

Description and Distribution
Habit Large shrub or small tree to 6 m; trunk smooth, pale brown; shoots terete or subterete, covered with fine, short dense hairs when young.

Leaves 4–8 × 2.4–4.5 cm, obovate, leathery, hairless, shiny, dark green above, dotted with glands beneath.

Flowers white, solitary in axils; bracteoles very small, caducous, ovate; calyx with 4–5 rounded lobes, 3–4 mm; petals *c.* 5 mm, elliptic.

Fruit 2.5–3.5 cm long, globose, reddish-purple, occasionally yellow; flesh usually purple, edible.

Seeds numerous [2, 65].

Invasive category 5.

Region of origin South America – Brazil [240]. Little is known about its ecology in its natural habitat.

Native climate trop. dry–moist (tropical moist forest).

Regions where introduced Oceania – Hawaii (invasive) [183], Tropical Polynesia (invasive); Australasia – Norfolk I. (invasive) [428]; Malagassia – Mauritius (invasive) [239, 240, 253].

Climate where invading Hawaii: wmtemp. wet, subtrop. wet, in areas at 100m–1300m in elevation with a wet aseasonal climate; Mauritius: wmtemp. moist–wet,

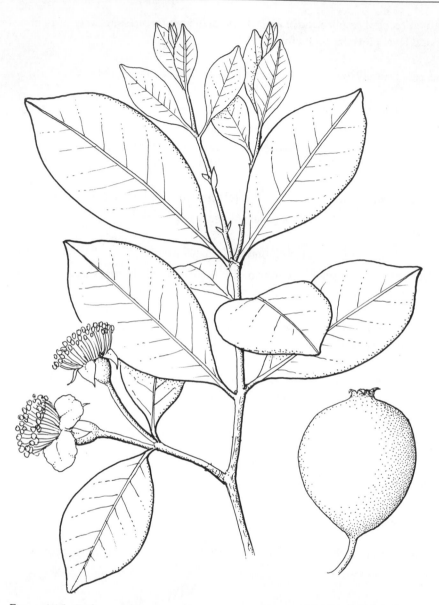

Figure 4.15 *Psidium cattleianum*

subtrop. moist–wet, relatively wet all year with maximum rainfall during the summer months and a brief (*c*. 1–2 months) dry period prior to the summer; Norfolk I.: subtrop. moist, relatively wet all year, with maximum rainfall during the winter months.

Psidium cattleianum is one of the most serious invaders of montane tropical

Figure 4.16 Relict native trees stand above a forest badly invaded by *Psidium cattleianum* on Mauritius. (Photo: Quentin Cronk)

rainforest on islands, and its effect on the native vegetation of Mauritius has been catastrophic. Surprisingly there have been no studies of its ecology in its native habitat. It is now a familiar cultivated plant throughout the tropics. *Psidium cattleianum* was introduced to Hawaii in 1821 for its fruit, but it soon escaped [361]. It is now invading a variety of native ecosystems, principally rainforest, where it is considered the worst pest [359]. It apparently invades intact and undisturbed rainforest, but also occurs along roadsides and in other disturbed habitats [183]. In Mauritius it was introduced around 1822 and is now invading upland evergreen wet forest, lower montane moist and wet forest, including areas with low disturbance [239, 240]. It has spread to nearly all areas on Norfolk Island.

Psidium cattleianum is a thicket-forming tree with rapid growth which shades out all other plants. It may occur in large numbers within dense forest, indicating that it is shade-tolerant. It can produce dense populations of suckers and seedlings, with dense mats of surface feeder roots, even in thickets with low light levels. It has broad environmental tolerances.

It flowers nearly all year round, although the peak of reproductive activity in Hawaii occurs from June to October. The prolifically produced seeds germinate rapidly under a wide range of environmental conditions. Feral pigs and non-native birds disperse the seeds. *Psidium cattleianum* seedlings occur on the same substrates as native woody species, such as bryophyte clumps, usually in undisturbed sites. Passage of the seeds through the guts of feral pigs has been found to have little effect on germination success, but does appear to shorten the time required for germination. Seedling establishment in the field seems to be independent of soil disturbance, such as that resulting from the rooting activity of pigs. However, dung piles of feral pigs may provide the same sort of protection from desiccation as bryophyte covered substrates. High densities of *Psidium cattleianum* seeds have been found in pig droppings [183].

Psidium cattleianum reproduces by seed and suckers, and the clonal offspring appear to have higher rates of growth and survival than the seedlings [183]. Native tree seedlings are often suppressed by litter from the canopy trees, but *Psidium cattleianum* can send up vigorous vegetative shoots. Both in Hawaii and Mauritius [183, 240] there are red and yellow fruited forms.

The following ecological characteristics of *Psidium cattleianum* may be suggested as reasons for its success as an invasive species:

1. effective dispersal of seeds over moderate distances by animals;
2. sprouting response of *Psidium cattleianum* to falling leaf litter, which is an important difference between this and many of the native species in Hawaii;
3. prolific seed production all year round;
4. broad environmental tolerances, including shade tolerance;
5. rapid growth, forming dense shade-casting thickets with dense mats of surface feeder roots, preventing the regeneration of native species.

Control and Management

Chemical control Chemical treatments are being tested in Hawaii Volcanoes and Haleakala National Parks [359].

Biological control No biological control program has been established to date in Hawaii. The prospects for biological control are relatively slim as it and the common guava, *Psidium guajava*, are cultivated widely for fruit. Any biological control agent would need to be very species-specific and not damage native endemic Myrtaceous trees [361]. However, the extent and success of *Psidium cattleianum* would suggest that biological control is the only viable method.

Prospects Psidium cattleianum is threatening the unique endemic floras of Hawaii, Mauritius and Norfolk Island, as well as other islands in tropical Polynesia. Control methods devised in one area would be of great interest elsewhere.

Rhododendron ponticum L. {R.lancifolium Moench, R. speciosum Salisb.} (Ericaceae)

Rhododendron

Figure 4.17   *Rhododendron ponticum*

Description and Distribution

Habit Evergreen shrub, 2–8 m high, when mature consisting of several major axes arising from a large irregular base, shoots hairless.

Leaves spirally arranged in lax clusters, oblong – elliptic, up to 22 cm long, leathery, hairless, entire, dark green above, paler below.

Inflorescence a compact raceme, protected by leafy scales in bud.

Flowers purple magenta, spotted with brown and orange; calyx small; corolla campanulate, 5-lobed, *c.* 5 cm across; stamens 10.

Fruit a woody capsule, persisting up to three years.

Seeds 1.5 × 0.5 mm, weighing 0.066 mg, dispersed by wind.

Invasive category 4.

Taxonomy Two subspecies are described from Europe [403]: ssp. *ponticum*, which has leaves 12–18 (–25) cm long, 2.5–3.5 times as long as wide and an inflorescence axes which are more or less hairless; and ssp. *baeticum* (Boiss. & Reuter) Hand.- Mazz., which has elliptic-oblong leaves 6–12 (–16) cm long and 3–5 times as long as wide, with tomentose inflorescence axes. The plants in the British Isles resemble ssp. *ponticum* [89] but Cox and Hutchinson [82] consider that they are mostly hybrids between *R. ponticum* and *R. catawbiense* Michaux; they have been considered to be nearer to ssp. *baeticum* by some authors [354]. *Rhododendron ponticum* in Britain has certainly been altered by hybridization [31].

Region of Origin Europe – a small area in the Stranja Mountains of northwest European Turkey and bordering parts of southeast Bulgaria (ssp. *ponticum*); parts of Portugal and southern Spain (ssp. *baeticum*) [89]; N. Asia – Turkey. *Rhododendron ponticum* has its main and most continuous distribution in the region of the Black sea (ssp. *ponticum*) [31]. It also occurs in the mountains of Lebanon and Syria (sometimes distinguished as ssp. *brachycarpum*).

Native climate Turkey: wmtemp. dry, temp. moist, seasonal, with a dry or drought summer period lasting from three to four months. In the colder months temperatures often drop below −10° C, and humidity is high [424]. Spain and Portugal: wmtemp. dry, a seasonal climate with a summer dry period lasting three to five months but with warmer winters than in the eastern part of the range.

Regions where introduced Europe – British Isles and Ireland (invasive) [88, 123, 339, 354, 386, 404], Belgium (naturalized) and France (naturalized) [89, 403].

Climate where invading temp. moist.

Rhododendron ponticum eliminates the ground flora of temperate deciduous woodlands and threatens rare species of Atlantic bryophytes in Ireland. Ironically there is fossil evidence that it occurred naturally in Ireland before the last ice age. In the present postglacial period it has, however, remained localized in refuges in southern Europe and Turkey. South of the Black Sea it grows in mixed deciduous forests of lime, oak and chestnut, and also in forests of beech, *Fagus orientalis*, [89] associated with species such as *Ilex aquifolium*, *Prunus laurocerasus*, *Vaccinium arctostaphylos*, *Buxus sempervirens* and *Daphne pontica* [423]. Similar vegetation types are found in SE Bulgaria [402]. In SW Iberia it grows in evergreen Mediterranean forest associated with other members of the family Ericaceae, such as *Erica arborea* and *Arbutus unedo*. East of the Black Sea *Rhododendron ponticum* is an important ingredient of the rich forests of western Transcaucasia (Colchis), growing under a canopy of *Fagus orientalis*, *Picea orientalis* or *Abies nordmanniana*. It ascends above the tree line as a dwarfed form well above 1800 m altitude [31] and grows right down to sea level in the neighborhood of Batum, forming thickets up to 6 m high in association with the cherry laurel (*Prunus laurocerasus*).

In Britain, *Rhododendron ponticum* was introduced as an ornamental. It became valued as game cover in large estates, from where it has invaded many seminatural woodlands on acid soils. It has been used as a rootstock for other Rhododendrons, which, when neglected, can then revert to *Rhododendron ponticum* [354, 386]. It came to Kew in 1793 [31] and was first distributed by the nurseryman Conrad Lodiges. Early introductions were probably of ssp. *baeticum* [31], but typical *Rhododendron ponticum* soon followed. Early hybridization with *Rhododendron maximum* has given rise to many garden forms. *Rhododendron ponticum* was probably introduced to Ireland in the late eighteenth century [90], and it now can be found invading western *Quercus petraea* woodlands dominated by *Quercus petraea* and *Ilex aquifolium* on acid soils with a rich bryophyte flora [199]. It also occurs in mixed oak woods, heaths, upland acid *Nardus* grassland and occasionally on dune heaths and bogs [89]. Invasion replaces the woodland understory with single species stands of *Rhododendron*. Reduction of light, along with the accumulating litter, eliminates bryophyte, herbaceous and dwarf shrub layers. Native trees and shrubs are unable to regenerate under the dense shade cast by *Rhododendron ponticum*. It can readily invade woods in which regeneration of native trees is inhibited by overgrazing of sheep and deer.

Rhododendron ponticum reproduces mainly by seed, although there is limited vegetative spread by layering, and cut stems sprout vigorously. It flowers after about 12 years and is predominantly an outbreeder, with the flowers mainly pollinated by members of the Hymenoptera and Syrphidae (this mining-bee group are specialized pollinators). *Rhododendron ponticum* flowers most profusely in the open or under a light canopy. It is a prolific seed producer and viable seeds, which are dispersed by wind, are produced every year. Light is essential for germination, the required temperature range for which is 10–15° C [89]. Shade cast by *Rhododendron ponticum* thickets reduces both the rate and quantity of germination of the ground flora compared to shade cast by an oak or holly canopy. Germination of *Rhododendron ponticum* seeds occurs on many substrates, including peat, mor humus and brown earth, but successful establishment of seedlings does not appear to occur where there is dense ground cover of litter or vegetation. The most favored sites are patches of bare mineral soil or humus, or on rotting wood.

Large mature *Rhododendron ponticum* bushes transmit only about 2% total daylight and growth of other species underneath is precluded [89]. Root competition is also likely to be important. In waterlogged conditions, growth is very slow and accompanied by signs of mineral deficiency. Like other ericaceous plants, *Rhododendron ponticum* has endotrophic mycorrhizae. Despite its presence in the British Isles for over 200 years very few insects are yet associated with this species. The most important disease is the fungus *Pycnostysanus azaleae*, which causes bud blast. This fungus occasionally attacks young stems and leaves. In Berkshire up to 50% of buds have been observed killed but in Ireland it is of minor importance only. *Rhododendron* produces an andromedo-toxin and the leaves are unpalatable to herbivores [121]. It has few associated animals or epiphytes and invasion causes a dramatic decline in ecosystem diversity at the species level [90].

The following ecological characteristics may be suggested as reasons for its success as an invasive species:

1. prolific annual production of small light seeds of high viability, which are dispersed efficiently by the wind;

2. toleration of a wide range of temperatures, including frost;

3. unpalatibility to herbivores, both vertebrate and invertebrate;

4. high competitive ability – its dense canopy shades out native trees preventing regeneration, while thick accumulation of litter which decomposes only slowly prevents the establishment of seedlings of native species;

5. ability to sprout vigorously after being cut or to send up shoots from fallen branches or stems;

6. rootstock rarely damaged by fire since it sprouts readily from underground buds;

7. disturbance of many native woodlands by people and grazing animals, providing sites for regeneration.

Control and Management

Physical and chemical control Cut stems of *Rhododendron ponticum* resprout vigorously, so all cut stems must be treated with herbicide and seedlings must be removed to prevent rerooting adventitiously [33, 386]. Control is labor-intensive and expensive. Spray treatment of cut stems with Amcide has been shown to be effective, although the surrounding vegetation may be affected [195]. Glyphosate is commonly used in Ireland and in English nature reserves.

Management Senescence of older *Rhododendron ponticum* bushes may allow native trees to regenerate and re-establish themselves, although this is unlikely to occur if the native vegetation is disturbed in any way. Management of woodlands for a rich ground flora (*Rhododendron ponticum* prefers bare patches for seedlings) helps, but the prevalent overgrazing by sheep and deer in many woods encourages invasion.

Biological control No biological control program has been initiated, and is anyway hampered by the low number of pests of *Rhododendron ponticum*, even in its natural range.

Salvinia molesta D.Mitch. {*Salvinia auriculata* auct.} (Pteridophyta: Salviniaceae)

Water fern, kariba weed, African payal

Description and Distribution

Habit Perennial, free-floating, aquatic fern, forming dense mats with plagiotropic shoots and tightly overlapping leaves [428].

Leaves floating leaves of different sizes, elliptic, entire, folded, light or brownish-green, becoming somewhat darker near the entire margins, densely covered on upper surface by hydrophobic papillae bearing groups of 2 or 4 uniseriate hairs united at their distal ends; papillae to 3 mm long; submerged leaf greatly dissected, hanging into the water, functioning as a root [336].

Sporocarps in long straight secund chains, hairy, about 1 mm in diameter, containing mostly empty sporangia [428].

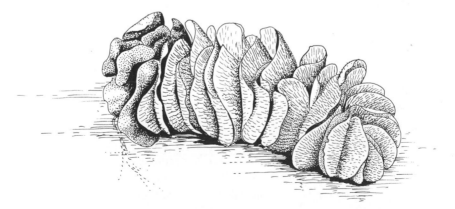

Figure 4.18 *Salvinia molesta*

Taxonomy morphologically plastic [278], it is distinguished from S. *auriculata*, S. *biloba* and S. *herzogii* by its small sporocarps bearing empty sporangia. It is sterile (pentaploid [391]) and probably of hybrid origin [277].

Invasive category 4.5.

Region of origin South America: *Salvinia molesta* has recently been discovered occurring naturally in southern Brazil [120]. It is found up to 200 km inland and at altitudes up to 500 m. *Salvinia molesta* occurs in natural lagoons, artificial dams, swamps, drains and along margins of rivers.

Native climate subtrop. dry-moist, trop. moist.

Regions where introduced Africa – Africa (invasive) [69, 247, 278]; S., E. and SE Asia – India (invasive) [389, 390], Sri Lanka (invasive) [352], Ceylon (invasive) [388]; Australasia – New Zealand (naturalized) [428], Australia (invasive) [337]; Malesia – Papua New Guinea (invasive) [278], Indonesia (invasive) [388], Singapore (invasive).

Climate where invading It is a serious pest in most tropical, subtropical and warm temperate regions of the Southern Hemisphere [389]. In the laboratory it is killed if the temperature drops below −3° C or rises above 43° C for 2–3 hours [439].

Salvinia molesta provides a good example of a case in which the control of an invasion sweeping the tropics was initially hampered by misidentification, as the species was not correctly named until 1972. It arrived in Asia via European botanical gardens [391], introduced as a botanical curiosity and aquarium plant. During the last 50 years it has spread widely through the tropics. In South Africa it has been widely distributed for aquaria and fish ponds and, although now proscribed as a noxious weed, it is still illegally grown in fish ponds and aquaria [148].

Salvinia molesta was first recorded in Australia in 1952, and first noticed as a pest in Kerala in 1956. By 1976 it had spread into many tropical and subtropical rivers and lakes in Australia and was more widespread than the other aquatic pest, *Eichhornia crassipes*. An infestation of *Salvinia molesta* leads to a decline in native plant species. In Kerala, for example, emergent hydrophytes with floating leaves (such as *Nymphaea stellata*, *Nelumbium speciosum* and *Limnanthemum cristatum*), 'suspended' hydrophytes (such as *Hydrilla verticillata*) and free-floating hydrophytes (such as *Pistia stratiotes*, *Azolla pinnata* and *Lemna minor*) are now rarely seen due to the invasion and spread of *Salvinia molesta* and *Eichhornia* [390].

In the early 1970s a few plants of *Salvinia molesta* were accidentally or intentionally introduced to a water body in the Sepik River floodplain, Papua New Guinea. By 1977 it had invaded many of the oxbow lakes associated with the river and it was continuing to spread [278]. By 1980 it covered $250 \, \text{km}^2$ of water surface [391]. *Salvinia molesta* impedes river transport, prevents fishing and the collection of sago palm in canoes (an essential source of carbohydrate in the diet of the people living near the floodplain of the Sepik River), blocks access to drinking water for people, domestic stock and wildlife, clogs irrigation and drainage canals during floods, invades rice fields and creates a habitat for hosts of human diseases such as schistosomiasis and bilharzia [148, 278, 390]. The detritus of *Salvinia molesta* infills ponds and leads to eutrophication of small water bodies.

Where it is native in Brazil its population density is generally lower than in Australia, where it is invading, presumably due to attack by natural enemies [120]. However, little is known of the ecology of *Salvinia molesta* in its native habitat. It rapidly colonizes tropical and subtropical waters which are sheltered from strong winds and currents [278], forming extensive and relatively stable mats. These mats are often colonized by sedges and other plants. By cutting off light to submerged plants, mats of *Salvinia molesta* depress oxygen concentrations and increase those of carbon dioxide and hydrogen sulphide in the waters below, which can lead to extinction of most of the benthic flora and fauna [391]. Not only does *Salvinia molesta* invasion affect the native flora, it dramatically alters the habitat for wildlife, including some types of invertebrates, birds and fish, which depend on open water. By depleting water of nutrients, it can cause a decline in fish production [389].

The doubling time in the biomass of *Salvinia molesta* may be as short as 2.2 days in summer and 40–60 days in winter [117]. It can cover lakes and slow moving rivers with mats up to 1 m thick [391], although its highest rate in terms of individual plants growth is in uncrowded conditions [342]. The rapid spread of *Salvinia molesta* depends not on any intrinsic photosynthetic advantage, compared with other plants, but on its free-floating habit and many-branched growth pattern, which enables it to remain in an active vegetative form until the water surface is covered. Intrinsic growth and net assimilation rates are generally significantly positively correlated with air temperature and NPK (nitrogen, phosphorus, potassium) contents of the plant [338]. The upper surface of the leaves is unwettable, thus helping flotation. *Salvinia molesta* is thus dispersed easily by wind and water. This species is capable of surviving severe winters and also tolerating saline water for some time [148].

Salvinia molesta exhibits three distinct growth forms (morphs) [9, 280]: (1) a delicate, fragile 'primary invading form' with long internodes and small leaves which are up to 1.5 cm in width and which float on the water surface; (2) an open water colonizing form with leaves more than about 2 cm in width, becoming deeply keeled and assuming a boat-shaped form, found on the margins of weed mats; (3) a 'mat form' with normally large floating leaves (up to 6 cm in width), found when the plants become compressed together.

The following ecological characteristics of *Salvinia molesta* may be suggested as reasons for its success as an invasive species:

1. morphological plasticity, shown by its ability to modify the shape of vegetative structures in response to environmental conditions;
2. rapid vegetative propagation;
3. potentially very high growth rates;
4. readily dispersed through pieces of the parent plant being broken off by the action of wind, waves or people (boats); long-distance dispersal can result if plant material is transported downstream and new colonies are initiated.

Control and Management

Chemical control Several chemicals have been tried that have remarkably toxic effects on *Salvinia molesta* [391]. However, the use of herbicides creates further problems of water pollution and threatens water supplies of the local people. Chemical control should therefore only be used in extreme circumstances in certain small and isolated water bodies.

Biological control Research into biological control was initiated following the appearance of the weed on Lake Kariba [391]. At the time, the plant was misidentified as *Salvinia auriculata* sensu stricto. The Commonwealth Institute for Biological Control was commissioned to find a suitable control agent and they made their collections for possible controlling agents in South America. Three insects were recommended, a moth, *Samea multiplicalis*, a grasshopper, *Paulinia acuminata*, and a beetle, apparently *Cyrtobagous singularis*. During the 1960s and 1970s, all three insects were released in several countries with varying levels of success and failure. It was not until 1970 that it was realized that the weedy *Salvinia* species was not *Salvinia auriculata* [277]. In 1978, apparently native populations of *Salvinia molesta* in southern Brazil were discovered [120] and collections of insects were made [337], including a new species, *Cyrtobagous salviniae* Calder and Sands. This beetle has successfully controlled *Salvinia molesta* in parts of Australia and Papua New Guinea, after earlier successes in Namibia [391]. It is now achieving control throughout southern Africa [69]. The snail, *Pila globosa*, has been found to feed voraciously on *Salvinia molesta* in Kerala [388]. Control has also been attempted using Khaki Campbell ducks (*Anas platyrhynchos*) imported into Kerala from Britain [389], but without much success.

Prospects Salvinia molesta is the only invasive representative of a complex of four closely related species [7, 9], distinguished by differences in the branching structure of sporocarp chains and chromosome number: S. *molesta* – 2n = 45; S. *auriculata* – 2n = 54; S. *herzogii* – 2n = 63; and S. *biloba* – unknown. Studies of the comparative ecology of these species might help in the formulation of control strategies.

Sesbania punicea (Cav.) Benth. (Leguminosae)

Coffeeweed, sesbania

Description and distribution

Habit Semideciduous shrub or small tree, up to 6 m tall [173].

Leaves 10–20 cm long, pendulous, pinnate, 10–40 pinnae per leaf; pinnae opposite, oblong and ending in pointed tips.

Inflorescence up to 25 cm long, pendulous, dense, a raceme of *c.* 14 flowers.

Flowers 2–3 cm long.

Fruit a legume, longitudinally 4-winged, oblong, 6–8 × 1 cm, short stalked, water dispersed, dehiscent, prolific.

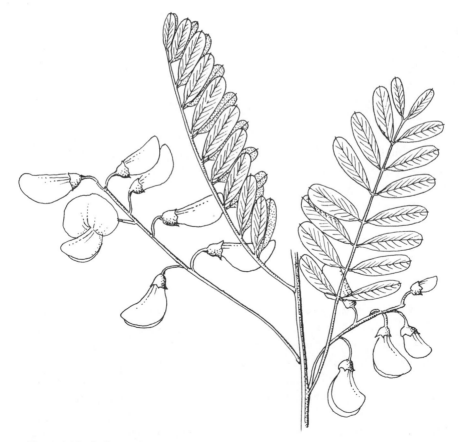

Figure 4.19 *Sesbania punicea*

Seeds 4–10 per pod [286, 315].

Invasive category 4.5.

Region of origin South America – northeast Argentina, Uruguay and southern Brazil [114, 315].

Native climate wmtemp. moist, subtrop. dry – moist.

Regions where introduced Africa – South Africa (invasive) [173, 315, 316]; North America – USA (Florida to Texas) (ruderal) [315].

Climate where invading wmtemp. dry – moist.

Sesbania punicea is another successful leguminous species invading South Africa. The nitrogen-fixing ability of these species may give them a significant advantage over the native vegetation. A native of riverside gallery forest vegetation in central South America [114], it is most common in areas frequently flooded. Initially introduced to South Africa as a garden ornamental, probably early in the present century, it now forms dense thickets along river banks, in wetlands and in damp lowland areas, posing a considerable conservation threat to native vegetation [173]. It invades various natural and seminatural vegetation types, including southern forest, eastern Cape forest, lowland fynbos and grassveld. In winter rainfall areas *Sesbania punicea* is mainly confined to major rivers, unable to survive the hot dry summers without perennial groundwater, but this is not the case in summer rainfall regions. The first mention of *Sesbania punicea* as a weed was in 1966. In the USA, it has spread from cultivation and invaded river banks, ditches and waste places [315].

Sesbania punicea seeds are readily water-dispersed, so the species poses a serious threat to riverside vegetation. *Sesbania punicea* infestations in the southwestern Cape are sometimes interspersed with other woody trees, in particular the Australian *Acacia* species and/or the native willow *Salix capensis*. Usually, however, the infestations take the form of almost impenetrable single-species stands, with dense interlocking canopies and lacking any grazing by native animals. The leaves and seeds of *Sesbania punicea* are highly poisonous to many mammals, birds and other animals [315]. The replacement of native vegetation by monotypic stands of *Sesbania punicea* affects native animals both by poisoning and by removing other food sources. The presence of *Sesbania punicea* in rivers obstructs the flow of water and this sometimes leads to erosion of water courses and widening of stream-beds, creating a perfect substrate for further lateral expansion of the infestations [173].

Sesbania punicea has a high growth rate [174], begins to set seed in its second growing season and does not usually survive for longer than 10 years [172]. Seeds germinate in the soil within about two years, but may persist longer if conditions are unfavorable for germination. Dormancy of seeds may pose a problem in weed control programs, as a source of re-infestation after clearance [139]. Crowding does not increase mortality in Sesbania punicea shrubs over two years of age but does decrease the number of seeds set, as well as the survival of seedlings and juveniles. This regulates plant density in herbivore-free populations [172].

The following ecological characteristics of Sesbania punicea may be suggested as reasons for its success as an invasive species:

1. prolific seed production;
2. adaptations for effective dispersal by water;
3. toxicity to many herbivores;
4. early reproductive maturity;
5. high growth rate;
6. seeds may remain dormant in the soil.

Control and Management

Biological control In 1982, four species of weevils, whose adults feed on the leaflets and buds of Sesbania punicea, were quarantined for screening tests in South Africa [173]. The smallest of the four weevil species, the bud-feeding apionid Trichapion lativentre, has so far proved to be the most successful biological control agent tested. Later it was discovered that T. lativentre was already present in Natal, probably inadvertently introduced by tourists from South America. It feeds on and damages the leaflets and growing points of the host [286] and has now been established over most of the range of Sesbania punicea in South Africa. Its presence also increases premature leaf abcission, reduces the growth of branches and greatly reduces the numbers of flowers, pods and seeds produced by the plants. Larval development of T. lativentre in the buds and flowers of Sesbania punicea results in a dramatic decrease in seed set, by more than 98%. Remarkably, Sesbania punicea populations are scarcely thinned by this, because of density dependent effects, although the ability of the plant to colonize new areas is severely reduced [175].

Trichapion lativentre, when used in combination with other weevil species which have been shown to be relatively effective such as Rhyssomatus marginatus and Neodiplogrammus quadrivittatus, may well result in complete control of Sesbania punicea [173]. These species and others are presently under investigation in South Africa. Models based on the population dynamics of Sesbania punicea show that a combination of a stem-boring weevil with two other weevils, which destroy the flower-buds and seeds respectively, would provide effective control. Ideally the stem-borer should be released around five years after the other two species [172].

5

Representative
invasive species

The following list is not intended to be exhaustive, but to be a representative sample of the world's invasive species to demonstrate the wide range of plant families, geographical areas, life forms and habitats associated with invasive plants. The accounts are of two types: (1) brief accounts, in which the salient facts of the plant's invasive behavior are given, together with references, and (2) listings, used in cases where detailed information is not known or not recorded, and only the basic geographical information is therefore given.

5.1 Notes on brief accounts of invasive species

The headings used at the beginning of each account are: species name, {synonyms}, (family) [242], common names.

Information given under the heading description
§Life form: Life form characteristics: herb, shrub, climber, tree, aquatic, moss; annual, biennial, perennial; deciduous, evergreen, semideciduous.
§Seed disp.: Seed dispersal mechanism: bird, mammal, wind, water, human, other.
§Seed prod.: Seed production: high, medium, low.
§Breeding syst.: Breeding system: hermaphrodite, monoecious, dioecious, seed apomixis, vegetative apomixis.
§Invasive category (scale of 0 to 5; 5 is most serious):

Category	Description
0	Not weedy or invasive
1	Minor weed of highly disturbed or cultivated land (man-made artificial landscapes)
1.5	Serious or widespread weeds of 1
2	Weeds of pastures managed for livestock, forestry plantations, or artificial waterways
2.5	Serious or widespread weeds of 2
3	Invading seminatural or natural habitats (of some conservation interest)

3.5	Serious or widespread invaders of 3
4	Invading important natural or seminatural habitats (i.e. species-rich vegetation, nature reserves, areas containing rare or endemic species)
4.5	Serious or widespread invaders of 4
5	Invasion threatening other species of plants or animals with extinction.

Regions of origin and invasion are recorded according to the following recognized areas on a practical rather than floristic basis:

1. **N. America** (United States, including Alaska and the Aleutian Is, Canada, Greenland)

2. **C. America** (= Central America and Caribbean) (Mexico including Baja California, Guatamala, Honduras, Costa Rica, Panama etc., Bahamas, Greater Antilles including Jamaica and Cuba etc., Lesser Antilles, Trinidad, Tobago)

3. **S. America** (Venezuela, the Guianas, Colombia and Ecuador south to Chile and Argentina)

4. **Australasia** (Australia, Tasmania, New Zealand, Lord Howe I., Norfolk I., Kermadecs, Chatham Is, Auckland Is and Campbell I.)

5. **Malagassia** (Madagascar, Comores, Mauritius, Réunion, Rodrigues, Seychelles, Aldabra)

6. **Africa** (North Africa and Egypt, south to the Cape of Good Hope, including Socotra and the Gulf of Guinea Is)

7. **Europe** (includes Iceland, Scandinavia, Russia to the Urals, Turkey-in-Europe and Greece to Portugal)

8. **N. Asia** (= north, central and west Asia) (Arabia, Levant including Turkey and Cyprus, Iranian Highlands including Afghanistan and Pakistan (part), Caucasus, Siberia, former Soviet Middle Asia, Chinese Central Asia including Mongolia and Tibet, former Soviet Far East including Kamchatka and Sakhalin)

9. **S. Asia** (= south, east and southeast Asia) (Pakistan (part), India, Sri Lanka, Bangladesh, Himalaya, China excluding Chinese Central Asia, Japan, Korea, Indochina including Vietnam, Burma and Thailand etc., Andaman Is, Nicobar Is)

10. **Malesia** (Peninsula Malaysia, Singapore, Sumatra, Borneo, Java, Sulawesi, Philippines, New Guinea, Solomon Is, Bismarcks etc.)

11. **Pacific** (= Oceania) (New Caledonia, south Central Pacific including Fiji and Samoa etc., Micronesia including Carolines and Marianas, Central Pacific Is including Tuvalu and Line Is, southeast Polynesia including Tahiti, Pitcairn and Marquesas etc., Hawaiian Is)

12. **Oceanic Is** (= most isolated oceanic islands) (Eastern Pacific Is: Clipperton, Cocos, Galápagos, Desventuradas, Juan Fernandez archipelago; Atlantic Is: Macaronesia, Bermuda, Fernando de Noronha and Trindade, Ascension, St Helena, Tristan da Cunha group, Gough I.; Indian Ocean Is: Laccadives, Maldives, Chagos, New Amsterdam and St Paul, Cocos (Keeling) Is, Christmas I.; Subantarctic Is: Macquarie, Kerguelen, Crozet, Marion, South Georgia)

Climatic zones. These are based only on mean annual precipitation and mean annual temperature [176] and do not take seasonality into account. They are intended as a rough guide to the climate of the areas in which the plants listed are found naturally or invade. In Table 5.1 the basic climatic information is given, including potential evapotranspiration (PET), which is a measure of the dryness of a climate taking both temperature and rainfall into account (higher values indicate greater dryness).

Table 5.1 Potential evapotranspiration values of the main climatic zones, with respect to temperature and rainfall

Climatic zone		PET	Precipitation (mm)	Temp (°C)
Temp. arid	Cool temperate arid	>2	<250	6–12
Temp. dry	Cool temperate dry	1–2	250–500	6–12
Temp. moist	Cool temperate moist	0.5–1	500–1000	6–12
Temp. wet	Cool temperate wet	<0.25	>1000	6–12
Wmtemp. arid	Warm temperate arid	>2	<500	12–18
Wmtemp. dry	Warm temperate dry	1–2	500–1000	12–18
Wmtemp. moist	Warm temperate moist	0.5–1	1000–2000	12–18
Wmtemp. wet	Warm temperate wet	<0.25	>2000	12–18
Subtrop. arid	Subtropical arid	>2	<500	18–24
Subtrop. dry	Subtropical dry	1–2	500–1000	18–24
Subtrop. moist	Subtropical moist	0.5–1	1000–2000	18–24
Subtrop. wet	Subtropical wet	<0.25	>2000	18–24
Trop. arid	Tropical arid	>2	<1000	>24
Trop. dry	Tropical dry	1–2	1000–2000	>24
Trop. moist	Tropical moist	0.5–1	2000–4000	>24
Trop. wet	Tropical wet	<0.25	>4000	>24

5.2 Species list

General References 9, 55, 57, 58, 81, 104, 110, 113, 119, 127, 143, 162, 166, 227, 239, 243, 254, 282, 314, 346, 347, 359, 361, 377, 445

Acacia cyclops A. Cunn. ex G. Don (Leguminosae)
Rooikrans

Description §Life form: shrub or shrubby tree (to 6 m), evergreen §Seed disp.: mammal (mouse, baboon), bird §Seed prod.: medium §Breeding syst.: hermaphrodite §Invasive category **4.5**.

Region of origin SW Australia. Climatic zone: wmtemp. arid, subtrop. arid. Grows scattered, rarely forming dense stands, typically on calcareous sands, with a rainfall of at least 250 mm.

Region invaded Africa (Cape Province, South Africa), N. America (California). Climatic zone: subtrop. dry–moist, wmtemp. arid–dry. It is the most widespread Australian wattle invading the lowland fynbos of Cape Province. It is also now well established in mountain fynbos and beginning to invade southern forest, eastern Cape forest and succulent karroo.

Notes Spread into natural vegetation by seed is particularly rapid after fire. It forms dense impenetrable stands with interlocking crowns, causing complete destruction of native vegetation.

Control Rooikrans rarely sprouts after intense burning or effective felling. Mechanical clearance is thus possible as long as the stems are cut low enough, preferably below the ground [48]. Biological control using seed-eating insects is under investigation in South Africa.

References 37, 48, 143, 209, 450.

Acacia dealbata Link (Leguminosae)

Blue wattle, silver wattle

Description shrub/tree

Region of origin Australasia (Australia)

Region invaded Africa (South Africa) [162]

Acacia longifolia (Andr.) Willd. (Leguminosae)
Long-leaved wattle, Sydney golden wattle

Description §Life form: shrub or tree (to 10 m), evergreen §Seed disp.: wind, water §Seed prod.: high §Breeding syst.: hermaphrodite §Invasive category **4.5**.

Region of origin Australasia (coastal areas of eastern Australia, New South Wales, Victoria and South Australia). Climatic zone: wmtemp. dry–moist, subtrop. moist. Characteristic of coastal areas, particularly sandy soils near creeks etc.

Region invaded Australasia (New Zealand), Africa (southwestern and eastern parts of Cape Province), N./W. Asia (Israel – especially the sand dunes of the coastal plain). Climatic zone: wmtemp. dry, subtrop. dry–moist. In South Africa it was originally planted on sand dunes but it has spread onto wet clay and dry sandy soils. It is one of the worst threats to mountain fynbos vegetation. It is established in lowland fynbos, southern forest, eastern cape forest and grassland vegetation.

Notes It produces large quantities of long-lived seed and regenerates rapidly after fire.

Control Mechanical clearance possible as long-leaved wattle does not sprout after cutting. The pteromalid gall wasp, *Trichilogaster acaciae longifoliae*, has been successfully used to reduce reproductive potential and vegetative growth [102] in South Africa by galling the reproductive buds.

References 46, 102, 196, 251.

Acacia mangium Willd. (Leguminosae)

Description shrub/tree

Region of origin Moluccas

Region invaded Sabah, Africa

Acacia mearnsii De Wild. {*Racosperma mearnsii* (De Wild.) Pedley} (Leguminosae)

Black wattle

Description §Life form: tree (to 20 m), evergreen §Seed disp.: mammal, water §Seed prod.: high §Breeding syst.: hermaphrodite §Invasive category **3.5**.

Region of origin Australasia (southern Queensland, southern New South Wales, Victoria, Tasmania and southeastern areas of South Australia). Climatic zone: wmtemp. dry–moist, subtrop. moist. It forms the understorey to *Eucalyptus* forest in areas with rainfall above 500 mm, typically on soils derived from sandstone, shale, granite or dolerite.

Region invaded Africa (Cape), Australasia (New Zealand), Pacific (Hawaii). Climatic zone: temp. moist, wmtemp. dry–moist, subtrop. moist. In South Africa it grows in fynbos vegetation, especially along rivers, streams and ditches, where it destroys the native vegetation and impedes water flow. In Hawaii it invades disturbed mesic habitats between 600 and 1700 m. It has been grown in the Cape since it was planted in the Cape Town Botanic Garden in the 1850s.

Notes It has a very high seed production, with a seed-bank of up to 20 000 per m^2 developing under a mature canopy. Fire stimulates germination and basal sprouting. It forms dense impenetrable thickets.

Control Mechanical control is only effective if the roots are removed or the stem is cut below the junction of the roots and stems. In South Africa, stems cut above the ground sprout and are treated with herbicide, such as 2,4,5-T in diesel oil [45]. Glyphosate controls seedlings and saplings.

References 45, 119, 161, 312, 359.

Acacia melanoxylon R.Br. (Leguminosae)
Australian blackwood, Australian ysterhout

Description §Life form: tree, evergreen §Seed disp.: bird, water §Seed prod.: high §Breeding syst.: hermaphrodite §Invasive category **3.5**.

Region of origin Australasia (South Australia, Victoria, New South Wales, southeastern Queensland). Climatic zone: subtrop. moist, wmtemp. dry–moist. Pioneer species in rainforest succession, usually on deep humic soils but tolerant.

Region invaded Africa (South Africa), S. America (Argentina), N. America (California). Climatic zone: wmtemp. dry. It is a timber tree in South Africa producing valuable wood, but it invades disturbed native forest and also fynbos.

Notes It produces abundant seed which remains dormant until fire or disturbance. It also suckers.

Control The roots must be grubbed up or herbicides applied when clearing an area to prevent resprouting from suckers [282].

Acacia nilotica (L.) Del. ssp. *indica* (Benth.) Brenan (Leguminosae)

Babul

Description shrub/tree

Region of origin Arabian peninsula, Pakistan, India, Burma

Region invaded Antigua, Barbuda, Anguilla, Ecuador, Australia (Queensland, Northern Territory), Indonesia (Baluran National Park).

Control The seed-feeding bruchid, *Bruchidius sahlbergi*, has been released in Australia [447].

Acacia saligna (Labill.) Wendl. (Leguminosae)

Description tree

Region of origin Australia

Region invaded South Africa, California [47]. See main account in Chapter 4.

Acer pseudoplatanus L. (Aceraceae)

Sycamore, great maple

Description §Life form: tree, deciduous §Seed disp.: wind §Seed prod.: high §Breeding syst.: monoecious §Invasive category **4**.

Region of origin Europe (south and central). Climatic zone: temp. moist. Common in woods, hedges, scree slopes and streamsides.

Region invading Australasia (New Zealand), Europe (Britain and Ireland), Oceanic Is (Madeira), S. America (Chile). Climatic zone: temp. moist, wmtemp. dry. It was introduced into Britain in Tudor times and invades strongly into seminatural woods and nutrient-rich waste land.

Notes It is one of the fastest growing of the European hardwood trees, tolerant of shade and exposure but preferring moist rich soils. It is mainly outbreeding, with nectar-bearing flowers; trees regularly produce c. 10 000 seeds annually.

Control Stems resprout unless treated with herbicides.

Reference 445.

Acorus calamus L. (Araceae)

Sweet-flag

Description herb

Region of origin S. Asia

Region invaded Europe

Ageratina adenophora (Spreng.) King & Robinson {Eupatorium adenophorum Spreng.} (Compositae)

Crofton weed, pamakani, white thoroughwort

Description §Life form: herb, perennial §Seed disp.: wind §Seed prod.: high §Breeding syst.: hermaphrodite §Invasive category **2.5**.

Region of origin C. America (Mexico). Climatic zone: subtrop. dry.

Region invaded S. Asia (N. India, N. Thailand, SE Asia), Australasia (subtropical E. Australia, New Zealand), Pacific Is including Hawaii, Africa (S. and W. Africa), N. America (California). Climatic zone: trop. arid–dry, subtrop. dry–moist, wmtemp. arid–moist. It invades rangelands, grasslands and woodland margins. It is unpalatable to cattle and tolerant of salinity.

Notes Agamospermous (triploid) with a high seed production, although low germination rates have been reported. It was introduced from Mexico to Britain in 1826 as an ornamental and from there was distributed around the world, escaping from cultivation in Australia around 1900 [13].

Control Easily removed by mechanical methods such as slashing. *Ageratina adenophora* is susceptible to a number of herbicides such as 2,4-D amine applied in a 0.6–0.8% solution [11]. Successful biological control has been achieved in Hawaii by the introduction of the Trypetid gallfly, *Procecidochares utilis* [11], a species which has also caused considerable mortality in parts of Australia, South Africa, New Zealand and India.

References 10–12, 14, 196.

Ageratina riparia King & Robinson {*Eupatorium riparium* Regel} (Compositae)

Description herb

Region of origin C. America

Region invaded Australia, New Zealand, Hawaii

Notes Biocontrol by a combination of the plume moth, *Oidaemaophorus beneficus*, a stem-galling fly, *Procecidochares alani*, and a pathogenic fungus, *Entyloma* sp., has been achieved in Hawaii [97].

Ailanthus altissima (Miller) Swingle {*Rhus cacodendron* Ehrh., *Albonia peregrina* Buc'hoz} (Simaroubaceae)

Tree of heaven

Description §Life form: tree, deciduous §Seed disp.: wind, water, bird §Seed prod.: high §Breeding syst.: dioecious §Invasive category **2.5**.

Region of origin E. Asia (temperate and subtropical China). Climatic zone: wmtemp. moist, subtrop. moist.

Region invaded Australia (Victoria), N. America (SE USA), C. America, S. America, Europe (France, Hungary, Greece). Climatic zone: temp. moist, wmtemp. arid–moist, subtrop. moist, trop. arid. Spreads rapidly on undisturbed grazing land, roadsides and waste places, on both clay and sandy soils.

Control Chemical control by spraying (using, for example, an 80% solution of 2,4,5-T) has proved successful in Australia [310]. Cut stumps are treated with herbicide to prevent reprouting, and for this Picloram is effective but expensive (as Tordon 50-D dilution 1 : 100).

References 310, 373.

Albizia lebbeck (L.) Benth. (Leguminosae)

East Indian walnut, kokko, siris

Description tree

Region of origin Tropical Asia

Region invaded Venezuela, Caribbean

Albizia lophantha (Willd.) Benth. (Leguminosae)

Description shrub

Region of origin W. Australia

Region invaded South Africa, California, New Zealand

Albizia procera (Roxb.) Benth. (Leguminosae)

Description tree

Region of origin NE Africa

Region invaded Venezuela

Alocasia macrorrhiza (L.) G.Don (Araceae)

Giant taro

Description herb

Region of origin Tropical Asia

Region invaded Kermadecs (Raoul)

Alternanthera philoxeroides (Mart.) Griseb. {Telanthera philoxeroides Moquin-Tandon} (Amaranthaceae)

Alligator weed

Description §Life form: herb, perennial, aquatic §Seed disp.: water, wind §Seed prod.: low §Breeding syst.: hermaphrodite §Invasive category **3.5**.

Region of origin S. America. Climatic zone: trop. arid. Widespread in freshwater habitats.

Region invaded S. Asia (India), N. America (southern USA – S. Carolina to Florida and Louisiana). Climatic zone: trop. arid, subtrop. moist. Forms dense mats in stagnant or slow-moving water.

Notes Seed set is rare; propagation is by vigorous production of below-surface shoots.

References 261, 343, 373.

Amaranthus spinosus L. (Amaranthaceae)

Description herb

Region of origin Tropics (including Vietnam)

Region invaded N. America

Ammophila arenaria (L.) Link {*A. arundinacea* Host, *Psamma arenaria* (L.) Roem. & Schult.} (Gramineae)

Marram grass

Description §Life form: herb, perennial, evergreen §Seed disp.: wind §Seed prod.: low §Breeding syst.: hermaphrodite §Invasive category **3.5**.

Region of origin Europe (coastal sand dunes of western Europe). Climatic zone: temp. moist, wmtemp. dry–moist. Dominant on foredunes, where it is often planted for stabilization, it colonizes bare sand with creeping underground stems.

Region invaded Australasia (New Zealand), N. America (California). Climatic zone: wmtemp. dry–moist, temp. wet.

Notes Vegetative reproduction predominant. It replaces native plants, altering the landscape significantly.

Control May be removed manually but care must be taken to remove all the rhizomes. Economic value for dune stabilization makes biological control unlikely.

Reference 445.

Andropogon glomeratus (Walt.) B.S.P. {*Schizachyrium condensatum* Nees} (Gramineae)

Bush beardgrass

Description herb

Region of origin USA, Mexico

Region invaded Hawaii

Andropogon virginicus L. (Gramineae)

Description herb

Region of origin SE USA

Region invaded Hawaii, Australia [140]. See main account in Chapter 4.

Anemone hupehensis (Lem. & Lem.f.) Lem. & Lem.f (Ranunculaceae)

Hupeh anemone

Description herb

Region of origin China

Region invaded Hawaii

Anredera cordifolia (Ten.) Steenis (Basellaceae)

Madeira vine, mignonette vine

Description climber

Region of origin Subtropical South America

Region invaded Australia (New South Wales)

Notes Tree-smotherer in rainforests with large underground tuber and clusters of aerial tubers.

Anthoxanthum odoratum L. (Gramineae)

Sweet vernal grass

Description herb

Region of origin Eurasia

Region invaded Chile, Hawaii

Antigonon leptopus H. & A. (Polygonaceae)

Coral vine, corallita

Description climber

Region of origin Mexico

Region invaded Guam

Ardisia crenata Sims (Myrsinaceae)

Description shrub

Region of origin NE India – Japan

Region invaded Mauritius, Réunion

Ardisia elliptica Thunb. {*A. solanacea* Roxb.} (Myrsinaceae)

Description tree

Region of origin S. Asia

Region invaded Hawaii

Ardisia humilis Vahl (Myrsinaceae)

Description climber

Region of origin Tropical Himalayas

Region invaded Cook Is

Aronia x prunifolia (Marshall) Rehder (Rosaceae)

Chokeberry

Description shrub

Region of origin hybrid

Region invaded Netherlands

Aster subulatus Michx (Compositae)

Description herb

Region of origin N. America

Region invaded Israel, Saudi Arabia

Baccharis halimifolia L. (Compositae)

Tree groundsel

Description dioecious shrub

Region of origin Eastern N. America

Region invaded Australia

Berberis darwinii Hook. (Berberidaceae)

Darwin's barberry

Description §Life form: shrub (to 4 m), evergreen §Seed disp.: mammal, bird. §Seed prod.: low §Breeding syst.: hermaphrodite §Invasive category 3.

Region of origin S. America (Southern Chile, Patagonia). Climatic zone: temp. arid–wet. Temperate forests dominated by *Saxegothaea* and *Nothofagus* at 0–500 m altitude.

Region invaded Australasia (New Zealand – Canterbury to Dunedin and the

Foveaux Strait). Climatic zone: temp. dry–wet. Remnant forest stands, scrub, along forest and plantation margins, roadsides. Locally common in Wellington and Wairarapa.

Notes It can invade undisturbed mature secondary woodland dominated by native species. Many tree species appear to be relatively unaffected, but *Kunzea ericoides* (with light-demanding seedlings) suffers, apparently from competition for seedling regeneration sites.

References [3, 322, 428, 445].

Boehmeria macrophylla D.Don (Urticaceae)

False nettle

Description herb

Region of origin subtrop. Himalayas and W. China

Region invaded Réunion

Brachiaria mutica (Forssk.) Stapf (Gramineae)

Description herb

Region of origin Tropical Africa and Brazil (wetlands)

Region invaded Hawaii, Australia (Northern Territory)

Bromus tectorum L. (Gramineae)

Downy brome, downy chess, cheatgrass

Description §Life form: herb, annual §Seed disp.: wind §Breeding syst.: hermaphrodite §Invasive category **2.5**.

Region of origin Europe, N. Asia. Herbivore adapted grass of the arid Eurasian steppes. Climatic zone: wmtemp. arid–dry.

Region invaded N. America., E. Asia (Japan), Oceanic Is (Tenerife). Climatic zone: wmtemp. arid–dry. In N. America it has replaced native colonizers such as *Festuca octoflora*, *F. microstachys* and *Bromus carinatus* in a variety of grassland types and along roadsides.

Figure 5.1 Invasive paper mulberry, *Broussonetia papyrifera*, a native of East Asia, growing over abandoned agricultural machinery, Budongo Forest, Uganda. (Photo: Doug Shiel)

Notes Cleistogamous and self-fertile, it is adapted to disturbance (trampling and grazing by large mammals). It behaves as a winter annual, surviving summer drought as seed.

References [105, 185, 257, 258].

Broussonetia papyrifera (L.) Vent. (Moraceae)
Paper mulberry

Description tree

Region of origin Tahiti

Region invaded N. America (SE USA), S. America (Peru), Africa (Ghana, Uganda – especially Budongo Forest Reserve), India

Caesalpinia decapetala (Roth.) Alston (Leguminosae)

Mysore thorn

Description shrub

Region of origin India

Region invaded Kermadecs (Raoul), South Africa (Transvaal) [162]

Calluna vulgaris L. (Ericaceae)

Heather, ling

Description shrub

Region of origin Europe

Region invaded New Zealand

Calotropis procera (Aiton) Aiton f. (Asclepiadaceae)

Apple of Sodom

Description shrub

Region of origin Old World tropics

Region invaded Pantropical Australia

Campylopus introflexus (Hedw.) Brid. (Dicranales – Bryophyta)

Description §Life form: moss §Spore disp.: wind, water §Breeding syst.: dioecious §Invasive category 3.

Region of origin S. America, Africa, Australia, Pacific. Climatic zone: temp. moist, wmtemp. moist.

Region invaded Europe. Climatic zone: temp. moist, wmtemp. moist. Invades and dominates dune bryophyte communities.

References [326].

Carduus nutans L. (Compositae)

Musk thistle

Description herb

Region of origin Europe

Region invaded Canadian and New Zealand pastures (agricultural ecosystems only, characteristic of overgrazed sward)

Notes Biocontrol by receptacle weevil, *Rhinocyllus conicus*, has proved moderately successful in Canada but unsuccessful in New Zealand.

Carpobrotus edulis (L.) N.E. Br. (Aizoaceae)
Hottentot fig

Description succulent herb

Region of origin South Africa (Cape)

Region invaded N. America (California) [92, 93], Europe (Portugal, SW England)

Casuarina equisetifolia L. (Casuarinaceae)
Common ironwood, common ru, Australian pine, horsetail tree (South Africa)

Description §Life form: tree (to 50 m), evergreen §Seed disp.: wind §Breeding syst.: dioecious (sometimes monoecious) §Invasive category **3.5**.

Region of origin Malesia (Melanesia, Polynesia), Australasia (Australia – N. and NE coastlines). Climatic zone: subtrop. dry–wet. Pioneer tree of tropical and subtropical coasts, forming dense stands on the foreshore, sometimes suckering from the roots, which possess nodules containing nitrogen fixing bacteria.

Region invaded Pacific (Hawaii), N. America (Florida), C. America (Bahamas), Africa (South Africa), Malagassia (Réunion), S. Asia (Japan). Climatic zone: wmtemp. arid–dry, subtrop. dry–moist, trop. arid. Where planted for shelter on sandy shores, it spreads to form monotypic stands with little understorey. In Hawaii it is now widely distributed on all the islands up to 500 m altitude, in all but the wettest and driest places. In Florida it has become so abundant on some sandy shores that it interferes with the nesting of sea turtles and American crocodiles. It regenerates from basal shoots after fire.

References [21, 115, 135, 359].

Figure 5.2 A South American scrambling shrub of the compositae (daisy family), *Chromolaena odorata*, is one of the most important alien invaders of the tropics and subtropics. Here it is shown dominating a woodland fringe in the South African savanna region. (Photo: I.A.W. Macdonald)

Cedrela odorata A.Juss (Meliaceae)

West Indian cedar

Description tree

Region of origin Central Mexico to Brazil

Region invaded Galápagos

Cenchrus ciliaris L. (Gramineae)

Buffel grass (Australia)

Description herb

Region of origin SW Asia

Region invaded Hawaii, Australia

Cestrum nocturnum L. (Solanaceae)

Lady of the night

Description shrub

Region of origin West Indies

Region invaded Rarotonga

Chromolaena odorata (L.) King & Robinson {*Eupatorium odoratum* L.} (Compositae)

Christmas bush, archangel (Jamaica), sam-solokh (India), awolowo weed, Siam weed (Nigeria)

Description Life form: woody herb or shrub scrambling to 20 m §Seed disp.: wind §Seed prod.: high §Breeding syst.: hermaphrodite §Invasive category **2.5**.

Region of origin N. America (Florida), C. America (West Indies), S. America (south to Paraguay). Climatic zone: subtrop. arid–dry, trop. arid. Common and variable species of roadside banks, fields, hillsides, clearings on limestone and wastelands.

Notes Apomictic. It does not grow in heavy shade but thrives on poor, rocky soils. It grows fast and regenerates from the roots after cutting or burning. It contains turpentines and is highly flammable, increasing the fire frequency often with disastrous results.

Control Chromolaena odorata rapidly recolonizes an area after physical clearing or application of herbicides [34]. However, in South Africa, Tordon 101 (0.75% in water) and Roundup (3%) have been used with some success. Biological control has been attempted in several countries but has not proved very successful. In Sri Lanka, partial control has been achieved by the introduction of *Pareuchaetes pseudoinsulara* Rego Barros (Lepidoptera), which causes defoliation. Management to reduce ecosystem disturbance reduces the spread of *C. odorata*.

References [34, 135, 219, 243, 340].

Chrysanthemoides monilifera (DC.) Norl. (ssp. *rotundata* and ssp. *monilifera*) (Compositae)

Bitou bush, bone-seed, salt bush, bietou

Description §Life form: shrub/tree (to 3 m) §Seed disp.: bird §Seed prod.: high, over an extended period §Breeding syst.: monoecious, outer florets female, inner florets male §Invasive category **3.5**.

Region of origin Africa (South Africa). Climatic zone: subtrop. dry–moist, wmtemp. dry. Widespread and occurs on coastal dunes.

Region invaded Australasia (Australia – southern Queensland, New South Wales, Victoria; New Zealand), Oceanic Is (St Helena), Europe (Mediterranean). Climatic zone: wmtemp. arid–moist, subtrop. moist. In New Zealand it invades coastal cliffs, waste places and scrubland. In Australia it invades littoral areas with native communities of *Acacia longifolia* and *Banksia integrifolia*, which it ousts.

Notes Mature individuals resprout after fire. Long decumbent branches can root at the nodes giving it sandbinding properties.

References [287, 429, 430].

Cinchona succirubra Pav. ex Klotsch (Rubiaceae)
Red quinine tree

Description §Life form: tree, evergreen §Seed disp.: wind §Seed prod.: high §Breeding syst.: hermaphrodite §Invasive category **4**.

Region of origin S. America (Ecuador). Climatic zone: trop. dry. It is not a dominant in its native forest habitats.

Region invaded Oceanic Is (Galápagos, St Helena). Climatic zone: wmtemp. dry, subtrop. moist. In the Galápagos it occurs in *Miconia*, *Robinsonia* and fern–sedge vegetation zones, with infestations covering some 4000 ha.

Notes Germination and seedling growth occur under a wide range of conditions, including deep shade. Regrowth after cutting is rapid and the plants have a wide ecological tolerance, mature early (flowering after 1–2 years) and can compete with and shade out native species.

Control Cinchona succirubra may be removed manually as has been done in 1000 ha of the Galápagos National Park [255]. It appears that it can regrow from root remnants [255]. Care must therefore be taken when removing roots that no fragments are left behind. In the Galápagos, painting the stump with herbicides such as Tordon 101, D.M.A.6., Certox 3,34 and Esterpac (concentration 1045 g/ha) was found to be effective in killing cut stumps [255].

References [151, 255, 347].

Cinnamomum camphora (L.) J. Presl (Lauraceae)

Camphor

Description tree

Region of origin China, Taiwan, Japan

Region invaded Australia, Japan, South Africa

Cinnamomum zeylanicum Nees (Lauraceae)

Cinnamon

Description tree

Region of origin East Indies

Region invaded Seychelles

Notes Introduced in the eighteenth century for spice cultivation and spread by the endemic blue pigeons (*Alectroenas pulcherrima*) into native vegetation.

Citrus limetta Risso (Rutaceae)

Sweet lime

Description tree

Region of origin Eurasia, North Africa

Region invaded Galápagos

Clematis vitalba L. (Ranunculaceae)

Description climber

Region of origin Europe

Region invaded New Zealand [200]. See main account in Chapter 4.

Clidemia hirta (L.) D. Don (Melastomataceae)

Description shrub

Region of origin Tropical America

Region invaded Hawaii, Guam, Fiji, Solomon Is, American Samoa, Vanuatu, Wallis and Futuna Is, Mascarene Is, Seychelles, Comores [435]. See main account in Chapter 4.

Coccinia grandis (L.) Voigt (Curcurbitaceae)

Description climber

Region of origin Tropical Africa

Region invaded Guam

Cortaderia selloana (Schultes & Schultes f.) Asch. & Graebner (Gramineae)

Pampas grass

Description herb, subdioecious

Region of origin S. America

Region invaded Australia, New Zealand

Crassula helmsii (T.Kirk) Cockayne {*Tillaea recurva* Hooker f.} (Crassulaceae)

Swamp stonecrop

Description §Life form: herb, perennial, aquatic §Seed disp.: water §Breeding syst.: hermaphrodite (probably self-pollinated) §Invasive category **4**.

Region of origin Australasia (SE Australia, Tasmania). Climatic zone: wmtemp. dry–moist. At altitudes up to 900 m in still shallow fresh water, swamps, edging streams, lagoons and channels up to 50 cm in depth. Occasionally occurs to 1m depth or terrestrially as dense mats on damp soil.

Region invaded Europe (southern England). Climatic zone: temp. moist. Wide range of habitats from shallow temporary pools to permanent water to depth of 3 m. Tolerant of a wide range of pH and nutrient status. Fast growing, readily dispersed by vegetative fragments, it now dominates many pools in the New Forest (England), excluding rare native plants such as *Ludwigia palustris* and *Galium debile*.

Notes Introduced as an aquarium plant. It is dispersed by people, birds (such as herons and geese) and ponies that drink from the pools.

References [71, 99, 369].

Crataegus monogyna Jacq. (Rosaceae)

Hawthorn

Description §Life form: shrub/tree (to 10 m), deciduous §Seed disp.: bird, mammal (possums in Australia) §Seed prod.: medium, hard seed coat promotes dormancy §Breeding syst.: hermaphrodite, the flowers are self-sterile and insect pollinated §Invasive category 3.

Region of origin Europe. Climatic zone: temp. moist–wet. Abundant in hedgerows and woods of northern Europe and invading abandoned pasture. It does not regenerate under shade but is an effective colonizing shrub of base-rich soils.

Region invaded Australasia (Australia – New South Wales; New Zealand – South Island). Climatic zone: temp. moist, wmtemp. dry. Invades wasteland, riverbeds, forest remnants and hill country farmland.

Notes In Britain colonization by *Crataegus monogyna* enriches the nutrient status of nutrient-poor grasslands, making restoration of the original grassland difficult.

Control Spread of *Crataegus monogyna* may be controlled by cutting, although it sprouts from cut stumps.

References [29, 142, 444, 445].

Cryptostegia grandiflora R. Br. (Asclepiadaceae (Periplocaceae))

Rubber vine (Australia)

Description climber

Region of origin Africa

Region invaded Australia (Queensland rainforest)

Cupressus lusitanica Miller (Cupressaceae)

Mexican cypress

Description tree, monoecious

Region of origin Mexico

Region invaded Malawi

Cytisus scoparius (L.) Link (Leguminosae)

Broom

Description §Life form: shrub (to 2.5 m), perennial, deciduous §Seed disp.: explosive dehiscence of the legume scatters seed, mammals (livestock and humans), water §Seed prod.: high §Breeding syst.: hermaphrodite §Invasive category **3.5**.

Region of origin Europe (southern Europe), N. Asia (Asia Minor, Russia). Climatic zone: wmtemp. arid–dry. Distribution limited by drought in the south and winter cold in the north. It occurs on heaths, rocky places and open places in woods.

Region invaded Australasia (New Zealand, Australia), Africa (South Africa), S. Asia (India). Climatic zone: wmtemp. dry–moist, subtrop. moist. In Australia it can invade eucalypt forest, suppressing herbaceous vegetation and the regeneration of trees. In New Zealand it invades river beds, native grasslands and previously forested hillsides.

Notes Tolerant of a wide range of soils, it fixes nitrogen and can grow all year in an equable climate. Seed set is little affected by altitude or drought. Drought adaptations include the xeromorphic photosynthetic stems.

Control Frustrated by long-lived soil seed-bank.

References [166, 426, 441].

Dactylis glomerata L. (Gramineae)

Cocks-foot

Description herb

Region of origin Eurasia

Region invaded Hawaii

Datura inoxia Mill. (Solanaceae)

Description herb

Region of origin Southern N. America

Region invaded Namibia

Digitaria decumbens Stent. (Gramineae)

Pangola grass

Description herb

Region of origin South Africa

Region invaded Galápagos

Dioscorea bulbifera L. {*D. sativa* Thunb.} (Dioscoreaceae)

Air potato, abobo (Malaysia)

Description §Life form: climber, perennial, herbaceous with a woody tuber §Seed disp.: water, wind (winged seeds) §Seed prod.: high §Breeding syst.: dioecious §Invasive category **4**.

Region of origin S. Asia (Japan), Pacific (Polynesia). Climatic zone: subtrop. wet, trop. arid–dry. Mountains (to 2000 m), disturbed woodland, coastal woodland where the rainfall is more than 700 mm during the wetter six months of the year.

Region invaded Malesia (Singapore). Climatic zone: trop. dry. Introduced to the Singapore Botanic Garden from where it has spread into the edges of the relatively

152

undisturbed primary rainforest. It has not spread far from the original point of introduction, although where it occurs it has a serious effect on the vegetation.

Notes It is cultivated for its edible bulbils and tubers. In Singapore it reproduces solely by means of vegetative axillary bulbils, borne aerially. Where both sexes occur it is probably pollinated by insects.

References [78, 152, 307, 372, 440].

Egeria densa Planchon (Hydrocharitaceae)

Description aquatic herb

Region of origin South America

Region invaded New Zealand (Lakes Rotorua, Rotoiti, Tarawera) [432]

Ehrharta calycina Sm. (Gramineae)

Description herb

Region of origin South Africa

Region invaded Australia

Ehrharta stipoides Lab. {*Microlaena stipoides* (Lab.) R. Br.} (Gramineae)

Description herb

Region of origin Australia

Region invaded Hawaii

Eichhornia crassipes (Mart.) Solms-Laub. {*E.speciosa* Kunth., *Piaropus mesomelas* Raf.} (Pontederiaceae)

Water hyacinth, aquape (Brazil), falkumbhi (India)

Description §Life form: herb, perennial, aquatic (free floating) §Seed disp.: water, wind §Seed prod.: high §Breeding syst.: hermaphrodite (tristyly) §Invasive category **4.5**.

Region of origin S. America (freshwater habitats in NE Brazil). Climatic zone: trop. arid–dry.

Region invaded S. Asia (India, Thailand, Malaysia), Africa (tropical and southern Africa), Australasia (Australia), N. America (Florida). Climatic zone: wmtemp. dry, subtrop. moist, trop. arid–dry. Widespread in the tropics and subtropics.

Notes Potential to produce high numbers of seeds (self-pollinated) but usually reproduces vegetatively. Tristylous and self-compatible populations are found and the flowers are insect pollinated. It grows rapidly in tropical freshwaters to form large floating mats of vegetation which cannot tolerate water temperatures above 34° C. The leaves are killed by frost but the plant is killed only if the rhizome tip is frozen.

Control Biological control, using the beetle *Neochetina eichhorniae* Warner (Coleoptera: Curculionidae), has been successful in some areas but not in others [196]. Inoculation of the plants with the fungus, *Cercospora rodmanii*, may improve success of the insect pest. Large areas of freshwater have been treated with 2,4-D in an attempt to control this pest but reinvasion from seed usually occurs.

References [9, 95, 137, 178, 181, 196, 313].

Elaeagnus angustifolia L. (Elaeagnaceae)

Russian olive, Trebizond date

Description shrub

Region of origin SE Europe, W. Asia

Region invaded N. America

Elettaria cardamomum (L.) Maton (Zingiberaceae)

Cardamom

Description herb

Region of origin India

Region invaded Sri Lanka, S. India

Elodea canadensis Michx. (Hydrocharitaceae)

Canadian pondweed

Description aquatic herb

Region of origin N. America

Region invaded C. Europe, Britain, New Zealand, Australia (New South Wales, Victoria)

Notes Introduced to Britain in 1840s initially as a female clone only, populations have now declined from the early massive infestations. Introduced to Australia sometime before 1960 [345].

Elodea nutallii (Planchon) St John (Hydrocharitaceae)

Nutall's pondweed

Description aquatic herb

Region of origin North America

Region invaded Britain

Erica lusitanica Rud. in Schrad. (Ericaceae)

Spanish heath

Description §Life form: shrub, evergreen §Seed disp.: wind §Seed prod.: high §Breeding syst.: hermaphrodite §Invasive category 2.

Region of origin Europe (south Portugal to SW France). Climatic zone: wmtemp. arid–moist. Damp heaths and woodland margins.

Region invaded Australasia (New Zealand). Climatic zone: wmtemp. dry–moist. Invades open disturbed areas and poor hill country pasture, replacing the native species *Leptospermum scoparium*.

Notes Has a high seed-bank (up to 480 000 per m^2) with germination stimulated by fluctuating temperatures. Fire creates ideal conditions for seed germination. It withstands grazing and trampling by producing abundant epicormic shoots. It is strongly mycorrhizal.

References [267, 403].

Eucalyptus camaldulensis Dehnh. (Myrtaceae)
Red gum

Description tree

Region of origin Australia

Region invaded South Africa (northern Cape savanna) [160]

Eucalyptus globulus Lab. (Myrtaceae)

Blue gum, fever tree

Description tree

Region of origin Australia

Region invaded California, USA

Eugenia jambos L. {Syzygium jambos (L.) Alston} (Myrtaceae)

Rose apple

Description shrub

Region of origin SE Asia

Region invaded Galápagos, Réunion, Cook Is, Hawaii

Flacourtia jangomas (Lour.) Rauschel (Flacourtiaceae)

Description shrub/tree

Region of origin Assam, Burma

Region invaded Cook Is

Fuchsia boliviana Carr. (Onagraceae)

Description shrub

Region of origin Bolivia

Region invaded Réunion

Fuchsia magellanica Lam. (Onagraceae)

Description shrub

Region of origin Chile, Argentina

Region invaded Réunion

Furcraea cubensis (Jacq.) Vent. {*F. hexapetala* (Jacq.) Urb.} (Agavaceae)

Cuban hemp, hemp, cabuya (Galápagos)

Description §Life form: shrub, evergreen §Breeding syst.: hermaphrodite §Invasive category **3**.

Region of origin C. America (Greater Antilles), S. America (NW S. America). Climatic zone: trop. arid, subtrop. moist. Common along roadsides and in waste places.

Region invaded Oceanic Is (Galápagos). Climatic zone: trop. arid. Habitats on Galápagos include the arid zone, fern–sedge vegetation (120–360 m), openings in forests, along trails and in abandoned settlements. Forms extensive thickets that exclude all other species.

Notes Reproduces vegetatively by means of bulbils and suckering.

References [2, 151, 347].

Furcraea foetida (L.) Haw. (Agavaceae)

Mauritius hemp

Description shrubby rosette

Region of origin Cuba S. America

Region invaded Kermadecs (Raoul), Hawaii, Mascarenes

Glyceria maxima (Hartm.) Holmb. (Gramineae)
Reed sweetgrass

Description water grass

Region of origin Europe

Region invaded Waterbodies up to 1m deep in southern Australia

Grevillea robusta Cunn. (Proteaceae)

Silky oak

Description tree

Region of origin E. Australia

Region invaded Hawaii

Hakea gibbosa (Sm.) Cav. (Proteaceae)
Rock hakea, downy hakea

Description §Life form: shrub/tree (up to 2 m where native, up to 4 m in South Africa) §Seed disp.: wind §Seed prod.: medium §Breeding syst.: hermaphrodite §Invasive category **4**.

Region of origin Australasia (Australia – New South Wales). Climatic zone: wmtemp. moist. Coastal heaths and scrub on sandy soil.

Region invaded Africa (South Africa – mountain fynbos), Australasia (New Zealand – gumlands and roadside scrub). Climatic zone: wmtemp. dry–moist. Forms dense thickets in which the native vegetation is suppressed. It was introduced into New Zealand as a hedge plant.

Control Hakea gibbosa can be removed from an area by cutting. Biological control using *Erytenna consputa* Pascoe (Coleoptera) has been tried since 1972 but consistent large scale fruit destruction has not been achieved [196].

Notes It is relatively long-lived with early reproductive maturity and shade tolerance.

References [116, 196, 301, 428].

Hakea sericea Schrad. (Proteaceae)

Description shrub

Region of origin Australia

Region invaded South Africa [303], Mediterranean. See main account in Chapter 4.

Hakea suaveolens R.Br. (Proteaceae)

Sweet hakea, fork-leaved hakea

Description §Life form: shrub/tree §Seed disp.: wind, water §Seed prod.: medium §Breeding syst.: hermaphrodite §Invasive category **4**.

Region of origin Australasia (endemic to Western Australia). Climatic zone: wmtemp. arid–dry. Shallow soils on rock outcrops.

Region invaded Africa (South Africa – mountain and lowland fynbos). Climatic zone: wmtemp. dry–moist. Forms fire adapted dense stands on granitic soils.

Notes Serotinous winged seeds which are not released from their capsules until after the death of the tree or branch. Fire usually leads to large-scale release of seeds.

Control Mechanical control is effective provided that all the plants are removed [302]. Potential biological control agents are under investigation.

Hedychium flavescens Carey ex Roscoe (Zingiberaceae)

Description large rhizomatous herb

Region of origin Himalayas

Region invaded New Zealand

Hedychium flavescens Carey ex Roscoe (Zingiberaceae)

Description large rhizomatous herb

Region of origin Himalayas

Region invaded New Zealand

Helianthus tuberosus L. (Compositae)

Jerusalem artichoke

Description herb

Region of origin USA

Region invaded C. Europe

Heracleum mantegazzianum Sommier & Levier (Umbelliferae)

Giant hogweed

Description herb

Region of origin Former USSR

Region invaded British Isles

Hieracium praealtum Gochnat (Compositae)

Description herb

Region of origin Europe

Region invaded New Zealand

Hieracium pilosella L. (Compositae)

Mouse-ear hawkweed

Description §Life form: herb, perennial §Seed disp.: wind §Seed prod.: low §Breeding syst.: hermaphrodite §Invasive category 2.

Region of origin Europe. Climatic zone: temp. moist–wet, wmtemp. arid–moist. Pasture, heaths, banks, rocks, walls.

Region invaded Australasia (New Zealand). Climatic zone: temp. moist, wmtemp. moist. Tussock grasslands, lawns, roadsides and pastures. Can displace tussock and fescue-tussock vegetation.

Notes Relies heavily on vegetative propagation by stolons. Variable, polyploid complex of sexually reproducing and partially apomictic forms. Produces allelopathic substances.

Control The herbicide 'Versatil' with 2,4-D esters gives relatively good control [349].

References [262, 349, 445].

Hiptage benghalensis (L.) Kurz (Malpighiaceae)

Description woody climber

Region of origin Indomalaysia

Region invaded Mauritius, Réunion

Holcus lanatus L. (Gramineae)

Yorkshire-fog

Description herb

Region of origin Eurasia

Region invaded Hawaii, New Zealand

Hydrilla verticillata (L.f.) Royle (Hydrocharitaceae)

Hydrilla, Florida elodea, water thyme

Description §Life form: herb, perennial, aquatic §Seed disp.: wind, water §Seed prod.: low §Breeding syst.: dioecious §Invasive category **3**.

Region of origin Australasia (NE Australia), E. and SE Asia, Africa (E.

Africa). Climatic zone: subtrop. moist–wet, trop. arid. Still or slow moving freshwater habitats.

Region invaded N. America (Florida – male plants, California – introduced by 1976, first to Sacramento Valley, now widespread), C. America (Panama), Pacific (Fiji), Australasia (New Zealand). Climatic zone: temp. moist, subtrop. moist, trop. arid. Forms dense submerged stands displacing native species.

Notes Mainly reproduces vegetatively. It is tolerant of a wide range of nutrient levels from oligotrophic to eutrophic and can overwinter as dormant shoots.

Control In the USA, *Paraponyx diminutalis* (Lepidoptera: Pyralidae) was introduced accidentally; it causes some damage but does not result in full control [196]. Other insects are under investigation as suitable biological control agents [24], as are fish such as the Chinese grass carp (a triploid strain of the fish has been used which lives to five years and dies without reproducing). Several herbicides such as diquat at 5 ppm or paraquat at 1–2 ppm, endothal and xylene have been used to control *Hydrilla*. Lowering the water level to expose *Hydrilla* to the sun for a number of days has been reported to control the weed. Manual weeding is used in the Philippines.

References [24, 196, 345, 385].

Hyparrhenia rufa (Nees) Stapf (Gramineae)

Jaragua grass

Description herb

Region of origin Tropical Africa

Region invaded Venezuela, Hawaii

Hypochoeris radicata L. (Compositae)

Cat's-ear

Description herb

Region of origin Europe

Region invaded Hawaii

Impatiens glandulifera Royle (Balsaminaceae)

Indian balsam, policeman's helmet

Description §Life form: herb, annual §Seed disp.: explosive dehiscence, water §Seed prod.: medium §Breeding syst.: hermaphrodite §Invasive category **3**.

Region of origin S. Asia (Himalayas). Climatic zone: subtrop. moist–wet. Riverine rainforest.

Region invaded Europe (Britain). Climatic zone: temp. moist. Along riverbanks and in wet disturbed habitats.

Notes Long cultivated in gardens and dispersed by people. The flowers are relatively large and pollinated by bumble-bees. The seeds sink in water.

References [96, 397].

Imperata conferta (J.S.Presl) Ohwi (Gramineae)

Description herb

Region of origin SE Asia

Region invaded Guam

Jacaranda mimosifolia D.Don (Bignoniaceae)

Description shrub

Region of origin NW Argentina

Region invaded Subtropical Africa

Kalanchoe pinnata (Lam.) Pers. {Bryophyllum pinnatum (Lam.) Kurz} (Crassulaceae)

Description succulent herb/shrub

Region of origin Madagascar

Region invaded Galápagos, Hawaii, Raoul

Lagarosiphon major (Ridl.) Moss (Hydrocharitaceae)

Description herb

Region of origin South Africa

Region invaded New Zealand, Mascarenes, Italy, Britain. See main account in Chapter 4.

Lantana camara L. (Verbenaceae)

Description shrub

Region of origin New World Tropics

Region invaded Pantropical, pansubtropical. See main account in Chapter 4.

Leptospermum laevigatum (Gaertn.) Muell. (Myrtaceae)
Australian myrtle, coastal tea-tree

Description §Life form: shrub/tree (to 12 m) §Seed disp.: wind, water §Seed prod.: high, but low viability reported §Breeding syst.: hermaphrodite §Invasive category 4.

Region of origin Australasia (Australia – Queensland, New South Wales, Victoria, South Australia to Tasmania). Climatic zone: wmtemp. dry–moist, subtrop. moist. Heath communities on calcareous or coastal sands. Characteristic of the closed-shrub stage of dune succession.

Region invaded Africa (SE Cape). Climatic zone: wmtemp. arid–moist. Sandy flats, lowland and mountain fynbos, southern forest. Introduced via the Cape Town Botanic Garden.

Notes Plants are killed by fire but the fruits open after burning to give prolific simultaneous germination. *Leptospermum laevigatum* has an efficient and extensive root system which competes for water with native plants.

Control In South Africa, the mature trees are cut and the area burnt about four years later to kill any seedlings that may have germinated from seed before they mature and produce fruit [193].

References [60, 193, 251, 428].

164

Leucaena leucocephala (Lam.) de Wit {*Leucaena glauca* Benth.} (Leguminosae)

Wild tamarind, lead tree, ko haole (Hawaii), guaje (Mexico)

Description §Life form: shrub/tree (2–7 m), evergreen §Seed disp.: gravity, insect activity on the ground §Seed prod.: high §Breeding syst.: hermaphrodite and largely self pollinated §Invasive category **3.5**.

Region of origin C. America (southern Mexico to Guatamala). Climatic zone: subtrop. moist, trop. arid–dry. Roadsides thickets and sandy scrub.

Region invaded Africa (Kenya, Tanzania), N. America (Florida), C. America (West Indies), S. America (south to Brazil), Pacific (Hawaii), S. Asia (Japan, Bonin Is), Malagassia (Mascarene Is), Australasia (N. Australia). Climatic zone: subtrop. dry–wet, trop. arid. It spread from Mexico to the Philippines as early as the seventeenth century and was widely introduced throughout the tropics for fodder in the nineteenth century. In the Hawaiian Is it is replacing native *Metrosideros–Diospyros* open forest and is possibly threatening *Erythrina sanwichensis* in parts of its range. It is found in dry to mesic habitats on all the Hawaiian Is to 700 m.

Notes Forms dense monospecific thickets. The stands are not very flammable but, if burning occurs, *Leucaena leucocephala* regenerates rapidly from basal shoots. Flowers and fruits continuously. Two subspecies are recognized, of which ssp. *leucocephala* is the shrubby form and the main invasive.

Control Biological control is frustrated by its economic importance. A psyllid insect pest, *Heteropsylla cubana*, which causes defoliation, spread by chance from Central America to Hawaii in 1984 and has recently spread through Asia into East Africa.

References [2, 79, 80, 237, 311, 422].

Ligustrum lucidum Aiton (Oleaceae)

Glossy privet

Description shrub or small tree

Region of origin China, Korea

Region invaded Australia, New Zealand, N. Argentina

Ligustrum robustum Blume ssp. *walkeri* (Decne.) P.S. Green {*L.walkeri* Decne., *L. ceylanicum* Decne.} (Oleaceae)

Privet

Description §Life form: shrub, evergreen §Seed disp.: bird §Seed prod.: medium §Breeding syst.: hermaphrodite §Invasive category **4.5**.

Region of origin S. Asia (India, Sri Lanka). Climatic zone: wmtemp. moist, subtrop. dry–wet. Characteristic of disturbed montane forest, often along streams, at 450–2000 m

Region invaded Malagassia (Mauritius, Réunion and Rodrigues). Climatic zone: subtrop. moist. Strongly invades the lower montane evergreen forest, with *Psidium cattleianum*. It is the most invasive species of the Mauritius uplands.

Notes In Mauritius it is widely dispersed by the introduced red-whiskered bulbul (*Pycnonotus jocosus*). Germination and growth are rapid and it forms dense monospecific thickets.

Control It is laboriously cleared by hand from special patches in nature reserves, an operation that has to be repeated yearly.

References [96, 239, 240, 381].

Ligustrum sinense Lour. (Oleaceae)

Chinese privet

Description shrub

Region of origin China

Region invaded Australia

Linaria genistifolia (L.) Mill. ssp. *dalmatica* (L.) Maire & Petitmengin (Scrophulariaceae)

Description herb

Region of origin Balkans

Region invaded USA

Lonicera japonica Thunb. (Caprifoliaceae)

Description climber

Region of origin E. Asia

Region invaded USA, Hawaii, Australia, New Zealand

Ludwigia peploides (Kunth) Raven (Onagraceae)

Description herb

Region of origin Australia

Region invaded Subtropical and Tropical America

Lupinus arboreus Sims (Leguminosae)

Tree lupin

Description shrub

Region of origin California

Region invaded New Zealand

Lupinus polyphyllus Lindley (Leguminosae)

Description herb

Region of origin Western N. America

Region invaded New Zealand

Lygodium japonicum (Thunb.) Sw. (Schizaeaceae – Pteridophyta)

Description fern

Region of origin Japan

Region invaded USA (Florida–Texas)

Lythrum salicaria L. (Lythraceae)

Purple loosestrife

Description herb

Region of origin Old World

Region invaded N. America

Maesopsis eminii Engl. (Rhamnaceae)

Musizi

Description §Life form: tree (to 40 m) §Seed disp.: bird (hornbills in the E. Usambaras) §Seed prod.: high §Breeding syst.: hermaphrodite, but protogynous and probably mainly outbreeding §Invasive category **4**.

Region of origin Africa (Uganda, Zaire, NW Tanzania, Zambia, Kenya, Angola, central Africa west to Liberia). In places it is a dominant canopy species in colonizing forest growing with an understorey of *Caloncoba schweinfurthii*. Climatic zone: subtrop. moist, trop.

Region invaded Africa (East Usambaras, E. Tanzania, Rwanda). It invades submontane (800–1200 m) evergreen forest of the East Usambaras, rich in endemics, as a gap-replacement species. It has spread from plantations into natural forest. It was first introduced to the East Usambaras by German foresters around 1913, with more planting being carried out in the 1960s and 70s. Climatic zone: subtrop. moist.

Notes Seeds are early and copiously produced and may remain dormant for some months in soil or damp litter. Seeds can germinate in shade but require a canopy gap within a few months of germination to survive.

References [38, 39].

Mangifera indica L. (Anacardiaceae)

Mango

Description tree

Region of origin Asia

Region invaded Antigua, Mauritius

Melaleuca quinquenervia (Cav.) Black (Myrtaceae)

Description tree

Region of origin Australia

Region invaded Florida [21], Hawaii, South Africa. See main account in Chapter 4.

Melia azedarach L. {M. dubia Cav.} (Meliaceae)

White cedar, Cape lilac, China berry, tulip cedar, syringa

Description §Life form: tree (10–20 m), deciduous §Seed disp.: bird §Seed prod.: high §Breeding syst.: hermaphrodite/monoecious §Invasive category **4.5**.

Region of origin Asia and Australasia (Australia). Climatic zone: wmtemp. dry–moist. On fertile soils in coastal rainforests

Region invaded Africa, Pacific. Climatic zone: subtrop. dry–wet. In South Africa it colonizes riparian habitats in subtropical veld and is one of the most widespread invaders in the Transvaal. It competes well with native plants.

Notes It flowers throughout the year and comes to reproductive maturity early. It is widely planted as an ornamental, growing rapidly. Its timber is used in cabinet making.

References [162, 247, 369].

Melinis minutiflora Beauv. {Panicum minutiflora (Beauv.) Rasp., P. melinis Trin.} (Gramineae)

Molasses grass, wynne grass

Description §Life form: herb, perennial §Seed disp.: wind §Breeding syst.: hermaphrodite §Invasive category **3.5**.

Region of origin Africa (Tropical Africa). Climatic zone: trop. arid–dry. Open grasslands.

Region invaded Pacific (Hawaii), C. America (Jamaica), S. America (Venezuela), Oceanic Is (Ascension). Climatic zone: subtrop. dry–wet. In Hawaii it occurs in dry habitats on all islands to 1500 m.

Notes Spreads mainly by means of runners. Apomictic. It forms dense monotypic stands, smothering surrounding vegetation. It is adapted to fire. Although relatively unpalatable to stock, its importance as a pasture grass prevents biological control.

References [359, 361].

Memecylon floribundum Blume (Melastomataceae)

Description shrub

Region of origin Indonesia

Region invaded Seychelles (Mahé)

Mesembryanthemum crystallinum L. {*Gasoul crystallinum* (L.) Rothm.} (Aizoaceae)

Ice-plant

Description §Life form: herb (succulent), annual §Seed disp.: wind §Breeding syst.: hermaphrodite §Invasive category **2.5**.

Region of origin Africa (probably native along west coast) trop. arid–dry. Locally frequent on saline soils in coastal areas.

Region invaded N. America. (California), Australasia (Australia, on samphire flats and saline ground), Europe – Africa – N./W. Asia (Mediterranean, including Israel). Climatic zone: wmtemp. arid wmtemp. dry, subtrop. arid, trop. arid. Invades degraded coastal pastures; it is encouraged by overgrazing. It is said to accumulate salt in the surface soil horizons, making grassland re-establishment more difficult after it has been removed.

References [204, 418].

Miconia calvescens (Schr. & Mart.) DC. (Melastomataceae)

Bush currant

Description shrub

Region of origin Tropical America

Region invaded Pacific Islands (Tahiti, Moorea)

Mikania micrantha H.B.K. (Compositae)

Description §Life form: climber, perennial §Seed disp.: wind §Seed prod.: medium §Breeding syst.: hermaphrodite §Invasive category **2.5**.

Region of origin S. America, C. America (including Caribbean). Climatic zone: subtrop. dry–moist, trop. arid. Damp clearings in forest from lowlands to 2000 m, streamsides and roadsides.

Region invaded S. Asia (India), Malesia (Malaysia, Philippines, Solomon Is), Pacific (Rarotonga). Climatic zone: subtrop. moist, trop. arid. It is mainly a weed of pasturelands but it invades forest margins.

Notes It is intolerant of deep shade; produces allelopathic substances. It combines effective seed production with vigorous vegetative reproduction.

References [178].

Mikania scandens (L.) Willd. (Compositae)

Description climber

Region of origin USA

Region invaded Guam, Rota, Saipan, Sri Lanka

Mimosa invisa Mart. (Leguminosae)

Description shrub

Region of origin Tropical America

Region invaded Pacific, Mariana Is, including Rota, Tinian, Saipan

Mimosa pigra L. {M. pellita Humb. & Bonpl. ex Willd., nom. rej.} (Leguminosae)

Description shrub

Region of origin Tropical America

Region invaded SE Asia, Tropical Africa, N. Australia [51, 234]. See main account in Chapter 4.

Myrica faya Ait. (Myricaceae)

Description shrub

Region of origin Azores

Region invaded Hawaii. See main account in Chapter 4.

Myriophyllum aquaticum (Vell. Conc.) Verdc. {M. brasiliense Cambess.} (Haloragidaceae)

Parrot's feather, water milfoil

Description §Life form: herb, perennial, aquatic §Seed disp.: wind, water §Breeding syst.: dioecious §Invasive category **3.5**.

Region of origin S. America (Brazil, Peru, Uruguay, Chile, Argentina). Climatic zone: subtrop. moist, trop. dry. Lakes, rivers and streams.

Region invaded N. America (E. Texas, Edwards Plateau), Australasia (Australia – Western Australia, Queensland, New South Wales, Victoria, Tasmania; New Zealand), Africa (South Africa). Climatic zone: temp. moist, wmtemp. dry–moist, subtrop. dry. Invades flowing and still water. Tolerant of a wide variety of environmental conditions and will persist in brackish or polluted water.

Notes In South Africa propagation is entirely vegetative.

References [149].

Myriophyllum spicatum L. (Haloragidaceae)

Description aquatic herb

Region of origin Eurasia

Region invaded USA (e.g. Lake George, NY [260]), Canada

Myroxylon toluiferum Humb. (Leguminosae)

Description tree

Region of origin Tropical America

Region invaded Sri Lanka

Myrsiphyllum asparagoides Willd. (Liliaceae)

Description climber to 3 m

Region of origin South Africa

Region invaded Australia (South Australia, Victoria)

Nassella trichotoma (Nees) Arech. {Stipa trichotoma Nees} (Gramineae)

Serrated tussock grass

Description §Life form: herb, perennial §Seed disp.: wind §Seed prod.: hermaphrodite §Invasive category **2.5**.

Region of origin S. America (Peru, Chile, Argentina, Uruguay). Climatic zone: temp. arid–wet, wmtemp. moist. Pampas where vegetation is sparse and in disturbed or cultivated areas. It is not abundant in its native region.

Region invaded Australasia (SE Australia), Africa (South Africa), Europe (Italy). Climatic zone: temp. moist, wmtemp. dry–moist, subtrop. dry. In Australia it invades the Tablelands grasslands and, in South Africa, grassveld. It is capable of replacing native grasslands once they have been disturbed.

Notes It is a drought resistant tussock-forming grass with a deep root system and seed which may remain viable in the soil for up to 20 years.

Control Burning at appropriate times to prevent seed production and release, and repeated plowing of stands. Improving pastures (addition of fertilizers) results in *Nassella trichotoma* diminishing with increasing competition. Herbicides (2,2-DPA or tetrapion) have been used in Australia, but they are uneconomical for use on large stands due to rapid re-infestation from buried seed. Minimizing disturbance in adjacent areas slows spread of *Nassella trichotoma*.

References [16, 20, 63, 431].

Nerium oleander L. (Apocynaceae)

Oleander

Description shrub

Region of origin Eurasia

Region invaded S. Africa

Nicotiana glauca Grah. (Solanaceae)

Wild tobacco

Description §Life form: shrub, perennial, evergreen §Seed disp.: wind, water §Seed prod.: high §Breeding syst.: hermaphrodite §Invasive category 3.

Region of origin S. America (northwestern and central Argentina, Paraguay, Bolivia). Climatic zone: wmtemp. arid, subtrop. dry–moist. Roadsides and along river banks, to 3000 m.

Region invaded C. America (Mexico), Africa (South Africa – Kruger National Park and the lower reaches of the Orange River; Namibia – lower reaches of the Ugab River), N./W. Asia (Israel), Australasia (Australia), Oceanic Is (St Helena). Climatic zone: wmtemp. arid–moist, subtrop. dry–moist. Waste places, dry river beds, roadsides and along river banks.

Notes Drought resistant, tolerant of a wide range of environmental conditions and poisonous to most stock. Where it grows vigorously, it forms dense monospecific stands.

Control In South Africa the plants are cut and the stumps treated with 2,4,5-T. Successful control of *Nicotiana glauca* has been achieved where the plants were sprayed with herbicide and then exposed to the beetle, *Malabris aculeata*.

References [58, 237, 254, 377].

Olea europaea L. ssp. africana Mill. (Oleaceae)

Olive

Description shrub

Region of origin Tropical and South Africa

Region invaded Norfolk I., Hawaii

Operculina ventricosa (Bert.) Peter (Convolvulaceae)

Description climber

Region of origin Tropical America

Region invaded Rota, Tinian, Saipan

Opuntia aurantiaca Lindley (Cactaceae)

Tiger pear

Description shrub

Region of origin South America, West Indies

Region invaded Australia [17], S. Africa

Opuntia ficus-indica (L.) Mill. (Cactaceae)

Common prickly pear, spiny pest pear

Description §Life form: shrub or small tree (to 5 m) §Seed disp.: mammals (including humans) §Seed prod.: medium §Breeding syst.: hermaphrodite §Invasive category 3.

Region of origin C. America (Mexico) Climatic zone: trop. arid–dry. Typically occurs in valley floodplains and at the mouths of small canyons.

Region invaded Africa (Red Sea coasts and South Africa), Pacific (Hawaii), N. America (California), Europe (Mediterranean), N. Asia (Arabia) Climatic zone: wmtemp. arid–dry. In South Africa it invades pastureland and native vegetation (karoo). It forms dense infestations and the seeds are dispersed by baboons.

Notes Widely introduced for its edible fruit. Pollinated by bees and beetles. It is intolerant of fire.

Control This cactus has been successfully controlled in most areas in Hawaii and South Africa by two introduced insects, *Dactylopius opuntiae* Cockerell (Hemiptera: Dactylopiidae) and *Cactoblastis cactorum* Bergroth (Lepidoptera: Pyralidae). Physical control is very difficult as it readily regenerates from spiny leaf pads.

References [36, 161, 453].

Opuntia imbricata (Haw.) DC. (Cactaceae)

Description shrub

Region of origin C. America

Region invaded S. Africa

Opuntia rosea DC. (Cactaceae)

Description shrub

Region of origin C. America

Region invaded S. Africa

Opuntia stricta (Haw.) Haw. {*Opuntia inermis* DC.} (Cactaceae)

Description §Life form: shrub (sprawling or weakly ascending, 0.5–2 m), perennial §Seed disp.: mammals (including humans), water §Seed prod.: medium §Breeding syst.: hermaphrodite §Invasive category **3**.

Region of origin N. America (Florida, Texas), C. America (Cuba). Climatic zone: wmtemp. arid, subtrop. dry–moist, trop. arid. On sandy soils, typically of coastal woodlands or stabilized dunes.

Region invaded Australasia (Australia – Queensland). Climatic zone: subtrop. moist, trop. arid. Invades *Acacia–Casuarina* scrubland and other habitats, converting open scrub into impenetrable *Opuntia stricta* thickets.

Control Opuntia stricta has been successfully controlled in Australia by the introduction of the cactus-consuming moth, *Cactoblastis cactorum* Bergroth (Lepidoptera: Pyralidae).

References [36, 308].

Opuntia vulgaris Mill. (Cactaceae)

Description shrub to 3–4 m

Region of origin C. America

Region invaded E. Africa (Uganda – Queen Elizabeth National Park), S. Africa, India

Orthodontium lineare Schwaegr. (Bryales – Bryophyta)

Description apocarpous moss

Region of origin Southern Hemisphere

Region invaded NW Europe

Ossaea marginata (Desr.) Triana (Melastomataceae)

Description shrub

Region of origin Brazil

Region invaded Mauritius

Panicum maximum Jacq. (Gramineae)

Guinea grass

Description herb

Region of origin Africa

Region invaded Antigua, Barbuda, Anguilla, S. America (Venezuela)

Parkinsonia aculeata L. (Leguminosae)

Jerusalem thorn (South Africa), parkinsonia (Australia)

Description shrub or small tree

Region of origin N. and S. America

Region invaded Australia (Northern Territory, Queensland)

Paspalum conjugatum L. (Gramineae)

Description herb

Region of origin West Indies

Region invaded Hawaii, Raoul

Paspalum digitatum (L.) Poiret (Gramineae)

Description herb

Region of origin S. America

Region invaded Hawaii

Passiflora mollissima (H.B.K.) Bailey (Passifloraceae)

Description climber

Region of origin S. America

Region invaded Hawaii [222], South Africa, New Zealand. See main account in Chapter 4.

Passiflora rubra L. (Passifloraceae)

Passion flower

Description climber

Region of origin Tropical America, West Indies

Region invaded Rarotonga

Passiflora suberosa L. (Passifloraceae)

Passion flower

Description climber

Region of origin C. and S. America, West Indies

Region invaded Hawaii

Pennisetum clandestinum Chiov. {P.longistylum Hochst. var. clandestinum (Chiov.) Leeke} (Gramineae)

Kikuyu grass

Description §Life form: herb, perennial (sward-forming) §Seed disp.: wind §Breeding syst.: hermaphrodite/monoecious §Invasive category **3.5**.

Region of origin Africa (tropical eastern Africa). Climatic zone: subtrop. dry–moist, wmtemp. dry–moist. Humid tropical highlands, 1400–3300 m, tolerant of some frost. An important fodder and pasture grass.

Region invaded Pacific (Hawaii), Africa (South Africa), Australasia (Australia, New Zealand). Climatic zone: wmtemp. moist. subtrop. moist. It prevents the regeneration of native trees and shrubs in degraded Hawaiian forests, 500–2000 m.

Notes Facultative apomict, reproducing vegetatively and rarely setting seed except at high elevations. It has been widely introduced around the world as a pasture and lawn grass. It is said to release allelopathic substances.

Control Two insect pests, *Sphenophorus ventus vestitus* and *Herpetogramma licarsicalis*, have caused severe injury to Kikuyu grass in Hawaii. Its economic importance prevents release of further biological control agents. The application of 0.5% glyphosate has proved effective.

References [72, 251, 359, 361, 445].

Pennisetum polystachion (L.) Schult. (Gramineae)

Mission grass (Australia)

Description herb

ROSEWARNE
LEARNING CENTRE

Figure 5.3 *Pinus patula*, a native of Mexico, invading herb-rich grassland in the Mazeka valley, Mount Mulanje, Malawi. Efforts have been made to control its spread out of forestry plantations, but control will depend not only on removal of young trees but also of the source seed trees in the plantations. (Photo: Alan Hamilton)

Region of origin Tropical Africa

Region invaded Guam, Sri Lanka, Australia (eucalypt forest)

Pennisetum purpureum Schumach. {*P. macrostachyum* Benth., *P. blepharideum* Gilli} (Gramineae)

Elephant grass, Napier grass

Description §Life form: herb, perennial (1–6 m) §Seed disp.: wind §Seed prod.: low §Breeding syst.: hermaphrodite/monoecious §Invasive category **4**.

Region of origin Africa (Tropical Africa). Climatic zone: subtrop. dry–moist, wmtemp. dry–moist. Riverine sites, perennial swamps and disturbed forest land (often associated with secondary forest), 0–500 m. In Uganda, for instance, it can replace semideciduous rainforest as a fire subclimax.

Region invaded Oceanic Is (Galápagos). Climatic zone: wmtemp. dry. In the *Scalesia* zone; its dense growth prevents regeneration of native species.

Notes Reproduction is mainly vegetative. It is tolerant of a wide range of environmental conditions, although it is easily killed by frost. It prefers rich well-drained soils. It is highly drought resistant.

References [72, 151, 178].

Pennisetum setaceum (Forsk.) Chiov. {*P. phalaroides* Schult.} (Gramineae)

Fountain grass

Description §Life form: herb, perennial §Seed disp.: wind §Seed prod.: low §Breeding syst.: hermaphrodite/monoecious §Invasive category **5.**

Region of origin Africa (North Africa) W. Asia. (Lebanon, Syria). Climatic zone: wmtemp. dry, trop. arid. Stony slopes and dry open places 300–1600 m.

Region invaded Pacific (Hawaii), Oceanic Is (St Helena – not invasive). Climatic zone: wmtemp. dry–moist, subtrop. moist–wet.

Notes Fountain grass is threatening species which are listed as endangered by the US wildlife service – *Gouania hillebradii, Haplostachys haplostacha, Kokia drynarioides, Lipochaeta venosa* and *Stenogyne angustifolia* var. *angustifolia*. It is a fire-adapted bunchgrass, and it both promotes fires and spreads as a result of them.

Control Physical control has prevented further spread of fountain grass in Hawaii. Biological control is hampered by opposition from the sugar cane industry.

References [235, 359, 361, 399, 422].

Peraserianthes falcataria (L.) Nielsen {*Albizia falcataria* (L.) Fosb.} (Leguminosae)

Batai wood, sau

Description tree

Region of origin Malesia

Region invaded Seychelles

Pereskia aculeata Miller (Cactaceae)

Barbados gooseberry

Description shrub

Region of origin S. America

Region invaded South Africa [207]

Persea americana Miller (Lauraceae)

Avocado pear, aguacate, alligator pear, palta

Description shrub

Region of origin C. America

Region invaded Galápagos

Pinus contorta Douglas (Pinaceae)

Lodge-pole pine

Description tree

Region of origin Western N. America

Region invaded New Zealand [188]

Figure 5.4 Throughout the world riparian vegetation is being replaced by alien species. In Namibia, some of the most important such invaders are Mesquite trees of the genus *Prosopis*. Ironically, these same species are often widely advocated for planting in land reclamation schemes in desertified areas. One possible solution to this potential conflict is the use of sterile forms. (Photo: H. Kolberg)

Pinus nigra Arnold (Pinaceae)

Black pine, Austrian pine

Description tree

Region of origin Europe

Region invaded New Zealand

Pinus patula Schiede & Deppe (Pinaceae)

Mexican weeping pine

Description §Life form: tree, evergreen §Seed disp.: wind §Seed prod.: high §Breeding syst.: monoecious §Invasive category **4**.

Region of origin C. America (Mexico). Climatic zone: wmtemp. arid. Highlands of the central and eastern states at 1500–3000 m elevation where *Pinus patula*, *P. pseudostrobus* and *Quercus reticulata* are characteristic species. In cool subtropical climates with winter temperatures often below freezing.

Region invaded Pacific (Hawaii), Africa (Malawi – Mulanje Mt). Climatic zone: wmtemp. moist–wet, subtrop. dry–moist. It threatens the unique flora of Mulanje Mt by forming dense monotypic stands. It was originally planted as a nurse to promote regeneration of the native *Widdringtonia nodiflora*. It occurs between 1800 and 2400 m in tussock grassland, *Brachystegia* woodland and *Widdringtonia* forest.

Notes Capable of some self-fertilization, it is partly serotinous, with a high growth rate.

Control Cutting, followed by burning once the seeds have germinated, may be effective.

References [110, 111, 275, 276, 359].

Pinus pinaster Ait. (Pinaceae)

Cluster pine, maritime pine

Description §Life form: tree (to 40 m), evergreen §Seed disp.: wind §Seed prod.: high §Breeding syst.: monoecious §Invasive category **4.5**.

Region of origin Europe (Mediterranean). Climatic zone: wmtemp. arid–dry. In a wide range of habitats from Atlantic coastal dunes to mountain woodland, generally on sandy infertile soils.

Region invaded Africa (South Africa), Pacific (Hawaii – 1600–2200 m on Maui I.), Australasia (New Zealand – Abel Tasman National Park). Climatic zone: wmtemp. arid–moist, subtrop. wet. Replaces native vegetation in mountain and lowland fynbos on acid, leached soils, as it generally survives fynbos fires and has greater growth rate and longevity than native fynbos plants.

Notes It is susceptible to frost damage, although its thick bark gives it resistance to fires. It has been widely introduced around the world as a commercial forestry tree.

Control Cutting followed by burning to kill any regrowth has been effective. Any biological control must involve a seed predator so as not to interfere with commercial plantings.

References [188, 214, 215, 327, 359].

Pinus radiata D.Don (Pinaceae)

Monterey pine

Description tree

Region of origin California

Region invaded Australia, New Zealand, South Africa [329]. See main account in Chapter 4.

Pistia stratiotes L. (Araceae)

Water lettuce

Description herb

Region of origin Pantropical

Region invaded South Africa, Zambia, Malaysia, Philippines, Thailand, Australia

Pittosporum undulatum Vent. (Pittosporaceae)

Cheesewood

Description tree

Region of origin Australia

Region invaded Jamaica, South Africa, Australia, Lord Howe I., Hawaii [130, 328]. See main account in Chapter 4.

Poa annua L. (Gramineae)

Annual meadow-grass

Description herb

Region of origin North Temperate

Region invaded South Georgia

Prosopis glandulosa Torrey {*P.chilensis* (Molina) Stuntz var. *glandulosa* (Torrey) Standley} (Leguminosae)

Mesquite

Description §Life form: shrub or small tree (to 15 m), deciduous (spiny) §Seed disp.: mammals §Seed prod.: high §Breeding syst.: hermaphrodite §Invasive category **3.5**.

Region of origin N. America (SW United States), C. America (NE Mexico). Climatic zone: wmtemp. arid–dry, subtrop. moist. Occurs naturally in valleys and dry uplands, but invades pasture and disturbed land vigorously.

Region invaded Africa (South Africa, Namibia), Australasia (Australia – Queensland). Climatic zone: wmtemp. arid, subtrop. dry–moist. In South Africa it invades karoo and thornveld, and is beginning to spread into mountain fynbos.

Notes Seeds may remain dormant in soil for up to 10 years but germination is enhanced by passage through the digestive tract of herbivores. It is tolerant of extreme temperatures, severe drought and overgrazing. It has been widely cultivated for fodder. The most invasive type appears to be var. *torreyana* (Benson) Johnston rather than var. *glandulosa* [160].

Control Mesquite resprouts vigorously after cutting from dormant buds below the soil, so the roots must be grubbed out and the clearing operation must be followed up in successive years. If herbicides are to be used, these should be applied during the peak growing season. Biological control has recently been attempted using the seed-feeding beetle, *Algarobius prosopis*.

References [153, 357, 369].

Prosopis pallida (Willd.) Kunth (Leguminosae)

Description shrub

Region of origin South America

Region invaded Hawaii

Prosopis velutina Wooten (Leguminosae)

Velvet mesquite

Description shrub

Region of origin SW N. America

Region invaded South Africa [160].

Prunus serotina Ehrh. (Rosaceae)

Black cherry

Description §Life form: shrub or tree (to 30 m), deciduous §Seed disp.: bird §Seed prod.: high §Breeding syst.: hermaphrodite §Invasive category **4**.

Region of origin N. America (Ontario and Quebec southwards to Texas and Florida). Climatic zone: temp. wet. Woods and clearings, floodplains and thickets by roadsides.

Region invaded Europe (Britain, Netherlands). Climatic zone: temp. moist. Invades seminatural woodland on acid sandy soil.

Notes Regenerates by seed in gaps after disturbance. Resprouts vigorously after cutting.

Control Chondrostereum purpureum (fungus: Basidiomycetes) is under field evaluation as a biological control agent.

References [196, 407].

Psidium cattleianum Sabine (Myrtaceae)

Description shrub

Region of origin Tropical S. America

Region invaded Hawaii, tropical Polynesia, Raoul, Norfolk I., Mascarenes (Réunion). See main account in Chapter 4.

Psidium guajava L. (Myrtaceae)

Guava, guayaba (Galápagos)

Description §Life form: shrub/tree (to 10 m) §Seed disp.: mammal, bird §Seed prod.: high §Breeding syst.: hermaphrodite §Invasive category **4.5**.

Region of origin S. America (tropical and subtropical S. America). Climatic zone: trop. arid–dry.

Region invaded Oceanic Is (Galápagos), Pacific (Hawaii), Africa (Natal, E. Transvaal, Zimbabwe) Australasia (New Zealand). Climatic zone: wmtemp. moist, subtrop. dry–wet. In Galápagos invades forest edge communities, reducing regeneration of native evergreen trees, with an infestation covering some 40 000 ha. In Hawaii it invades *Acacia* forest at high elevations.

Notes It flowers and produces fruit nearly all the year round under favorable conditions, often being dispersed by introduced mammals and birds. It is intolerant of frost and deep shade but regenerates and grows quickly in gaps.

Control As *Psidium guajava* regenerates readily from underground parts by suckering, it is extremely difficult to kill. Penetration by herbicides is limited by the waxy cuticle.

References [65, 162, 183, 243, 251, 347].

Pueraria lobata (Willd.) Ohwi. {*P.thunbergiana* (Sieb. & Zucc.) Benth., *P.hirsuta* Schnied.} (Leguminosae)

Kudzu vine, Japanese arrowroot

Description §Life form: climber, perennial §Seed disp.: bird, mammal §Seed prod.: high §Breeding syst.: hermaphrodite §Invasive category **3.5**.

Region of origin N. Asia (China, Korea and Japan). Climatic zone: temp. wet. Climber of forest margins (up to 2000 m), common in tropical and subtropical regions.

Region invaded Africa (Eastern Transvaal), Australasia (Papua New Guinea), Pacific (Hawaii and Western Pacific Is), N. America (S. United States), C. America. Climatic zone: subtrop. dry, wmtemp. moist. In the United States it has been widely planted as an erosion control and green fodder. It has spread to forest margins where it is able to smother whole trees.

Notes It appears to be outbreeding and bee-pollinated. The aerial parts are damaged by frost but it is drought tolerant. It grows poorly where the temperature and humidity are high.

Control In Hawaii the herbicide Garlon 4 appears to be effective in controlling Kudzu vine.

References [61, 211, 408].

Ravenala madagascariensis Sonn. (Strelitziaceae)

Traveller's palm

Description §Life form: tree §Seed disp.: birds (fleshy aril) §Invasive category **4**.

Region of origin Malagassia (Madagascar). Climatic zone: trop. arid, subtrop. moist. characteristic of secondary forest.

Region invaded Malagassia (Mauritius) Climatic zone: subtrop. moist. Dominates large areas of marsh, mountain slopes and valleys, forming dense stands.

Notes Reproduces vegetatively by suckering. It was introduced to Mauritius in 1768.

References [238, 239].

Reynoutria japonica Houtt. {*Polygonum cuspidatum* Siebold & Zucc, *P. compactum* Hook f.} (Polygonaceae)

Japanese knotweed

Description §Life form: herb, perennial §Seed disp.: wind, water §Seed prod.: low §Breeding syst.: dioecious §Invasive category **3.5**.

Region of origin N. Asia (Japan, Korea and northern China). Climatic zone: temp. wet, wmtemp. moist–wet, subtrop. moist. Characteristically a colonist of bare volcanic soils, very common in open places on hills and high mountains, and in *Miscanthus sinensis* grassland.

Region invaded Europe (British Isles and N. Europe to E. Germany). Climatic zone: temp. moist, temp. wet. River and railway embankments, roadsides and waste ground. Introduced to Britain in 1825 and cultivated as an ornamental.

Notes Fruit is rarely seen in the British Isles, where spread is by vigorous rhizomatous growth. The flowers are functionally dioecious. It is intolerant of extreme frost, drought or high temperatures. A variable species.

Control Control can prove extremely difficult as *Reynoutria japonica* is fairly resistant to herbicides; when cleared manually, all the rhizomes must be removed to prevent resprouting. This usually proves impossible.

References [71, 76, 307, 383].

Reynoutria sachalinensis (Petrop.) Nakai (Polygonaceae)

Description herb

Region of origin Asia

Region invaded N. and C. Europe

Rhododendron ponticum L. (Ericaceae)

Description shrub

Region of origin Turkey, Spain, Portugal

Region invaded British Isles. See main account in Chapter 4.

Ricinus communis L. (Euphorbiaceae)

Castor bean, castor oil plant, jarak (Malaya)

Description §Life form: shrub, evergreen §Seed disp.: mammal (including humans), bird §Seed prod.: high §Breeding syst.: monoecious §Invasive category **3.5**.

Region of origin Africa (Tropical Africa). Climatic zone: trop. arid–dry.

Region invaded Africa (South Africa – Natal), N./W. Asia (Israel), Pacific (Hawaii), Australasia (Queensland, New South Wales), C. America (Antigua). Climatic zone: wmtemp. moist, subtrop. dry–moist. In South Africa it is widespread in the native vegetation of Natal where disturbance has occurred. In Hawaii it is present in dry disturbed habitats from sea level to 1200 m on all the major islands.

Notes A fast growing thicket-forming plant, widely cultivated for its oil and naturalized in most subtropical countries, easily destroyed by fire. It fruits all the year round under favorable conditions.

References [79, 251, 359].

Robina pseudacacia L. (Leguminosae)

False acacia, black locust

Description shrub

Region of origin N. America

Region invaded Netherlands, France, Germany, Switzerland, Hungary, Greece, Turkey, Cyprus, Israel, Australia, New Zealand

Reference [210].

Rosa rubiginosa L. (Rosaceae)

Sweet-briar

Description shrub

Region of origin Europe

Region invaded Argentina (Nahuel Huapi National Park)

References [94, 100].

Rubus argutus Link {*R. penetrans* Bailey} (Rosaceae)

Florida prickly blackberry

Description §Life form: shrub (thorny), perennial §Seed disp.: bird §Seed prod.: medium §Breeding syst.: possibly dioecious §Invasive category 3.

Region of origin N. America (Prince Edward I. to Georgia and Alabama). Climatic zone: temp. moist, wmtemp. moist, subtrop. moist. Common in well drained sites.

Region invaded Pacific (Hawaii). Climatic zone: wmtemp. moist. Disturbed mesic to wet forests, 1000–2300 m, forming impenetrable thickets by tip rooting of the arching stems.

Notes Resprouts from basal and subterranean shoots after fire. Dispersed by alien birds in Hawaii.

Control Some biological control agents previously introduced to control blackberry in Hawaii have had adverse affects on two native *Rubus* species. Two rust diseases are under investigation for their biological control potential.

References [357, 359, 361].

Rubus cuneifolius Pursh. (Rosaceae)

Description shrub

Region of origin SE Asia

Region invaded South Africa

Rubus ellipticus Sm. {R. *flavus* Hamilton ex D.Don} (Rosaceae)
Yellow Himalayan raspberry

Description §Life form: shrub, semideciduous §Seed disp.: bird, mammal §Seed prod.: medium §Breeding syst.: hermaphrodite §Invasive category **4**.

Region of origin S. Asia (India, Sri Lanka, Burma, Tropical China, Philippines). Climatic zone: wmtemp. moist–wet. Evergreen oak–laurel forest, generally at altitudes of 1700–2300 m, in places associated with *Castanopsis* species; spreading into cultivated areas.

Region invaded Pacific (Hawaii), Africa (Mulanje Mt). Climatic zone: wmtemp. moist, subtrop. dry–moist. In Hawaii it invades pig-disturbed wet forest at 700–1700 m. In Malawi it often forms impenetrable thickets at forest margins or in clearings, having been introduced to the Zomba Botanic Garden between 1898 and 1900.

Notes It spreads rapidly by root suckers and regenerates from underground shoots after fire or cutting.

Control If physical clearance is undertaken, the roots must be grubbed out and burned. Alternatively, cut stumps may be treated with a herbicide: 2,4,5-T or a mixture of 2,4,5-T and 2,4-D are generally employed against *Rubus* species.

References [110, 111, 152, 359].

Rubus fruticosus L. sensu lato (Rosaceae)

Bramble, blackberry

Description shrub

Region of origin Europe

Region invaded Australia

Rubus moluccanus L. {Rubus alceifolius} (Rosaceae)

Description shrub

Region of origin Himalayas – Australasia

Region invaded Mauritius, Réunion

Rudbeckia lacinata L. (Compositae)

Coneflower, black-eyed Susan

Description herb

Region of origin N. America

Region invaded Japan

Saccharum spontaneum L. (Gramineae)

Description herb

Region of origin E. Africa

Region invaded Guam

Salix fragilis L. (Salicaceae)

Crack willow

Description shrub

Region of origin Eurasia

Region invaded New Zealand.

Salvinia molesta D.Mitch. (Salviniceae)

Water fern, kariba weed, African payal

Description herb

Region of origin Brazil

Region invaded Africa (South Africa, Namibia), India, Sri Lanka, Singapore, Malaysia, Philippines, Indonesia, New Guinea, Australia, New Zealand, Fiji, French Polynesia [148]. See main account in Chapter 4.

Sapium sebiferum (L.) Roxb. (Euphorbiaceae)

Chinese tallow

Description tree

Region of origin China, Japan

Region invaded SE USA (Louisiana to South Carolina) [75]

Scaevola plumieri (L.) Vahl. (Goodeniaceae)

Description shrub

Region of origin Australia

Region invaded Paraguay, Venezuela

Schinus terebinthifolia Raddi (Anacardiaceae)

Schinus, Florida holly, Brazilian pepper, Christmas berry

Description §Life form: shrub/tree, perennial, evergreen §Seed disp.: bird §Seed prod.: high §Breeding syst.: dioecious §Invasive category **3.5**.

Region of origin S. America (Brazil, Paraguay, Argentina). Climatic zone: wmtemp. dry, subtrop. dry, trop. arid–dry. Occurs in riverine forest and on damp soils, it thrives on disturbance but, in its native region, does not become a serious pest.

Region invaded N. America (Florida), Pacific (Hawaii), Australasia (Norfolk I.), Malagassia (Mauritius), Oceanic Is (St Helena). Climatic zone: wmtemp. dry, subtrop. moist–wet. Where invasive it has a broad ecological tolerance, for instance in Florida from mangrove swamp to pinelands. It thrives in disturbed habitats resulting from drainage or farming.

Notes A stand of *Schinus terebinthifolia* casts deep shade and lacks an herbaceous understorey. After burning, it resprouts from the base. It is said to release allelopathic chemicals. In Florida it is pollinated by flies (*Palpada vinetorum*). It produces its berries in winter, unlike many of the native Florida trees.

Control Several native pests from Brazil have been released in Hawaii to control *Schinus* but have not as yet been successful. Two have become established (*Bruchus atronotatus*–Coleoptera, *Episimus utilus*–Lepidoptera), but their effects are negligible.

References [21, 115, 196].

Sesbania punicea (Cav.) Benth. (Leguminosae)

Description shrub

Region of origin Argentina, Uruguay, Brazil

Region invaded South Africa [114, 173, 315]. See main account in Chapter 4.

Setaria palmifolia (Koenig) Stapf (Gramineae)

Description herb

Region of origin India

Region invaded Hawaii

Solanum mauritianum Scop. {syn. Solanum auriculatum Ait.} (Solanaceae)

Description shrub

Region of origin Tropical Asia

Region invaded South Africa, Uganda (Mabira Forest Reserve), Réunion, Norfolk I., New Zealand, Polynesia

Solidago canadensis L. (Compositae)

Canadian goldenrod

Description herb

Region of origin N. America

Region invaded C. Europe

Sorghum halepense (L.) Pers. (Gramineae)

Johnson grass

Description herb

Region of origin Mediterranean

Region invaded USA (Mediterranean climate areas)

Spartina anglica C.E.Hubbard (Gramineae)

Common cord-grass

Description herb

Region of origin uk. c. 1890 from *s.* x *townsendii* Groves and J. Groves

Region invaded British Isles [393], Netherlands, France, C. Europe, China, New Zealand.

Swietenia macrophylla King {*S. candollei* Pittier, *S. belizensis* Lundell} (Meliaceae)

Honduras mahogany, broadleaved mahogany

Description §Life form: tree, deciduous §Seed disp.: wind §Seed prod.: high §Breeding syst.: hermaphrodite §Invasive category **4**.

Region of origin C. America (S. Mexico to British Honduras), S. America (Panama, Colombia, Venezuela, Peru, Bolivia, Brazil). Climatic zone: subtrop. moist–wet, trop. dry.

Region invaded S. Asia (Sri Lanka). Climatic zone: trop. dry. It has been planted along skid-trails in previously logged tropical forest, in order to reforest areas of the Sinharaja Biosphere Reserve. Most of this reserve is relatively undisturbed, but *Swietenia macrophylla* threatens to dominate in places if not cleared, as it has a higher growth rate than native trees and is long-lived.

Notes Swietenia macrophylla becomes reproductively mature after 15 years and has a high seed production with good germination success.

Control Swietenia macrophylla has been logged near to roads in order to eradicate it. Further logging is planned. It has some ability to sprout after cutting.

References [79, 101].

Tamarindus indica L. (Leguminosae)

Tamarind

Description tree

Region of origin Tropical Africa

Region invaded Antigua

Tamarix aphylla (L.) Karsten (Tamaricaceae)

Athel pine (Australia)

Description tree

Region of origin Mediterranean

Region invaded Australia, Hawaii

Tamarix ramosissima Ledeb. (Tamaricaceae)

Description shrub

Region of origin Eurasia

Region invaded California, Australia (Finke River south of Alice Springs)

Thunbergia grandiflora (Rottler) Roxb. (Acanthaceae)
Blue thunbergia (Australia)

Description climber

Region of origin India

Region invaded Singapore, Australia (Queensland rainforest)

Tradescantia fluminensis Vell. Conc. (Commelinaceae)
Wandering jew

Description §Life form: herb §Seed prod.: low §Breeding syst.: hermaphrodite §Invasive category 3.

Region of origin S. America (Brazil). Climatic zone: trop. arid–dry.

Region invaded Australasia (New Zealand). Climatic zone: wmtemp. dry=moist. Invades disturbed lowland forest, producing a dense mat up to 60 cm deep, inhibiting the regeneration of native trees.

Notes Spreads rapidly by vegetative growth. Grows most rapidly under high light and is inhibited by deep shade.

Control Ecosystem management to keep the forest canopy unbroken and casting deep shade is probably the best preventive measure against this plant. Paraquat at 2 kg active ingredient per hectare has been used in New Zealand and reduces the standing crop of *Tradescantia fluminensis* by over 50% within 10 weeks [198], but it also damages native plants.

References [197, 198, 445].

Ugni molinae Turcz. (Myrtaceae)

Chilean guava

Description shrub

Region of origin Chile

Region invaded Juan Fernandez Is, Chatham Is

Ulex europaeus L. (Leguminosae)

Gorse, whin, furze

Description §Life form: shrub (spiny), evergreen §Seed disp.: Explosive dehiscence §Seed prod.: high §Breeding syst.: hermaphrodite §Invasive category **3.5**.

Region of origin Europe (western Europe). Climatic zone: temp. dry–wet. Heaths, upland pasture on mildly acidic soil.

Region invaded Pacific (Hawaii), S. Asia (India, Japan), N. America (USA), Australasia (New Zealand, Australia), Africa (South Africa). Climatic zone: temp. moist, wmtemp. moist, subtrop. moist. In New Zealand it vigorously invades pasture, wasteland, roadsides, fernland, scrubland and montane snow tussock. In Hawaii it is regarded as a threatening invader of open habitats.

Notes Although it is not tolerant of shade, in open areas it forms dense monospecific thickets. It regenerates rapidly after fire, both by resprouting and by growing from a persistent soil seed-bank.

Control Biological control using the weevil, *Exapion ulicis* Forster (Coleoptera: Apionidae), has been attempted in New Zealand, Australia and Chile, but has not been successful despite widespread establishment [196]. In New Zealand gorse has been suggested to help re-establishment of native trees as a nurse, in the anticipation that the gorse will disappear in the course of succession over a period of 50–60 years. Seed set of gorse is facilitated in Hawaii by the introduced honey-bee. The weevil, *Apion sculletone*, and the butterfly, *Lampides boeticus*, have been tested as gorse biological control agents in Hawaii.

References [196, 228, 235, 359].

Undaria pinnatifida (Harvey) Suringer (Phaeophyta: Laminariales)

Japanese kelp (Australia), japweed (British)

Description seaweed (kelp)

Region of origin Japan

Region invaded Tasmania, France, Britain

Vinca major L. (Apocynaceae)

Greater periwinkle

Description perennial herb, apparently only spreading vegetatively

Region of origin Europe

Region invaded New Zealand

Appendices

Appendix A – Use of herbicides: some environmental cautions

WWF policy is that herbicide use should be kept to a minimum. WWF cannot endorse the use of any particular herbicide, and it advises all potential users to check on current knowledge about the environmental consequences of particular formulations. Summary notes about the adverse effects of some common herbicides are given below to illustrate some of the issues. No claim is made that all toxic effects are listed.

2,4-D and 2,4,5-T
These substances are very poisonous to humans and there is evidence that they are carcinogenic. Dioxin, a contaminant of 2,4,5-T, is known to be a potent carcinogen. Fears have also been raised of a link between 2,4,5-T and birth defects. 2,4,5-T is persistent in the soil. It has been banned in over 10 countries; its use should be completely avoided (Martlew and Silver, 1991). 2,4-D is toxic to insects (Hurst *et al.*, 1991).

Bromacil (*Hyvar* X; *Krovar II*; *Uragan*)
A soil-acting herbicide. Care must be taken to keep it out of the rooting zone of native plants. Bromacil can be irritating to the skin, eyes and respiratory system. It is considered unlikely to cause an acute hazard to humans under normal use. However, it is dangerous to wildlife (Watterson, 1988).

Dalapon (as sodium/magnesium salts) (*Dowpon*; *Radapon*; *Basfapon*)
Effective for the control of grasses and usually applied as a foliar spray. It leaches readily but breaks down fairly rapidly in soil, persisting some two to four weeks. There is some evidence that Dalapon can cause skin and eye irritation, and it has moderate oral toxicity. It is said to be unlikely to be an acute health hazard to humans under normal use, although possible adverse effects on animal kidneys have been reported (Watterson, 1988).

Dicamba (*Banvel*; *Fallowmaster*)
Supplied as an amine or sodium salt, it is effective against woody plants and may be applied as foliar spray or on cut surfaces. It is mobile in soils and fairly persistent, with a half-life in soil of two weeks or more. It is a mammalian skin and eye irritant of moderate toxicity.

Diquat (as dibromide salt) (*Reglone; Reglox*)
It is highly toxic, although less toxic, and less effective as a herbicide, than paraquat. It is inactivated quickly in soils by adsorption onto clay minerals. Diquat can be fatal if swallowed, inhaled or absorbed through the skin, and can induce serious adverse effects on mammals (Watterson, 1988). There is no known antidote. It may also cause severe eye and skin irritation (Martlew and Silver, 1991).

Endothall (*Des-I-Cate; Aquathol*)
Highly toxic to people and wildlife, but less so to fish and occasionally used as an aquatic herbicide.

Glyphosate (*Round-up* (Monsanto); *Tumbleweed*)
A glycine derivative supplied as an amine salt. Herbaceous species are susceptible to foliar treatment, and some woody species are susceptible to cut-surface treatment or bark injection. It is inactivated immediately in soil by adsorption and decomposes relatively quickly with a half-life of some 60 days. It is said that it is unlikely to represent an acute health hazard to humans under normal use. Can cause nausea and eye irritation. Harmful to fish (Watterson, 1988).

Paraquat (as dichloride salt) (*Gramoxone, Dextrone X; Pillarxone*)
Foliar contact herbicide, highly toxic to plants and people. In soil it is immediately adsorbed to clay minerals in a persistent but biologically inactive form. This is an acutely poisonous chemical responsible for a significant number of deaths. It may also encourage Parkinson's disease, and can be fatal to small mammals (Watterson, 1988; Hurst *et al.*, 1991). There is no known antidote. The use of Paraquat is not advised (Martlew and Silver, 1991).

Picloram (as potassium salt) (*Tordon 22K* (Dow); *Amdan; Grazon*)
It is highly effective against woody plants and may be applied as foliar spray on cut surfaces or as soil-active granules. However, as it is persistent and mobile in soils, it should be used with caution. It is said that it is unlikely to present an acute health hazard to humans under normal use. Of moderate oral toxicity, it is an irritant to the skin, eyes and respiratory tract. High doses produce chronic renal disease in animals. Carcinogenic in animals and harmful to fish (Watterson, 1988).

Triclopyr (as amine salt or ester) (*Garlon* (Dow); *Crossbow*)
Forbs and woody plants are susceptible but grasses are tolerant. However, it is mobile in soil and persistent over a half-life of *c.* 46 days. Mild eye and skin irritant, slightly hazardous to humans and dangerous to fish (Watterson, 1988).

Sources:

Hurst, P., Hay, A. and Dudley, N. (1991) *The Pesticide Handbook*, Journeyman, London (UK) and Concord (USA).
Martlew, G. and Silver, S. (1991) *The Green Home Handbook*, Fontana, London.
Watterson, A. (1988) *Pesticide User's Safety Handbook*, Gower Technical, Aldershot (UK).

Appendix B – A selection of relevant addresses

Australia

CSIRO Division of Entomology,
Long Pocket Laboratories,
Private Bag 3, PO,
Indooroopilly,
Queensland 4068

CSIRO Division of Plant Industry,
GPO Box 1600,
Canberra,
ACT 2601

CSIRO Tropical Ecosystems Research Centre,
PMB 44,
Winellie,
Darwin NT08,
Northern Territory

Netherlands

Research Institute for Nature,
Kemperbergerweg 67,
6816 RM Arnhem

Dept of Vegetation Science, Plant Ecology and Weed Science,
Agricultural University,
Bornsesteeg 69,
6708 PD Wageningen

New Zealand

Land Care Research NZ Ltd,
PO Box 40,
Lincoln,
Canterbury

Department of Conservation,
PO Box 12–240,
Wellington

South Africa

National Botanical Institute,
Private Bag X101,
Pretoria 0001

Percy Fitzpatrick Institute of Ornithology,
University of Cape Town,
Private Bag,
Rondebosch 7700

Switzerland

Plants Officer,
IUCN – The World Conservation Union
Rue Mauverney 28
CH-1196 Gland

WWF International
Avenue du Mont Blanc
CH-1196 Gland

United Kingdom

Royal Botanic Gardens,
Kew,
Richmond,
Surrey TW9 3AA

Botanic Garden Conservation International,
Descanso House,
199 Kew Road,
Richmond,
Surrey TW9 3BW

International Institute for Biological Control,
Silwood Park,
Buckhurst Road,
Ascot,
Berkshire
SL5 7TA

WWF Plants Conservation Officer,
Panda House,
Weyside Park,
Godalming,
Surrey GU7 1XR

World Conservation Monitoring Centre,
219 Huntingdon Road,
Cambridge CB3 0DL

USA

WWF – United States
1250 24th Street NW
Washington DC 20037-1175
USA

USA – Hawaii

Hawaii Volcanoes National Park,
US National Park Service,
PO Box 52,
Honolulu,
Hawaii 96712

Cooperative Parks Study Unit,
University of Hawaii at Manoa,
90 Maile Way,
Honolulu,
Hawaii 96822

National Tropical Botanic Garden,
PO Box 340,
Lawai,
Kauai,
Hawaii 96765

Glossary

adventive	an immigrant, a plant recently arrived and not yet established
agamospermy	seed production without sexual fusion, a type of apomixis (q.v.)
alien	not native, exotic (adj.), a non-native organism (noun)
allelopathy	release by plants of chemicals into soil which inhibit the growth of others
apomixis	asexual reproduction
autecology	study of the relationship between an organism and its environment
biological control	control of pests by use of their predators or pathogens
biotype	a biologically distinct population or variant
cross-fertilization	fusion of the sex-cells of different organisms
cross-pollination	transfer of pollen from a different plant onto the stigma
database	source of organized information, generally held on a computer
dicotyledon	one of the two divisions of flowering plants, characteristically with reticulate venation and two seed-leaves, e.g. Leguminosae, Compositae
dioecy	separation of sexes, with male and female flowers on different plants
dispersal	process by which seeds, or other reproductive units, are carried away from the parent plant
endemic	(of an organism) restricted to a particular place, usually used of organisms which are not widespread
eutrophication	increase of availability or mineral nutrients (usually nitrates and phospates) in an ecosystem
evapotranspiration	loss of water from soil by evaporation from surface and from plant leaves (transpiration)
exotic	not native, alien (adj.), a non-native organism (noun)
facilitation	change in environmental conditions aiding or enabling invasion
facultative apomixis	reproduction sexual or asexual depending on conditions

feral	naturalized, not native
focus	point of introduction from which spread occurs (plural: foci)
fynbos	open scrubland of Cape Province, South Africa
genotype	the particular genetic constitution of an organism
germplasm	living material capable of propagation
grassveld	grassland of large perennial grasses characteristic of parts of South Africa
herbivore	plant-eating animal
hermaphrodite	having both male and female organs in each flower
inbreeding	reproduction by self-fertilization (q.v.)
indigenous	native
invasion	spread of an organism, without human assistence, into natural or seminatural habitats to produce a significant ecosystem change (of composition, structure or processes)
karoo	dry open vegetation of low shrubs and succulents, characteristic of parts of Cape Province, South Africa
mattock	implement with blade and handle for removal of small tree roots
monocotyledon	one of the two divisions of flowering plants, characteristically with parallel leaf-veins and one seed-leaf, e.g. grasses, orchids, palms (cf. dicotyledons)
monoecy	separation of male and female organs in different flowers but on the same plant
mycoherbicide	fungal spores in suspension used as a weedkiller
native	naturally occurring in an area
naturalization	process of establishment of an introduction in native vegetation from some point of introduction (e.g. a garden or plantation). An early stage in the process of invasion
obligate apomixis	inability to reproduce sexually
outbreeding	reproduction by cross-fertilization (q.v.)
polyploid	having more than two sets of chromosomes
propagule	a plant part or plant organ, such as a seed or stem fragment, capable of reproducing the plant after dispersal
remote sensing	collection of ground information by satellite or aircraft
ruderal	plant associated with human activity or disturbed sites
savanna	tropical grassland of tall grasses and sparse low trees, characteristic of much of Africa but also occurring in N. Australia and in Venezuela, Colombia ('ilanos') and Brazil ('campos')
sclerophyll	plant with tough, rigid leaves, such as *Eucalyptus*. Such plants are typical of Mediterranean-type ecosystems
seed-bank	reservoir of viable seed in soil capable of remaining dormant for some time, and usually germinating after disturbance

self-compatible	able to self-fertilize
self-fertilization	fusion of the sex-cells of the same organism
self-incompatible	not able to self-fertilize because of genetic and physiological factors
self-pollination	transfer of pollen from the same plant onto the stigma
serotiny	delayed seed release (often stimulated by fire)
subdioecy	incomplete separation of sexes between different plants
succession	change of plant communities over time following an environmental perturbation
syndrome	a collection of characteristics of a plant that are associated with particular ecological behavior
tannin	type of plant chemical that deters grazing and is used to tan leather
translocation	(of organism) movement of germplasm (q.v.) from one place to another; (of herbicide) movement of chemical from one part of the plant to another
triploid	having three sets of chromosomes, one set being unpaired

References

1. Abbott, R.J. (1992) Plant invasion, interspecific hybridization and the evolution of new plant taxa, *Trends in Ecology and Evolution*, **7**, 401–5.
2. Adams, C.D. (1972) *Flowering Plants of Jamaica*, University of the West Indies, Jamaica.
3. Allen, R.B. (1991) A preliminary assessment of the establishment and persistence of *Berberis darwinii* Hook., a naturalised shrub in secondary vegetation near Dunedin, New Zealand, *New Zealand Journal of Botany*, **29**, 353–60.
4. Amor, R.L. and P.L. Stevens (1975) Spread of weeds from a roadside into sclerophyll forests at Dartmouth, Australia, *Weed Research*, **16**, 111–18.
5. Andres, L.A. (1981) Conflicting interests and the biological control of weeds, in *Proceedings of the Fifth International Symposium on Biological Control of Weeds*, (ed. E.S. Del Fosse), CSIRO, Brisbane, Australia, pp. 11–20.
6. Anon. (1985) Ecology of Biological Invasions, *SCOPE Newsletter*, **23**, 1–5.
7. Arthington, A.H. and D.S. Mitchell (1986) Aquatic invading species, in *Ecology of Biological Invasions*, (ed. R.H. Groves and J.J. Burdon), Cambridge University Press, Cambridge, pp. 34–56.
8. Ashton, D.H. (1981) Tall open forests, in *Australian Vegetation*, (ed. R.H. Groves), Cambridge University Press, Cambridge, pp. 121–51.
9. Ashton, P.J. and D.S. Mitchell (1989) Aquatic plants: patterns and modes of invasion, attributes of invading species and assessment of control programs, in *Biological Invasions: a global perspective*, (ed. J.A. Drake *et al.*), John Wiley & Sons, Chichester, pp. 111–54.
10. Auld, B.A. (1969) The distribution of *Eupatorium adenophorum* Spreng. on the far north coast of New South Wales, *Journal and Proceedings of the Royal Society of New South Wales*, **102**, 159–61.
11. Auld, B.A. (1970) *Eupatorium* weed species in Australia, *PANS*, **16**, 82–6.
12. Auld, B.A. (1975) The autecology of *Eupatorium adenophorum* Spreng. in Australia, *Weed Research*, **15**, 27–31.
13. Auld, B.A. (1977) The introduction of *Eupatorium* species to Australia, *Journal of the Australian Institute of Agricultural Science*, September/December, 146–7.
14. Auld, B.A. (1981) Invasive capacity of *Eupatorium adenophorum*, in *Proceedings of the 8th Asian-Pacific Weeds Science Conference*, pp. 145–7.
15. Auld, B.A. and B.G. Coote (1980) A model of a spreading plant population, *Oikos*, **34**, 287–92.
16. Auld, B.A. and B.G. Coote (1981) Prediction of pasture invasion by *Nassella trichotoma* (Gramineae) in south east Australia, *Protection Ecology*, **3**, 271–7.
17. Auld, B.A., J. Hosking and R.E. McFadyen (1982/1983) Analysis of the spread of tiger pear and parthenium weed in Australia, *Australian Weeds*, **2**, 56–60.
18. Auld, B.A., K.M. Menz and N.M. Monaghan (1978/1979) Dynamics of weed spread: implications for policies of public control, *Protection Ecology*, **1**, 141–8.
19. Auld, B.A., K.M. Menz and C.A. Tisdell (1987) *Weed Control Economics*, Academic Press, London.

20. Auld, B.A., D.T. Vere and B.G. Coote (1982) Evaluation of control policies for the grassland weed, *Nassella trichotoma*, in south-east Australia, *Protection Ecology*, **4**, 331–8.

21. Austin, D.F. (1978) Exotic plants and their effects in south east Florida, *Environmental Conservation*, **5**, 25–34.

22. Baker, H.G. (1965) Characteristics and modes of origin of weeds, in *The Genetics of Colonizing Species*, (ed. H.G. Baker and C.L. Stebbins), Academic Press, New York, pp. 147–69.

23. Baker, H.G. (1986) Genetic characteristics of invasive plants, in *Ecology of Biological Invasion of North America and Hawaii*, (ed. H.A. Mooney and J.A. Drake), Springer-Verlag, New York, pp. 147–68.

24. Balloch, G.M., S. Ullah and A.A. Shah (1980) Some promising insects for the biological control of *Hydrilla verticillata* in Pakistan, *Tropical Pest Management*, **26**, 194–200.

25. Bannister, M.H. (1965) Variation in the breeding system of *Pinus radiata*, in *The Genetics of Colonizing Species*, (ed. H.G. Baker and G.L. Stebbins), Academic Press, New York, pp. 353–73.

26. Barneby, R.C. (1989) Reflections on typification and application of the names *Mimosa pigra* L. and *M. asperata* L. (Mimosaceae), in *The Davis and Hedge Festschrift*, (ed. K. Tan), Edinburgh University Press, Edinburgh, pp. 137–47.

27. Barrett, S.C.H. (1988) Evolution of breeding systems in *Eichhornea* (Pontederiaceae): a review, *Annals of the Missouri Botanical Garden*, **75**, 741–60.

28. Barrows, E.M. (1976) Nectar robbing and pollination of *Lantana camara* (Verbenaceae), *Biotropica*, **8**, 132–5.

29. Bass, D.A. (1990) Dispersal of an introduced shrub (*Crataegus monogyna*) by the brush-tailed possum (*Trichosurus vulpecula*), *Australian Journal of Ecology*, **15**, 227–9.

30. Bawa, K.S. (1980) Evolution of dioecy in flowering plants, *Annual Review of Ecology and Systematics*, **11**, 15–39.

31. Bean, W.J. (1976) *Trees and Shrubs Hardy in the British Isles*, 8th edn, John Murray, London, pp. 741–4.

32. Beard, J. (1976) Alien shrub runs riot in Hawaii, *New Scientist*, **1708**, 30.

33. Becker, D. (1988) *Management techniques: the control and removal of Rhododendron ponticum on RSPB reserves in England and Wales*, The Royal Society for the Protection of Birds. Sandy, UK.

34. Bennett, F.D. and V.P. Rao (1968) Distribution of an introduced weed *Eupatorium odoratum* Linn. (Compositae) in Asia and Africa and possibilities of its biological control, *Pest Articles and News Summaries, Section C*, **14**, 277–81.

35. Bennett, K.D. (1986) The rate of spread and population increase of forest trees during the postglacial, *Philosophical Transactions of the Royal Society, London, Series B*, **314**, 523–9.

36. Benson, L. (1982) *The Cacti of the United States and Canada*, Stanford University Press, Stanford.

37. Bentham, G. (1875) Revision of the suborder Mimosae, *Transactions of the Linnean Society*, **30**, 335–664.

38. Binggeli, P. (1989) The ecology of *Maesopsis* invasion and dynamics of the evergreen forest of the East Usambaras and their implications for forest conservation and forestry practices, in *Forest Conservation in the East Usambara Mountains Tanzania*, (ed. A.C. Hamilton and R. Bensted-Smith), IUCN, Gland, pp. 269–300.

39. Binggeli, P. and A.C. Hamilton (1990) Tree species invasions and sustainable forestry in the East Usambaras, in *Research for Conservation of Tanzanian Catchment Forests*, (ed. I. Hedberg and E. Persson), Uppsala Universitet Reprocentralen HSC, Uppsala, pp. 39–47.

40. Birks, H.J.B. and J. Deacon (1973) A numerical analysis of the past and present flora of the British Isles, *New Phytologist*, **72**, 877–902.

41. Booth, T. *et al.* (1987) Grid matching: a new method of homoclime analysis, *Agricultural and Forest Meteorology*, **39**, 241–55.
42. Booth, T.H. (1985) A new method for assisting species selection, *Commonwealth Forestry Review*, **64**, 241–50.
43. Booth, T.H. and T. Jovanovic (1988) Assaying natural climatic variability in some Australian species with fuelwood and agroforestry potential, *Commonwealth Forestry Review*, **67**, 27–34.
44. Bottrell, D.G. and R.F. Smith (1982) Integrated Pest Management, *Environmental Science and Technology*, **16**, 282A–8A.
45. Boucher, C. (1980) Black wattle, in *Plant Invaders: beautiful but dangerous*, 2nd edn, (ed. C.H. Stirton), The Department of Nature and Environmental Conservation of the Cape Provincial Administration, Cape Town, pp. 48–51.
46. Boucher, C. and C.H. Stirton (1980) Long-leaved wattle, in *Plant Invaders: beautiful but dangerous*, 2nd edn, (ed. C.H. Stirton), Department of Nature and Environmental Conservation of the Cape Provincial Administration., Cape Town, pp. 44–7.
47. Boucher, C. and C.H. Stirton (1980) Port Jackson, in *Plants Invaders: beautiful but dangerous*, 2nd edn, (ed. C.H. Stirton), Department of Nature and Environmental Conservation of the Cape Provincial Administration, Cape Town, pp. 60–3.
48. Boucher, C. and C.H. Stirton (1980) Rooikrans, in *Plant Invaders: beautiful but dangerous*, 2nd edn, (ed. C.H. Stirton), Department of Nature and Environmental Conservation of the Cape Provincial Administration, Cape Town, pp. 40–3.
49. Boyette, C.D., G.E. Templeton and L.R. Oliver (1984) Texas gourd (*Cucurbita texana*) control with *Fusarium solani* f. sp. *cucurbitae*, *Weed Science*, **32**, 649–55.
50. Bradley, J. (1988) *Bringing Back the Bush*, Landsdowne Press, Sydney.
51. Braithwaite, R.W., W.M. Lonsdale and J.A. Esthbergs (1989) Alien vegetation and native biota in tropical Australia: the impact of *Mimosa pigra*, *Biological Conservation*, **48**, 189–210.
52. Bramwell, D. and Z.I. Bramwell (1974) *Wild Flowers of the Canary Islands*, Stanley Thornes, London.
53. Brenan, J.P.M. (1959) *Leguminosae Subfamily Mimosoideae, Flora of Tropical East Africa*, (ed. C.E. Hubbard and E. Milne-Redhead), Crown Agents, London.
54. Bridgewater, P.B. and D.J. Backshall (1981) Dynamics of some Western Australian ligneous formations with special reference to the invasion of exotic species, *Vegetatio*, **46**, 141–8.
55. Brockie, R.E. *et al.* (1988) Biological invasions of island nature reserves, *Biological Conservation*, **44**, 9–36.
56. Brockway, L.H. (1979) *Science and Colonial Expansion*, Academic Press, New York.
57. Brown, C.J., I.A.W. Macdonald and S.E. Brown, ed. (1985) *Invasive Alien Organisms in South West Africa/Namibia*, CSIR, Pretoria.
58. Buckley, R. (1981) Alien plants in central Australia, *Botanical Journal of the Linnean Society*, **82**, 369–80.
59. Burdon, J.J. and G.A. Chilvers (1977) Preliminary studies on a native eucalypt forest invaded by exotic pines, *Oecologia*, **31**, 1–12.
60. Burrell, J.P. (1981) Invasion of coastal heaths of Victoria by *Leptospermum laevigatum* (J.Gaertn.) F. Muell., *Australian Journal of Botany*, **29**, 747–64.
61. Burrows, J.E. (1989) Kudzu vine – a new plant invader of South Africa, *Veld & Flora*, **75**, 116–17.
62. Buxton, J.M. (1985) The potential for biological control of *Clematis vitalba* L., M.Sc. Thesis, Imperial College, Ascot.
63. Campbell, M.H. (1982) The biology of Australian weeds 9. *Nassella trichotoma* (Nees) Arech., *The Journal of the Australian Institute of Agricultural Science*, **48**, 76–84.
64. Cassani, J.R., T.W. Miller and M.L. Beach (1981) Biological control of aquatic weeds in southwest Florida, *Journal of Aquatic Plant Management*, **19**, 49–50.

65. Cattley, W. (1821) *Psidium cattleianum*, *Transactions of the Royal Horticultural Society*, **4**, 314–17.
66. Chapman, V.J. (1967) Conservation of maritime vegetation and the introduction of submerged freshwater aquatics, *Micronesica*, **3**, 31–5.
67. Charudattan, R. (1986) Integrated control of water hyacinth (*Eichhornea crassipes*) with a pathogen, insects and herbicides, *Weed Science*, **34**, (Suppl.1), 26–30.
68. Chilvers, G.A. and J.J. Burdon (1983) Further studies on a native Australian eucalypt forest invaded by exotic pines, *Oecologia*, **59**, 239–45.
69. Cilliers, C.J. (1991) Biological control of water fern, *Salvinia molesta* (Salviniaceae), in South Africa, *Agriculture, Ecosystems and Environment*, **37**, 219–24.
70. Cilliers, C.J. and S. Neser (1991) Biological control of *Lantana camara* (Verbenaceae) in South Africa, *Agriculture, Ecosystems and Environment*, **37**, 57–75.
71. Clapham, A.R., T.G. Tutin and E.F. Warburg (1962) *Flora of the British Isles*, 2nd edn, Cambridge University Press, Cambridge.
72. Clayton, W.D. and S.A. Renvoize (1982) Gramineae, part 3, in *Flora of Tropical East Africa*, (ed. R.M. Polhill), A.A. Balkema, Rotterdam.
73. Coblentz, B.E. (1990) Exotic organisms: A dilemma for conservation biology, *Conservation Biology*, **4**, 261.
74. Coffey, B.T. and J.S. Clayton (1988) Changes in the submerged macrophyte vegetation of Lake Rotoiti, central North Island, New Zealand, *New Zealand Journal of Marine and Freshwater Research*, **22**, 215–23.
75. Conner, W.H. and G.R. Askew (1993) Impact of saltwater flooding on red maple, redbay, and Chinese tallow seedlings, *Castanea*, **58**, 214–19.
76. Conolly, A.P. (1977) The distribution and history in the British of some alien species of *Polygonum* and *Reynoutria*, *Watsonia*, **11**, 291–311.
77. Cooper, R.C. (1956) The Australian and New Zealand species of *Pittosporum*, *Annals of the Missouri Botanical Garden*, **43**, 87–188.
78. Corlett, R.T. (1988) The naturalized flora of Singapore, *Journal of Biogeography*, **15**, 657–63.
79. Corner, E.J.H. (1988) *Wayside Trees of Malaya*, Vol. 1, 3rd edn, The Malayan Nature Society, Kuala Lumpur.
80. Correll, D.S. and M.C. Johnston (1970) *Manual of the Vascular Plants of Texas*, Series 1, (ed. C.L. Lundell), Texas Research Foundation., Texas.
81. Cowie, I.D. and P.A. Werner (1993) Alien plant species in the Kakadu National Park, tropical northern Australia, *Biological Conservation*, **62**, 127–35.
82. Cox, P. and P. Hutchinson (1963) Rhododendrons in north east Turkey, *Rhododendron Yearbook*, **17**, 64–7.
83. Crawley, M.J. (1987) What makes a community invasible?, in *Colonization, Succession and Stability*, (ed. M.J. Crawley, P.J. Edwards and A.J. Gray), Blackwell, Oxford, pp. 629–54.
84. Cronk, Q.C.B. (1986) The decline of the St Helena Ebony *Trochetiopsis melanoxylon*, *Biological Conservation*, **35**, 159–72.
85. Cronk, Q.C.B. (1987) Combating the invasive plant threat: the feasibility, structure and role of an action-oriented database, IUCN: unpublished report.
86. Cronk, Q.C.B. (1989) The past and present vegetation of St Helena, *Journal of Biogeography*, **16**, 47–64.
87. Crosby, A.W. (1986) *Ecological Imperialism: The biological expansion of Europe, 900–1900*, Cambridge University Press, Cambridge.
88. Cross, J.R. (1973) The ecology and control of *Rhododendron ponticum* L., Ph.D. Thesis, University of Dublin.
89. Cross, J.R. (1975) Biological Flora of the British Isles, no. 137. *Rhododendron ponticum* L., *Journal of Ecology*, **63**, 345–64.
90. Cross, J.R. (1982) The invasion and impact of *Rhododendron* in native Irish vegetation, in *Studies on Irish Vegetation*, (ed. J. White), Royal Dublin Society, Dublin, pp. 209–20.

91. Cruz, F.J. Cruz and J. Laweson (1986) *Lantana camara* L., a threat to native plants and animals, *Noticias de Galapagos*, **43**, 10–11.

92. D'Antonio, C.M. (1993) Mechanisms controlling invasion of coastal plant communities by the alien succulent *Carpobrotus edulis*, *Ecology*, **74**, 83–95.

93. D'Antonio, C.M. and B.E. Mahall (1991) Root profiles and competition between the invasive exotic perennial, *Carpobrotus edulis*, and the two native shrub species in California coastal scrub, *American Journal of Botany*, **78**, 885–94.

94. Damascos, M.A. and G.G. Gallopin (1992) Ecología de un arbusto introducido (*Rosa rubiginosa* L. = *Rosa eglanteria* L.): riesgo de invasión y efectos en las comunidades vegetales de la región andino-patagónica de Argentina, *Revista Chilena de Historia Natural*, **65**, 395–407.

95. Das, R. (1969) A study of reproduction in *Eichhornia crassipes*, *Tropical Ecology*, **10**, 195–8.

96. Dassanayake, M.D. and F.R. Fosberg, ed. (1985) *A Revised Handbook to the Flora of Ceylon*, Vol. 5, Amerind Publishing Company, New Delhi.

97. Davis, C.J., E. Yoshioka and D. Kageler (1992) Biological control of lantana, prickly pear, and hamakua pamakani in Hawaii: a review and update, in *Alien Plant Invasions in Native Ecosystems of Hawaii: management and research*, (ed. C.P. Stone, C.W. Smith and J.T. Tunison), University of Hawaii Cooperative National Park Resources Studies Unit, Honolulu, pp. 411–31.

98. Davis, D.R. *et al.* (1991) Systematics, morphology, biology, and host specificity of *Neurostrota gunniella* (Busck) (Lepidoptera: Gracillariidae), an agent for the biological control of *Mimosa pigra* L., *Proceedings of the Entomological Society of Washington*, **93**, 16–44.

99. Dawson, F.H. and E.A. Warman (1987) *Crassula helmsii* (T.Kirk) Cockayne: Is it an aggressive alien aquatic plant in Britain?, *Biological Conservation*, **42**, 247–72.

100. De Pietri, D.E. (1992) Alien shrubs in a national park: can they help in the recovery of natural degraded forest?, *Biological Conservation*, **62**, 127–30.

101. de Zoysa, N.D., C.V.S. Gunatilleke and I.A.U.N. Gunatilleke (1986) Vegetation studies of a skid-trail planted with mahogany in Sinharaja, *The Sri Lanka Forester*, **17**, 142–7.

102. Dennill, G.B. (1990) The contribution of a successful biocontrol project to the theory of agent selection in weed biocontrol – the gall wasp *Trichilogaster acaciaelongifoliae* and the *Acacia longifolia*, *Agriculture, Ecosystems and Environment*, **31**, 147–54.

103. Denton, G.R.W., and R. Muniappan (1991) Status and natural enemies of the weed, *Lantana camara*, in Micronesia, *Tropical Pest Management*, **37**, 338–44.

104. Devine, W.T. (1977) A programme to exterminate introduced plants on Raoul Island, *Biological Conservation*, **11**, 193–207.

105. Dickson, J.H., J.C. Rodriguez and A. Machado (1987) Invading plants at high altitudes on Tenerife especially in the Teide National Park, *Botanical Journal of the Linnean Society*, **95**, 155–79.

106. Downward, P. (1986) Herbicides for control of old man's beard, in *Proceedings of the 39th New Zealand Weed and Pest Control Conference*, pp. 108–9.

107. Du Cane, G. (1870) *Natural History of the Azores*, John van Voorst, London.

108. Duggen, K.J. and L. Henderson (1981) Progress with a survey of exotic woody plant invaders of the Transvaal, in *Proceedings of the Fourth National Weeds Conference of South Africa*, (ed. H.A. van de Venter and M. Mason), A.A. Balkema, Capetown, pp. 7–20.

109. Dyer, C. and D.M. Richardson (1992) Population genetics of the invasive Australian shrub *Hakea sericea* (Proteaceae) in South Africa, *South African Journal of Botany*, **58**, 117–24.

110. Edwards, I.D. (1982) Plant invaders on Mulanje Mountain, *Nyala*, **8**, 89–94.

111. Edwards, I.D. (1985) Conservation of plants on Mulanje Mountain, Malawi, *Oryx*, **19**, 86–90.

112. Ellenberg, H. (1974) Indicator values of vascular plants in central Europe, *Scripta Geobotanica*, **9**, 1–86.
113. Elton, C.S. (1958) *The Ecology of Invasions by Animals and Plants*, Chapman & Hall, London.
114. Erb, H.E. (1979) The natural enemies and distribution of *Sesbania punicea* (Cav.) Benth. in Argentina, in *Proceedings of the Third National Weeds Conference of South Africa, Pretoria*, pp. 205–10.
115. Ewel, J.J. (1986) Invasibility: lessons from South Florida, in *Ecology of Biological Invasion of North America and Hawaii*, (ed. H.A. Mooney and J.A. Drake), Springer-Verlag, New York, pp. 214–30.
116. Fairley, A. and P. Moore (1989) *Native Plants of the Sydney District: An Identification Guide*, Kangaroo Press, New South Wales.
117. Farell, T.P. (1979) Control of *Salvinia molesta* and *Hydrilla verticillata* in Lake Moondarra, Queensland, in *Australian Water Resources Council Seminar on Management of Aquatic Weeds*, pp. 57–71.
118. Flanagan, G.J., C.G. Wilson and J.D. Gillett (1990) The abundance of native insects on the introduced weed *Mimosa pigra* in Northern Australia, *Journal of Tropical Ecology*, **6**, 219–30.
119. Floyd, A.G. (1990) *Australian Rainforests in New South Wales*, Vol. 1, Surrey Beatty & Sons Pty Limited, New South Wales.
120. Forno, I.W. and K.L.S. Harkey (1979) The occurrence of *Salvinia molesta* in Brazil, *Aquatic Botany*, **6**, 185–7.
121. Forsyth, A.A. (1954) British poisonous plants, *Bulletin of the Ministry of Agriculture, Fisheries and Food, London*, No. 161.
122. Fuller, J.L. (1991) The threat of invasive plants to natural ecosystems, M.Phil. Thesis, University of Cambridge.
123. Fuller, R.M. and L.A. Boorman (1977) The spread and development of *Rhododendron ponticum* L. on dunes at Winterton, Norfolk, in comparison with invasion by *Hippophae rhamnoides* L. at Saltfleeby, Lincolnshire, *Biological Conservation*, **12**, 83–94.
124. Gardner, D.E. and V.A.D. Kageler (1982) *Herbicidal control of firetree in Hawaii Volcanoes National Park: a new approach*, Ecological Services Bulletin, No. 7, US Department of the Interior, Washington.
125. Gardner, D.E. and C.W. Smith (1985) Plant biocontrol quarantine facility at Hawaii Volcanoes, *Park Science*, **6**, 3–4.
126. Geldenhuys, C.J. (1982) The management of the southern Cape forests, *South African Forestry Journal*, **121**, 1–7.
127. Geldenhuys, C.J., P.J. Le Roux and K.H. Cooper (1986) Alien invasion in the indigenous evergreen forest, in *Ecology and Management of Biological Invasions in South Africa*, (ed. I.A.W. Macdonald, F.J. Kruger and A.A. Ferrar), Oxford University Press, Cape Town, pp. 275–82.
128. Gill, L.T. (1989) Perspectives on environmental education in Hawaii, in *Conservation Biology in Hawaii*, (ed. C.P. Stone and D.B. Stone), University of Hawaii Cooperative National Park Resources Studies Unit, Honolulu, pp. 177–8.
129. Gleadow, R.M. (1982) Invasion by *Pittosporum undulatum* of the forests of Central Victoria. 2, Dispersal, germination and establishment, *Australian Journal of Botany*, **30**, 185–98.
130. Gleadow, R.M. and D.H. Ashton (1981) Invasion by *Pittosporum undulatum* of the forests of Central Victoria. 1, Invasion patterns and morphology, *Australian Journal of Botany*, **29**, 705–20.
131. Gleadow, R.M., and K.S. Rowan (1982) Invasion by *Pittosporum undulatum* of the forests of Central Victoria. 3, Effects of temperature and light on growth and drought resistance, *Australian Journal of Botany*, **30**, 347–57.
132. Gleason, H.A. (1939) The genus *Clidemia* in Mexico and Central America, *Brittonia*, **3**, 97–140.

133. Godwin, Sir H. (1975) *The History of the British Flora*, 2 edn, Cambridge University Press, Cambridge.
134. Golley, F.B. (1965) Structure and function of an old-field broomsedge community, *Ecological Monographs*, **35**, 113–37.
135. Gooding, E.G.B., A.R. Loveless and G.R. Proctor (1965) *Flora of Barbados*, Her Majesty's Stationary Office, London.
136. Goodland, T. (1990) A report on the spread of an invasive tree species *Pittosporum undulatum* into the forests of the Blue Mountains, Jamaica, B.Sc. report, University College of North Wales.
137. Gopal, B. (1987) *Water Hyacinth: The most troublesome weed in the world*, Hindasia Publishers, Delhi.
138. Gowda, M. (1951) The genus *Pittosporum* in the Sino-Indian Region, *Journal of the Arnold Arboretum*, **32**, 263–343.
139. Graaf, J.L. and J. van Staden (1984) The germination characteristics of two *Sesbania* species, *South African Journal of Botany*, **3**, 59–62.
140. Griffen, J.L., V.H. Watson and W.F. Strachan (1988) Selective broomsedge (*Andropogon virginicus* L.) control in permanent pastures, *Crop Protection*, **7**, 80–3.
141. Griffin, G.F. *et al.* (1989) Status and implications of the invasion of Tamarisk (*Tamarix aphylla*) on the Finke River, Northern Territory, Australia, *Journal of Environmental Management*, **29**, 297–315.
142. Grime, J.P. (1979) *Plant Strategies and Vegetation Processes*, John Wiley & Sons, Chichester.
143. Groves, R.H. (1985) Invasion of weeds in mediterranean ecosystems, in *Resilience in Mediterranean Climatic Ecosystems*, (ed. B. Dell), Dr.W.Junk, The Hague.
144. Groves, R.H. (1986) Plant invasion of Australia: an overview, in *Ecology of Biological Invasions*, (ed. R.H. Groves and J.J. Burdon), Cambridge University Press, Cambridge, pp. 137–49.
145. Groves, R.H. and J.J. Burdon, ed. (1986) *Ecology of Biological Invasions*, Cambridge University Press, Cambridge.
146. Groves, R.H. and J.D. Williams (1975) Growth of Skeleton Weed (*Chondrilla juncea* L.) as affected by growth of subterranean clover (*Trifolium subterraneum* L.) and infected by *Puccinia chondrillina* Bubak & Syd., *Australian Journal of Agricultural Research*, **26**, 975–83.
147. Grubb, P.J. and E.V.J. Tanner (1976) The montane forest and soils of Jamaica: a re-assessment, *Journal of the Arnold Arboretum*, **57**, 313–68.
148. Guillarmod, A.J. (1980) Kariba weed, in *Plant Invaders: beautiful but dangerous*, 2nd ed, (ed. C.H. Stirton), Department of Nature and Environmental Conservation of the Cape Provincial Administration, Cape Town, pp. 132–5.
149. Guillarmod, A.J. (1980) Parrot's feather, in *Plant Invaders: beautiful but dangerous*, 2nd ed, (ed. C.H. Stirton), The Department of Nature and Environmental Conservation of the Cape Provincial Administration, Cape Town, pp. 96–9.
150. Haggar, J.P.C. (1988) The structure, composition and status of the cloud forests of the Pico Island in the Azores, *Biological Conservation*, **46**, 7–22.
151. Hamann, O. (1984) Changes and threats to the vegetation, in *Key Environments: Galapagos*, (ed. R. Perry), Pergamon Press, Oxford, pp. 115–31.
152. Hara, H. (1966) *Flora of the Eastern Himalaya*, University of Tokyo Press, Tokyo.
153. Harding, G. (1980) Mesquite, in *Plant Invaders: beautiful but dangerous*, (ed. C.H. Stirton), Department of Nature and Environmental Conservation for the Cape Provincial Administration, Cape Town, pp. 128–31.
154. Harper, J.L. (1977) *Population Biology of Plants*, Academic Press, New York.
155. Harris, P. (1979) Cost of biological control of weeds by insects, *Weed Science*, **27**, 242–50.
156. Harris, P. (1984) Current approaches to biological control of weeds, in *Biological*

217

Control Programmes Against Insects and Weeds, (ed. J.S. Kelleher and M.A. Hulme), CAB, Slough, pp. 95–104.

157. Harris, P. (1984) *Euphorbia esula-virgata* complex, Leafy Spurge and *E. cyparissias* L., Cypress spurge (Euphorbiaceae), in *Biological Control against Insects and Weeds in Canada 1969–1980*, (ed. J.S. Kelleher and M.A. Hulme), CAB, Slough, pp. 159–69.

158. Haslewood, E.L. and G.G. Motter, ed. (1984) *Handbook of Hawaiian Weeds*, University of Hawaii Press, Honolulu.

159. Hathaway, D.E. (1989) *Molecular Mechanisms of Herbicide Selectivity*, Oxford University Press, Oxford.

160. Henderson, L. (1991) Invasive alien woody plants of the northern Cape, *Bothalia*, **21**, 177–89.

161. Henderson, L. (1992) Invasive alien woody plants of the eastern Cape, *Bothalia*, **22**, 119–43.

162. Henderson, L. and K.J. Musil (1984) Exotic woody plant invaders of the Transvaal, *Bothalia*, **15**, 297–313.

163. Hengeveld, R. (1987) Theories on biological invasions, *Proceedings of the Koninklijke Nederlandse Akademie van Wetenschappen*, **C90**, 45–9.

164. Hengeveld, R. (1988) Mechanisms of biological invasions, *Journal of Biogeography*, **15**, 819–28.

165. Heywood, V.H. (1987) The changing role of the botanic garden, in *Botanic Gardens and the World Conservation Strategy*, (ed. D. Bramwell *et al.*), Academic Press, London, pp. 3–18.

166. Heywood, V.H. (1989) Pattern, extent and modes of invasions by terrestrial plants, in *Biological Invasion: a global perspective*, (ed. J.A. Drake *et al.*), John Wiley & Sons, Chichester, pp. 31–60.

167. Higashino, P.K., W. Guyer and C.P. Stone (1983) The Kilauea Wilderness marathon and Crater Rim runs: sole searching experiences, *Newsletter Hawaiian Botanical Society*, **22**, 25–8.

168. Hislop, E.C. (1987) Requirements for effective and efficient pesticide application, in *Rational Pesticide Use*, (ed. K.J. Brent and R.K. Atkin), Long Ashton Symposium Series (No. 9), Cambridge University Press, Cambridge.

169. Hobbs, R.J. (1989) The nature and effects of disturbance relative to invasions, in *Biological Invasions: a global perspective*, (ed. J.A. Drake *et al.*), John Wiley & Sons, Chichester, pp. 389–406.

170. Hodges, C.S. and D.S. Gardner (1985) Myrica faya: *potential biological contral agents*, Cooperative National Park Resources Studies Unit, University of Hawaii at Manoa, Department of Botany, Honolulu.

171. Hoffman, M.T. and D.T. Mitchell (1986) The root morphology of some legume spp. in the south-western Cape and the relationship of vesicular-arbuscular mycorrhizas with dry mass and phosphorus content of *Acacia saligna* seedlings, *South African Journal of Botany*, **52**, 316–20.

172. Hoffmann, J.H. (1990) Interactions between three weevil species in the biocontrol of *Sesbania punicea* (Fabaceae): the role of simulation models in evaluation, *Agriculture, Ecosystems, and Environment*, **32**, 77–87.

173. Hoffmann, J.H. and V.C. Moran (1988) The invasive weed *Sesbania punicea* in South Africa and prospects for its control, *South African Journal of Science*, **4**, 740–3.

174. Hoffmann, J.H. and V.C. Moran (1989) Novel graphs for depicting herbivore damage on plants: the biological control of *Sesbania punicea* (Fabaceae) by an introduced weevil, *Journal of Applied Ecology*, **26**, 353–60.

175. Hoffmann, J.H. and V.C. Moran (1991) Biocontrol of a perennial legume, *Sesbania punicea*, using a florivorous weevil, *Trichapion lativentre*: weed population dynamics with a scarcity of seeds, *Oecologia*, **88**, 574–6.

176. Holdridge, L.R. (1967) *Life Zone Ecology*, Tropical Science Center, Costa Rica.

177. Holm, L. *et al.* (1979) *A Geographical Atlas of World Weeds*, John Wiley & Sons, New York.
178. Holm, L.G. *et al.* (1977) *The World's Worst Weeds*, University Press of Hawaii, Honolulu.
179. Holmes, P.M., H. Dallas and T. Phillips (1987) Control of *Acacia saligna* in the south western Cape – are clearing treatments effective?, *Veld & Flora*, **73**, 98–100.
180. Holmes, P.M., I.A.W. Macdonald and J. Juritz (1987) Effects of clearing treatment on seed banks of the alien invasive shrubs *Acacia saligna* and *Acacia cyclops* in the Southern and South Western Cape, South Africa, *Journal of Applied Ecology*, **24**, 1045–51.
181. Horn, C.N. (1987) Pontederiaceae, in *Flora del Paraguay*, (ed. R. Spichiger), Missouri Botanical Garden, pp. 1–28.
182. Howard-Williams, C. and J. Davies (1988) The invasion of Lake Taupo by the submerged water weed *Lagarosiphon major* and its impact on the native flora, *New Zealand Journal of Ecology*, **11**, 13–19.
183. Huenneke, L.F. and P.M. Vitousek (1990) Seedling and clonal recruitment of the invasive tree *Psidium cattleianum*: implications for management of native Hawaiian forests, *Biological Conservation*, **53**, 199–211.
184. Hughes, C.E. and B.T. Styles (1989) The benefits and risks of woody legume introductions, *Monographs in Systematic Botany*, Missouri Botanic Garden, 505–31.
185. Hulbert, L.C. (1955) Ecological studies of *Bromus tectorum* and other annual brome-grasses, *Ecological Monographs*, **25**, 181–213.
186. Humbert, H., ed. (1951) *Flore de Madagascar et des Comores: Mélastomatacées*, Muséum National d'Histoire Naturelle, Paris.
187. Humphries, S.E., R.H. Groves and D.S. Mitchell (1991) *Plant Invasions of Australian Ecosystems: a status review and management directions*, Endangered Species Program, Project No. 58, Australian National Parks and Wildlife Service, Canberra.
188. Hunter, G.G. and M.H. Douglas (1984) Spread of exotic conifers on South Island Rangelands, *New Zealand Journal of Forestry*, **29**, 78–96.
189. IUCN (1987) *The IUCN Position Statement on Translocation of Living Organisms*, IUCN, Gland.
190. Janzen, D.H., ed. (1983) *Costa Rican Natural History*, The University of Chicago Press, Chicago.
191. Jarvis, P.J. (1977) The ecology of plant and animal introductions, *Progress in Physical Geography*, **3**, 187–214.
192. Joenje, W., K. Bakker and L. Vlijm, ed. (1986) *The Ecology of Biological Invasions*, Proceedings of the Koninklijke Nederlandse Akademie van Wetenschappen, **C90**.
193. Johnson, C. (1980) Australian Myrtle, in *Plant Invaders: beautiful but dangerous*, 2nd ed, (ed. C.H. Stirton), The Department of Nature and Environmental Conservation of the Cape Provincial Administration, Cape Town.
194. Johnstone, I.M. (1986) Plant invasion windows: a time-based classification of invasion potential, *Biological Reviews*, **61**, 369–94.
195. Jones, W.I. (1974) *A Rhododendron eradication trial*, Nature Conservancy Council, Information Paper No. 1.
196. Julien, M.H., ed. (1987) *Biological Control of Weeds: a world catalogue of agents and their target weeds*, CAB International Institute of Biological Control, Ascot.
197. Kelly, D. and J.P. Skipworth (1984) *Tradescantia fluminensis* in a Manawatu (New Zealand) forest I, *New Zealand Journal of Botany*, **22**, 393–7.
198. Kelly, D. and J.P. Skipworth (1984) *Tradescantia fluminensis* in a Manawatu (New Zealand) forest II, *New Zealand Journal of Botany*, **22**, 399–402.
199. Kelly, D.L. (1981) The native forest vegetation of Killarney, south-west Ireland: an ecological account, *Journal of Ecology*, **69**, 437–72.
200. Kennedy, P.C. (1984) The general morphology and ecology of *Clematis vitalba*, in *The Clematis vitalba Threat*, DSIR, Wellington, pp. 26–35.

201. Kenney, D.S. (1986) De Vine – The way it was developed – An industrialist's view, *Weed Science*, **34**, (Suppl. 1), 15–16.
202. Khoshoo, T.F. and C. Mahal (1967) Versatile reproduction of *Lantana camara*, *Current Science*, **36**, 201–3.
203. Killip, E.P. (1938) The American species of Passifloraceae, *Publications of the Field Museum Natural History, Botanical Series*, **19**, 613.
204. Kloot, P.M. (1983) The role of the common iceplant (*Mesembryanthemum crystallinum*) in the deterioration of mesic pastures, *Australian Journal of Ecology*, **8**, 301–6.
205. Kloot, P.M. (1987) The invasion of Kangaroo Island by alien plants, *Australian Journal of Ecology*, **12**, 263–6.
206. Kluge, R.L. (1983) Progress in the fight against hakea, *Veld & Flora*, **69**, 136–8.
207. Kluge, R.L. and P.M. Caldwell (1991) Alarming new records of *Pereskia*, *Veld & Flora*, **77**, 39.
208. Kluge, R.L. and S. Neser (1991) Biological control of *Hakea sericea* (Proteaceae) in South Africa, *Agriculture, Ecosystems and Environment*, **37**, 91–113.
209. Knight, R.S. and I.A.W. Macdonald (1991) Acacias and korhans: an artificially assembled seed dispersal system, *South African Journal of Botany*, **57**, 220–5.
210. Kohler, A., and H. Sukopp (1964) Uber die soziologische Struktur einiger Robinienbestände im Stadtgebiet von Berlin, *Sonderdruck aus Sitzungsberichte der Gesellschaft Naturforschender Freunde zu Berlin*, **4**(2), 74–88.
211. Koopowitz, H. and H. Kaye (1990) *Plant Extinction: A Global Crisis*, Christopher Helm, London.
212. Kornas, J. (1982) Man's impact upon the flora: processes and effects, *Memorabilia Zoologica*, **37**, 11–30.
213. Kornberg, H. and M.H. Williamson, ed. (1986) Quantitative aspects of the ecology of biological invasions, *Philosophical Transactions of the Royal Society, London, Series B*, **341**.
214. Kruger, F.J. (1977) Invasive woody plants in the Cape fynbos with special reference to the biology and control of *Pinus pinaster*, Proceedings of the Second National Weeds conference in South Africa, Balkema, Cape Town, pp. 57–74.
215. Kruger, F.J. (1980) Cluster Pine, in *Plant Invaders: beautiful but dangerous*, 2nd ed, (ed. C.H. Stirton), The Department of Nature and Environmental Conservation of the Cape Provincial Administration, Cape Town, pp. 124–7.
216. Kruger, F.J. *et al.* (1989) The characteristics of invaded mediterranean-climate regions, in *Biological Invasions: a global perspective*, (ed. J.A. Drake *et al.*), John Wiley & Sons, Chichester, pp. 181–214.
217. Kruger, F.J., D.M. Richardson and B.W. van Wilgen (1986) Processes of invasion by plants, in *The Ecology and Management of Biological Invasions in South Africa*, (ed. I.A.W. Macdonald, F.J. Kruger and A.A. Ferrar), Oxford University Press, Cape Town, pp. 145–55.
218. Kugler, H. (1980) Zur Bestäubung von *Lantana camara* L. (On the pollination of *Lantana camara* L.), *Flora*, **169**, 524–9.
219. Kushwaha, S.P.S., P.S. Ramakrishnan and R.S. Tripathi (1981) Population dynamics of *Eupatorium odoratum* in successional environments following slash and burn agriculture, *Journal of Applied Ecology*, **18**, 529–35.
220. Laroche, F.B. and A.P. Ferriter (1992) The rate of expansion of *Melaleuca* in South Florida, *Journal of Aquatic Plant Management*, **30**, 62–5.
221. LaRosa, A. (1987) Note on the identity of the introduced passion flower vine 'banana poka' in Hawaii, *Pacific Science*, **39**, 369–71.
222. LaRosa, A.M. (1984) The biology and ecology of *Passiflora mollissima* in Hawaii, Technical Report No.50, Cooperative National Park Resources Studies Unit, Hawaii.
223. LaRosa, A.M. (1992) The status of Banana Poka in Hawaii, in *Alien Plant Invasions in Native Ecosystems of Hawaii: management and research*, (ed. C.P. Stone, C.W. Smith

and J.T. Tunison), University of Hawaii Cooperative National Park Resources Studies Unit, Honolulu, pp. 000–000.

224. LaRosa, A.M., C.W. Smith and D.E. Gardner (1985) Role of alien and native birds in the dissemination of fire tree (*Myrica faya* Ait. – Myricaceae) and associated plants in Hawaii, *Pacific Science*, **39**, 372–7.

225. Lawton, J.H. (1988) Biological control of bracken in Britain: constraints and opportunities, *Philosophical Transactions of the Royal Society, London, Series B*, **318**, 335–54.

226. Leader-Williams, N., R.I.L. Smith and P. Rothery (1987) Influence of introduced reindeer on the vegetation of South Georgia: results from a long-term exclusion experiment, *Journal of Applied Ecology*, **24**, 801–22.

227. Lee, M.A.B. (1974) Distribution of native and invader plant species on the island of Guam, *Biotropica*, **6**, 158–64.

228. Lee, W.G., R.B. Allen and P.W. Johnson (1986) Succession and dynamics of gorse (*Ulex europaeus* L.) communities in the Dunedin ecological district, South Island, New Zealand, *New Zealand Journal of Botany*, **24**, 279–92.

229. Lewis, G.P. (1987) *Legumes of Bahia*, Royal Botanic Gardens, Kew.

230. Lock, M. (1989) *Legumes of Africa: a check-list*, Royal Botanic Gardens, Kew.

231. Lonsdale, W.M. (1988) Litterfall of an Australian population of *Mimosa pigra* an invasive tropical shrub, *Journal of Tropical Ecology*, **4**, 381–92.

232. Lonsdale, W.M. and D.G. Abrecht (1989) Seedling mortality in *Mimosa pigra*, an invasive tropical shrub, *Journal of Ecology*, **77**, 372–85.

233. Lonsdale, W.M., K.L.S. Harley and J.D. Gillet (1988) Seed bank dynamics in *Mimosa pigra*, an invasive tropical shrub, *Journal of Applied Ecology*, **25**, 963–76.

234. Lonsdale, W.M., I.L. Miller and I.W. Forno (1989) The biology of Australian weeds 20. *Mimosa pigra* L., *Plant Protection Quarterly*, **4**, 119–31.

235. Loope, L.L., O. Hamann and C.P. Stone (1988) Comparative conservation biology of oceanic archipelagos: Hawaii and the Galapagos, *Bioscience*, **38**, 272–82.

236. Loope, L.L. and D. Mueller-Dombois (1989) Characteristics of invaded islands with special reference to Hawaii, in *Biological Invasions: a global perspective*, (ed. J.A. Drake *et al.*), John Wiley & Sons, Chichester, pp. 257–80.

237. Loope, L.L. *et al.* (1988) Biological invasions of arid land nature reserves, *Biological Conservation*, **44**, 95–118.

238. Lorence, D.H. (1978) The pteridophytes of Mauritius (Indian Ocean): ecology and distribution, *Botanical Journal of the Linnean Society*, **76**, 207–47.

239. Lorence, D.H. and R.W. Sussman (1986) Exotic species invasion into Mauritius wet forest remnants, *Journal of Tropical Ecology*, **2**, 147–62.

240. Lorence, D.H. and R.W. Sussman (1988) Diversity, density, and invasion in a Mauritian wet forest, *Monographs of Systematics of the Missouri Botanical Garden*, **25**, 187–204.

241. Lucas, G. and H. Synge (1978) *The IUCN Red Data Book*, IUCN, Switzerland.

242. Mabberley, D.J. (1987) *The Plant-Book*, Cambridge University Press, Cambridge.

243. Macdonald, I.A.W. (1983) Alien trees, shrubs and creepers invading indigenous vegetation in the Hluhluwe-Umfolozi Game Reserve Complex in Natal, *Bothalia*, **14**, 949–59.

244. Macdonald, I.A.W. (1986) Range expansion in the pied barbet and the spread of alien tree species in southern Africa, *Ostrich*, **57**, 75–94.

245. Macdonald, I.A.W. (1987) Banana poka in the Knysna forest, *Veld & Flora*, **73**, 133–4.

246. Macdonald, I.A.W. (1987) State of the art in the science of wildlife management: a North–South comparison, *South African Journal of Science*, **83**, 397–9.

247. Macdonald, I.A.W. (1988) The history, impacts and control of introduced species in the Kruger National Park, South Africa, *Transactions of the Royal Society South Africa*, **46**, 252–76.

248. Macdonald, I.A.W. and G.W. Frame (1988) The invasion of introduced species into nature reserves in tropical savannas and dry woodlands, *Biological Conservation*, **44**, 67–93.

249. Macdonald, I.A.W. and W.P.D. Gertenbach (1988) A list of alien plants in the Kruger National Park, *Koedoe*, **31**, 137–50.

250. Macdonald, I.A.W. *et al.* (1988) Introduced species in nature reserves in Mediterranean-type climatic regions of the world, *Biological Conservation*, **44**, 37–66.

251. Macdonald, I.A.W. and M.L. Jarman (1985) *Invasive Alien Plants in the Terrestrial Ecosystems of Natal, South Africa*, South African National Scientific Programmes Report No. 118, CSIR, Pretoria.

252. Macdonald, I.A.W., F.J. Kruger and A.A. Ferrar, ed. (1986) *The Ecology and Management of Biological Invasions in Southern Africa*, Oxford University Press, Cape Town.

253. Macdonald, I.A.W. *et al.* (1989) Wildlife conservation and the invasion of nature reserves by introduced species: a global perspective, in *Biological Invasions: a global perspective*, (ed. J.A. Drake *et al.*), John Wiley & Sons, Chichester, pp. 215–56.

254. Macdonald, I.A.W. and T.B. Nott (1987) Invasive alien organisms in central south west Africa/Namibia: results of a reconnaisance survey conducted in November 1984, *Madoqua*, **15**, 21–34.

255. Macdonald, I.A.W. *et al.* (1988) The invasion of highlands in Galápagos by the red quinine tree *Cinchona succirubra*, *Environmental Conservation*, **15**, 215–20.

256. Macdonald, I.A.W. and C. Wissel (1992) Determining optimal clearing treatments for the alien invasive shrub *Acacia saligna* in the southwestern Cape, South Africa, *Agriculture, Ecosystems and Environment*, **39**, 169–86.

257. Mack, R.N. (1981) Invasion of *Bromus tectorum* L. into western North America: an ecological chronicle, *Agro-Ecosystems*, **7**, 145–65.

258. Mack, R.N. (1984) Invaders at home on the range, *Natural History*, **2**, 40–7.

259. Mack, R.N. (1985) Invading plants: their potential contribution to population biology, in *Studies on Plant Demography: a Festschrift for John L. Harper*, (ed. J. White), Academic Press, London, pp. 127–41.

260. Madsen, J.D. *et al.* (1991) The decline of native vegetation under dense Eurasian watermilfoil canopies, *Journal of Aquatic Plant Management*, **29**, 94–9.

261. Maheshwari, J.K. (1965) Alligator weed in Indian lakes, *Nature*, **206**, 1270.

262. Makepeace, W. (1981) Polymorphism and the chromosomal number of *Hieracium pilosella* L. in New Zealand, *New Zealand Journal of Botany*, **19**, 255–7.

263. Markin, G.P. (1989) Alien plant management by biological control, in *Conservation Biology in Hawaii*, (ed. C.P. Stone and D.B. Stone), Cooperative National Park Resources Studies Unit, Hawaii, pp. 70–3.

264. Martin, F.W. and H.Y. Nakasone (1970) The edible species of *Passiflora*, *Economic Botany*, **24**, 333–43.

265. Maslin, B.R. (1974) Studies in the genus *Acacia*, 3. The taxonomy of *Acacia saligna* (Labill.) H.Wendl., *Nuytsia*, **2**, 332–40.

266. Mason, R. (1960) Three waterweeds of the family Hydrocharitaceae in New Zealand, *New Zealand Journal of Science*, **3**, 383–95.

267. Mather, L.J. and P.A. Williams (1990) Phenology, seed ecology, and age structure of Spanish heath (*Erica lusitanica*) in Canterbury, New Zealand, *New Zealand Journal of Botany*, **28**, 207–15.

268. Mathur, G. and H.H. Mohan Ram (1978) Significance of petal colour in thrips-pollinated *Lantana camara* L., *Annals of Botany*, **42**, 1473–6.

269. McClune, B. (1988) Ecological diversity in North American pines, *American Journal of Botany*, **75**, 353–68.

270. McLoughlin, L. and J. Rawling (1990) *Making Your Garden Bush Friendly: how to recognise and control garden plants which invade Sydney's bushland*, McLoughlin-Rawling, Killara, NSW.

271. Meurk, C.D. (1977) Alien plants in Campbell Island's changing vegetation, *Mauri Ora*, **5**, 93–118.
272. Miller, I.L. (1983) The distribution and threat of *Mimosa pigra* in Australia, International Plant Protection Center, Corvallis, Oregon, USA.
273. Miller, I.L. and W.M. Lonsdale (1987) Early records of *Mimosa pigra* in the Northern Territory, *Plant Protection Quarterly*, **2**, 140–2.
274. Milton, S.J. (1980) Australian Acacias in the south western Cape: preadaption, predation and success.
275. Miranda, F. and A.J. Sharp (1950) Characteristics of the vegetation in certain temperate regions of eastern Mexico, *Ecology*, **31**, 313–33.
276. Mirov, N.T. (1967) *The Genus* Pinus, The Ronald Press Company, New York.
277. Mitchell, D.S. (1972) The kariba weed: *Salvinia molesta*, *British Fern Gazette*, **10**, 251–2.
278. Mitchell, D.S. (1980) The water fern *Salvinia molesta* in the Sepick River, Papua New Guinea, *Environmental Conservation*, **7**, 115–22.
279. Mitchell, D.S. and B. Gopal (1991) Invasion of tropical freshwaters by alien aquatic weeds, in *Ecology of Biological Invasion in the Tropics*, (ed. P.S. Ramakrishnan), International Scientific Publications, New Delhi, pp. 139–56.
280. Mitchell, D.S. and N.N. Tur (1975) The rate and growth of *Salvinia molesta* (*S. auriculata*) in laboratory and in natural conditions, *Journal of Applied Ecology*, **12**, 212–25.
281. Mohan Ram, H.Y. and G. Mathur (1984) Flower colour changes in *Lantana camara*, *Journal of Experimental Botany*, **35**, 1656–62.
282. Moll, E.J. (1980) Blackwood, in *Plant Invaders: beautiful but dangerous*, 2nd ed, (ed. C.H. Stirton), Department of Nature and Environmental Conservation of the Cape Provincial Administration, Cape Town, pp. 52–5.
283. Mollison, D. (1986) Modelling biological invasion: chance, explanation, prediction, *Philosophical Transactions of the Royal Society, London, Series B*, **314**, 675–92.
284. Moody, M.E. and R.N. Mack (1988) Controlling the spread of plant invasions: the importance of nascent foci, *Journal of Applied Ecology*, **25**, 1009–21.
285. Mooney, H.A. and J.A. Drake, ed. (1986) *Ecology of Biological Invasions of North America and Hawaii*, Springer-Verlag, New York.
286. Moran, V.C. and J.H. Hoffmann (1989) The effects of herbivory by a weevil species acting alone and unrestrained by natural enemies on growth and phenology of the weed *Sesbania punicea*, *Journal of Applied Ecology*, **26**, 967–77.
287. Moriarty, A. (1982) *Outeniqua Tsitsikamma & Eastern Little Karoo*, Botanical Society of South Africa, Kirstenbosch.
288. Morris, J.M. (1982) Biological control of hakea by a fungus, *Veld & Flora*, **68**, 51–2.
289. Morris, M.J. (1982) Gummosis and die-back of *Hakea sericea* in South Africa, in *Proceedings of the Fourth National Weeds Conference of South Africa*, (ed. H.A. van der Venter and M. Mason), Balkema, Cape Town, pp. 51–4.
290. Motooka, P., G. Nagai and L. Ching (1982) Weed and brush control in pasture and ranges of Hawaii 1–5, *HITAHR Brief*, 16–20.
291. Mueller-Dombois, D. (1973) A non-adapted vegetation interferes with water removal in a tropical rainforest area in Hawaii, *Tropical Ecology*, **14**, 1–16.
292. Mueller-Dombois, D. *et al.* (1980) Ohi'a rainforest study: investigation of the Ohi'a dieback problem in Hawaii, *Hawaii Agricultural Experimental Station Miscellaneous Publications*, **183**, 64.
293. Mueller-Dombois, D. and L.D. Whiteaker (1990) Plants associated with *Myrica faya* and two other pioneer trees on a recent volcanic surface in Hawaii Volcanoes National Park, *Phytocoenologia*, **19**, 29–41.
294. Munton, P. (1988) *The Role, Impact and Management of the Translocation of Living Organisms in the Context of Wildlife Resources (Draft Guidelines)*, Report of the Introduction Specialist Group of the Species Survival Commission,

295. Munz, P.A. (1959) *A California Flora*, University of California Press, Berkeley.
296. Myers, R.L. (1983) Site susceptibility to invasion by the exotic tree *Melaleuca quinquenervia* in southern Florida, *Journal of Applied Ecology*, **20**, 645–58.
297. Nakahara, L.M., R.M. Burkhart and J.Y. Funasaki (1992) Review and status of biological control of *Clidemia* in Hawaii, in *Alien Plant Invasions in Native Ecosystems of Hawaii: management and research*, (ed. C.P. Stone, C.W. Smith and J.T. Tunison), University of Hawaii Cooperative National Park Resources Studies Unit, Honolulu.
298. Natarajan, A.T. and M.R. Ahuja (1947) Cytotaxonomical studies of the genus *Lantana*, *Journal of the Indian Botanical Society*, **36**, 35–45.
299. National Trust, NSW (1991) *Bush Regenerators Handbook*, National Trust of Australia (NSW), New South Wales.
300. Naveh, Z. (1967) Mediterranean ecosystems and vegetation types in California and Israel, *Ecology*, **48**, 443–59.
301. Neser, S. (1980) Rock hakea, in *Plant Invaders: beautiful but dangerous*, 2nd ed, (ed. C.H. Stirton), The Department of Nature and Environmental Conservation of the Cape Provincial Administration, Cape Town, pp. 72–5.
302. Neser, S. (1980) Sweet hakea, in *Plant Invaders: beautiful but dangerous*, 2nd ed, (ed. C.H. Stirton), The Department of Nature and Environmental Conservation of the Cape Provincial Administration, Cape Town, pp. 80–3.
303. Neser, S. and S.R. Fugler (1980) Silky hakea, in *Plant Invaders: beautiful but dangerous*, 2nd ed, (ed. C.H. Stirton), The Department of Nature and Environmental Conservation of the Cape Provincial Administration, Cape Town, pp. 76–7.
304. Newbold, C. (1975) Herbicides in aquatic systems, *Biological Conservation*, **7**, 97–118.
305. Newbold, C. (1977) Aquatic herbicides: possible future developments, in *Ecological Effects of Pesticides*, (ed. F.H. Perring and K. Mellanby), Academic Press, London, Linnean Society Symposium Series, Number 5, pp. 000–000.
306. Noble, I.R. (1989) Attributes of invaders and the invading process: terrestrial and vascular plants, in *Biological Invasions: a global perspective*, (ed. J.A. Drake *et al.*), John Wiley & Sons, Chichester, pp. 301–14.
307. Ohwi, J. (1965) *Flora of Japan*, Smithsonian Institution, Washington DC.
308. Osmond, C.B. and J. Monro (1981) Prickly pear, in *Plants and Man in Australia*, (ed. D.J. Carr and S.G.M. Carr), Academic Press, Sydney, pp. 194–222.
309. Parham, J.W. (1964) *Plants of the Fiji Islands*, Government Press, Suva.
310. Parsons, W.T. (1973) *Noxious Weeds of Victoria*, Inkata Press, Melbourne.
311. Pathak, P.S., R. Debroy and P. Rai (1974) Autecology of *Leucaena leucocephala* (Lam.) de Wit 1. Seed production and germination, *Tropical Ecology*, **15**, 1–11.
312. Pedley, L. (1986) Derivation and dispersal of *Acacia* (Legumisosae), with particular reference to Australia, and the recognition of *Senegalia* and *Racosperma*, *Botanical Journal of the Linnean Society*, **92**, 219–54.
313. Penfound, W.T. (1948) The biology of the water hyacinth, *Ecological Monographs*, **18**, 447–72.
314. Pickard, J. (1984) Exotic plants on Lord Howe Island: distribution in space and time, 1853–1981, *Journal of Biogeography*, **11**, 181–208.
315. Pienaar, K. (1980) Sesbania, in *Plant Invaders: beautiful but dangerous*, 2nd ed, (ed. C.H. Stirton), The Department of Nature and Environmental Conservation of the Cape Provincial Administration, Cape Town, pp. 136–9.
316. Pienaar, K.J. (1977) *Sesbania punicea* (Cav.) Benth. The handsome plant terrorist, *Veld & Flora*, **63**, 17–18.
317. Popay, A.I. (1984) Prospects for herbicidal control of *Clematis vitalba*, in *The* Clematis vitalba *Threat*, DSIR, Wellington, pp. 43–6.
318. Popay, A.I. (1986) *Old Man's Beard* Clematis vitalba: *control measures*, Farm Production and Practice Report, Ministry of Agriculture and Fisheries, New Zealand.

319. Proctor, V.W. (1968) Long-distance dispersal of seeds by retention in the digestive tract of birds, *Science*, **160**, 321–2.

320. Ramakrishnan, P.S. (1991) Biological invasion in the tropics: an overview, in *Ecology of Biological Invasions in the Tropics*, (ed. P.S. Ramakrishnan), International Scientific Publications, New Delhi, pp. 1–20.

321. Ramakrishnan, P.S. and P.M. Vitousek (1989) Ecosystem-level processes and the consequences of biological invasions, in *Biological Invasions: a global perspective*, (ed. J.A. Drake *et al.*), John Wiley & Sons, Chichester, pp. 281–300.

322. Reiche, C. (1896) *Flora de Chile*, Vol. 1, Bandera, Santiago de Chile.

323. Reimer, N.J. (1988) Predation on *Liothrips urichi* Karny (Thysanoptera: Phlaeothripidae): a case of biotic interference, *Environmental Entomology*, **17**, 132–4.

324. Rejmanek, M. (1989) Invasibility of plant communities, in *Biological Invasions: a global perspective*, (ed. J.A. Drake *et al.*), John Wiley & Sons, Chichester, pp. 369–88.

325. Richards, A.J. (1986) *Plant Breeding Systems*, George Allen & Unwin, London.

326. Richards, P. W. and A. J. E. Smith (1975) A progress report on *Campylopus introflexus* (Hedw.) Brid. and C. *polytrichoides* De Not. in Britain and Ireland. *Journal of Bryology*, **8**, 293–8.

327. Richardson, D.M. and W.J. Bond (1991) Determinants of plant distribution: evidence from pine invasions, *The American Naturalist*, **137**, 639–68.

328. Richardson, D.M. and M.P. Brink (1985) Notes of *Pittosporum undulatum* in the south western Cape, *Veld & Flora* **71**, 75–7.

329. Richardson, D.M. and P.J. Brown (1986) Invasion of mesic mountain fynbos by *Pinus radiata*, *South African Journal of Botany*, **52**, 529–36.

330. Richardson, D.M. and R.M. Cowling (1992) Why is mountain fynbos invasible and which species invade?, in *Fire in South African Mountain Fynbos*, (ed. B.W. van Wilgen *et al.*), Springer-Verlag, Berlin, pp. 161–81.

331. Richardson, D.M., R.M. Cowling and D.C. Le Maitre (1990) Assessing the risk of invasive success in *Pinus* and *Banksia* in South African mountain fynbos, *Journal of Vegetation Science*, **1**, 629–42.

332. Richardson, D.M. and P.T. Manders (1985) Predicting pathogen-induced mortality in *Hakea sericea* (Proteacea) an aggressive alien plant invader in South Africa, *Annals of Applied Biology*, **106**, 243–54.

333. Richardson, D.M. and B.W. van Wilgen (1984) Factors affecting the regeneration success of *Hakea sericea*, *South African Forestry Journal*, **131**, 63–8.

334. Ridings, W.H. (1986) Biological control of strangler vine in citrus – A researcher's view, *Weed Science*, **34**(Suppl. 1), 31–2.

335. Ridley, H.N. (1923) *Flora of the Malay Peninsula*, Vol. 1, L. Reeves, London.

336. Room, P.M. (1983) 'Falling apart' as a lifestyle: the rhizome architecture and population growth of *Salvinia molesta Journal of Ecology*, **71**, 349–65.

337. Room, P.M. *et al.* (1981) Successful biological control of the floating weed *Salvinia*, *Nature*, **294**, 78–80.

338. Room, P.M. and P.A. Thomas (1986) Population growth of the floating weed *Salvinia molesta*: field observation and a global model based on temperature and nitrogen, *Journal of Applied Ecology*, **23**, 1013–28.

339. Rotherham, I.D. (1986) The introduction, spread and current distribution of *Rhododendron ponticum* in the Peak district and Sheffield area, *The Naturalist*, **111**, 61–7.

340. Rouw, A. De (1991) The invasion of *Chromolaena odorata* (L.) King & Robinson (ex *Eupatorium odoratum*), and competition with the native flora, in a rain forest zone, south-west Cote d'Ivoire, *Journal of Biogeography*, **18**, 13–23.

341. Sagar, G.R. (1974) On the ecology of weed control, in *Biology in Pest and Disease Control*, (ed. D. Price Jones and M.E. Solomon), Symposium of the British Ecological Society (13), Blackwell Scientific Publications, Oxford.

342. Sale, P.J.M. *et al.* (1985) Photosynthesis and growth rates on *Salvinia molesta* and *Eichhornia*, *Journal of Applied Ecology*, **22**, 125–37.

343. Sankaran, T. and E. Narayanan (1971) Occurrence of the alligator weed in South India, *Current Science*, **40**, 641.

344. Santos, G.L. et al. (1986) *Herbicidal control of selected alien plant species in Hawaii Volcanoes National Park*, Cooperative National Park Resources Studies Unit, University of Hawaii at Manoa, Technical Report 60, Honolulu.

345. Sauer, J.D. (1988) *Plant Migration: the dynamics of geographic patterning in seed plant species*, University of California Press, Berkeley.

346. Schofield, E.K. (1973) Galápagos flora: the threat of introduced plants, *Biological Conservation*, **5**, 48–51.

347. Schofield, E.K. (1989) Effects of introduced plants and animals on island vegetation: examples from the Galapagos archipelago, *Conservation Biology*, **3**, 227–38.

348. Schreiber, M.M. (1982) Modelling the biology of weeds for integrated weed management, *Weed Science*, **30** (Suppl.), 13–16.

349. Scott, D., J.S. Robertson and W.J. Archie (1990) Plant dynamics of New Zealand tussock grassland infested with *Hieracium pilosella*. 1. Effects of seasonal grazing, fertiliser, and overdrilling, *Journal of Applied Ecology*, **27**, 224–34.

350. Scowcroft, P.G. and K.T. Adee (1991) *Site Preparation Affects Survival, Growth of Koa on Degraded Montane Forest Land*, Pacific Southwest Research Station, Forest Service, USDA, Research Paper PSW-205, Berkeley, California.

351. Scowcroft, P.G. and P.G. Nelson (1976) *Disturbance After Logging Stimulates Regeneration of Koa*, Pacific South West Forest and Range Experimental Station, USDA Forest Research Notes 306.

352. Seratna, J.E. (1943) *Salvinia auriculata* Aublet – a recently introduced free-floating water weed, *Tropical Agriculture Magazine*, **99**, 146–9.

353. Shaughnessy, G. (1980) Historical Ecology of Alien Woody Plants in the Vicinity of Cape Town, South Africa, Ph.D. Thesis, Research Report No. 23, School of Environmental Studies, University of Cape Town, Cape Town.

354. Shaw, M.W. (1984) *Rhododendron ponticum* – ecological reasons for the success of an alien species in Britain and features that may assist in its control, *Aspects of Applied Biology*, **5**, 231–42.

355. Shimizu, Y. and H. Tabata (1985) Invasion of *Pinus lutchuensis* and its influence on the native forest on a Pacific island, *Journal of Biogeography*, **12**, 195–207.

356. Sinha, S. and A. Sharma (1984) *Lantana camara* L. – a review, *Feddes Repertorium*, **95**, 621–33.

357. Small, J.K. (1913) *Flora of the South-Eastern States*, Published by the Author, New York.

358. Smathers, G.A. and D.E. Gardner (1979) Stand analysis of an invading firetree (*Myrica faya* Aiton) population, Hawaii, *Pacific Science*, **33**, 239–55.

359. Smith, C.W. (1985) Impact of alien plants on Hawaii's native biota, in *Hawaii's Terrestrial Ecosystems: preservation and management*, (ed. C.P. Stone and J.M. Scott), Cooperative National Park Resources Studies Unit, University of Hawaii, Honolulu.

360. Smith, C.W. (1989) Controlling the flow of non-native species, in *Conservation Biology in Hawaii*, (ed. C.P. Stone and Stone D.B.), University of Hawaii Cooperative National Park Resources Studies Unit, Honolulu, pp. 139–45.

361. Smith, C.W. (1989) Non-native plants, in *Conservation Biology in Hawaii*, (ed. C.P. Stone and D.B. Stone), University of Hawaii Cooperative National Park Resources Studies Unit, Honolulu, pp. 60–9.

362. Smith, C.W. (1992) Distribution, status, phenology, rate of spread, and management of *Clidemia* in Hawaii, in *Alien Plant Invasions in Native Ecosystems of Hawaii: management and research*, (ed. C.P. Stone, C.W. Smith and J.T. Tunison), University of Hawaii Cooperative National Park Resources Studies Unit, Honolulu.

363. Smith, D. (1984) *Clematis vitalba* – a paper on past control, in *The* Clematis vitalba *Threat*, DSIR, Wellington, pp. 47–9.

364. Smith, L.S. and D.A. Smith (1982) *The Naturalised* Lantana camara *Complex in*

Eastern Australia, Queensland Botany Bulletin, Report No. 1, Department of Primary Industries, Brisbane.

365. Soulé, M.E. (1990) The onslaught of alien species, and other challenges in the coming decades, *Conservation Biology*, **4**, 233–9.

366. Specht, R.L. (1970) Vegetation, in *The Australian Environment*, 4th ed, (ed. G.W. Leeper), CSIRO, Melbourne, pp. 44–67.

367. Spongberg, S.A. (1990) *A Reunion of Trees*, Harvard University Press, Cambridge, Mass.

368. Sprankle, P., W.F. Meggitt and E. Penner (1975) Rapid inactivation of glyphosate in the soil, *Weed Science*, **23**, 224–8.

369. Stanley, T.D. and T.M. Ross (1983) *Flora of South-eastern Queensland*, Vol. 1, Queensland Department of Primary Industries, Brisbane.

370. State Forester, Hawaii (c. 1980) *The Banana Poka Caper*, Department of Land and Natural Resources, Hawaii, Honolulu.

371. Stebbins, G.L. (1971) Adaptive radiation of reproductive characteristics in angiosperms, II: Seeds and seedlings, *Annual Review of Ecology and Systematics*, **2**, 237–60.

372. Steenis, C.G.G.J., ed. (1954) *Flora Malesiana*, Vol. 4, Noordhoff-Kolff N.V., Djakarta.

373. Steenis, C.G.G.J., ed. (1972) *Flora Malesiana*, Vol. 6, Wolters-Noordhoff Publishing Company, Groningen.

374. Steyermark, J.A. (1963) *Flora of Missouri*, The Iowa State University Press, Iowa.

375. Stirton, C.H. (1977) Some thoughts on the polyploid complex *Lantana camara* L. (Verbenaceae), in *Proceedings of the Second National Weeds Conference of South Africa*, Balkema, Cape Town, pp. 321–40.

376. Stirton, C.H. (1980) *Lantana*, in *Plant Invaders: beautiful but dangerous*, 2nd ed, (ed. C.H. Stirton), The Department of Nature and Environmental Conservation, Cape Provincial Administration, Cape Town, pp. 88–91.

377. Stirton, C.H., ed. (1980) *Plant Invaders: beautiful but dangerous*, Department of Nature and Environmental Conservation of the Cape Provincial Administration, Cape Town.

378. Stockard, J., B. Nicholson and G. Williams (1985) An assessment of a rainforest regeneration program at Wingham Brush, *Victorian Naturalist*, **103**, 85–93.

379. Stone, C.P., L.W. Cuddihy and J.T. Tunison (1992) Responses of Hawaiian ecosystems to removal of feral pigs and goats, in *Alien Plant Invasions in Native Ecosystems of Hawaii: management and research*, (ed. C.P. Stone, C.W. Smith and J.T. Tunison), University of Hawaii Cooperative National Park Resources Studies Unit, Honolulu, pp. 666–704.

380. Strahm, W. (1988) The Mondrain Reserve and its conservation management, *Proceedings of the Royal Society of Arts and Science, Mauritius*, **5**, 139–77.

381. Strahm, W. (1990) Conservation of Endemic Plants of Mauritius and Rodrigues, Unpublished Progress Report of Project 3149, WWF/IUCN.

382. Sukopp, H. (1962) Neophyten in naturlichen Pflanzengesellschaften Mitteleuropas, *Sonderabdruck aus den Berichten der Deutschen Botanischen Gesellschaft*, **75**(6), 193–205.

383. Sukopp, H. and U. Sukopp (1988) *Reynoutria japonica* Houtt. in Japan und in Europa, *Veröffentlichungen des Geobotanisches Institut, Eidgenössiche Technische Hochschule, Stiftung Rübel, Zürich*, **98**, 354–72.

384. Sutherst, R.W. and G.F. Maywald (1985) A computerised system for matching climates in ecology, *Agriculture, Ecosystems and Environment*, **13**, 281–99.

385. Swarbrick, J.T., C.M. Finlayson and A.J. Cauldwell (1981) The biology of Australian weeds 7. *Hydrilla verticillata* (L.f.) Royle, *The Journal of the Australian Institute of Agricultural Science*, **47**, 183–90.

386. Tabbush, P.M. and D.R. Williamson (1987) *Rhododendron ponticum* as a forest weed, *Forestry Commission Bulletin*, **73**, 1–7.

387. Thaman, R.R. (1974) *Lantana camara*: its introduction, dispersal and impact on islands of the tropical Pacific Ocean, *Micronesica*, **10**, 17–39.

388. Thomas, K.J. (1975) Biological control of *Salvinia molesta* by the snail *Pila globosa* Swainson, *Biological Journal of the Linnean Society*, **18**, 263–78.

389. Thomas, K.J. (1979) The extent of *Salvinia* infestation in Kerala (South India): its impact and suggested methods of control, *Environmental Conservation*, **6**, 63–9.

390. Thomas, K.J. (1981) The role of aquatic weeds in changing the pattern of ecosystems in Kerala, *Environmental Conservation*, **8**, 63–6.

391. Thomas, P.A. and P.A. Room (1986) Taxonomy and control of *Salvinia molesta*, *Nature*, **320**, 581–4.

392. Thompson, D.Q., R.L. Stuckey and E.B. Thompson (1987) Spread, impact, and control of purple loosestrife (*Lythrum salicaria*) in North American wetlands, *Fish and Wildlife Research*, **2**, 1–55.

393. Thompson, J.D. (1991) The biology of an invasive plant: what makes *Spartina anglica* so successful?, *Bioscience*, **41**, 393–401.

394. Timmins, S. and P.A. Williams (1989) Reserve design and management for weed control, in *Alternatives to the Chemical Control of Weeds*, (ed. C. Bassett, L.J. Whitehouse and J. Zabkiewicz), FRI Bulletin 155, Ministry of Forestry, Rotorua, New Zealand, pp. 133–8.

395. Timmins, S.M. and P.A. Williams (1987) Characteristics of problem weeds in New Zealand's protected natural areas, in *Nature Conservation: the role of remnants of native vegetation*, (ed. D.A. Saunders *et al.*), Surrey Beatty/CSIRO/CALM, pp. 241–7.

396. Tisdell, C.A., B.A. Auld, and K.M. Menz (1984) On assessing the value of biological control of weeds, *Protection Ecology*, **6**, 169–79.

397. Trewick, S. and P.M. Wade (1986) The distribution and dispersal of two alien species of *Impatiens*, waterway weeds in the British Isles, in *7th Symposium on Aquatic Weeds*, pp. 351–6.

398. Trujillo, E.E. (1986) *Colletotrichum gloeosporioides*, a possible control agent for *Clidemia hirta* in Hawaiian forests, *Plant Disease*, **70**, 974–6.

399. Tunison, J.T. (1992) Fountain grass control in Hawaii Volcanoes National Park: management considerations and strategies, in *Alien Plant Invasions in Native Ecosystems of Hawaii: management and research*, (ed. C.P. Stone, C.W. Smith and J.T. Tunison), University of Hawaii Cooperative National Park Resources Studies Unit, Honolulu.

400. Tunison, J.T. and C.P. Stone (1992) Special ecological areas: an approach to alien plant control in Hawaii Volcanoes National Park, in *Alien Plant Invasions in Native Ecosystems of Hawaii: management and research*, (ed. C.P. Stone, C.W. Smith and J.T. Tunison), University of Hawaii Cooperative National Park Resources Studies Unit, Honolulu, pp. 781–98.

401. Turner, D.R. and P.M. Vitousek (1987) Nodule biomass of the nitrogen-fixing alien *Myrica faya* Ait. in Hawaii Volcanoes National Park, *Pacific Science*, **41**, 186–90.

402. Turrill, W.B. (1929) *Plant Life of the Balkan Peninsula*, Clarendon Press, Oxford.

403. Tutin, T.G. *et al.*, ed. (1972) *Flora Europaea. Vol. 3*, Cambridge University Press, Cambridge.

404. Usher, M.B. (1986) Invasibility and wildlife conservation: invasive species on nature reserves, *Philosophical Transactions of the Royal Society, London, Series B*, **314**, 695–709.

405. Usher, M.B. (1988) Biological invasions of nature reserves: a search for generalisations, *Biological Conservation*, **44**, 119–35.

406. Usher, M.B. (1991) Biological invasion into tropical nature reserves, in *Ecology of Biological Invasion in the Tropics*, (ed. P.S. Ramakrishnan), International Scientific Publications, New Delhi, pp. 21–34.

407. van den Tweel, P.A. and H. Eijsackers (1987) Black cherry, a pioneer species or 'forest pest', *Proceedings of the Koninklijke Nederlandse Akademie van Wetenschappen*, **C90**, 59–66.

408. van der Maesen, L.J.G. (1985) Revision of the genus *Pueraria* DC. with some notes on *Teylreia* Backer, *Agricultural University Wageningen Papers*, **85**, 3–132.
409. Van Wilgen, B.W. and D.M. Richardson (1985) The effects of alien shrub invasions on vegetation structure and fire behaviour in South African fynbos shrublands: a simulation study, *Journal of Applied Ecology*, **22**, 955–66.
410. van Wilgen, B.W. and W.R. Siegfried (1986) Seed dispersal properties of three pine species as a determinant of invasive potential, *South African Journal of Botany*, **52**, 546–8.
411. Veblen, T.T. (1975) Alien weeds in the tropical highlands of Western Guatemala, *Journal of Biogeography*, **2**, 19–26.
412. Vere, D.T. and B.A. Auld (1982) The cost of weeds, *Protection Ecology*, **4**, 29–42.
413. Vitousek, P.M. (1988) Diversity and biological invasions of oceanic islands, in *Biodiversity*, (ed. E.O. Wilson), National Academy Press, Washington, DC, pp. 181–92.
414. Vitousek, P.M. (1989) Biological invasion by *Myrica faya* in Hawaii: plant demography, nitrogen fixation, ecosystem effects, *Ecological Monographs*, **59**, 247–65.
415. Vitousek, P.M. (1990) Biological invasions and ecosystems processes: towards an integration of population biology and ecosystem studies, *Oikos*, **57**, 7–13.
416. Vitousek, P.M., L.L. Loope and C.P. Stone (1987) Introduced species in Hawaii: biological effects and opportunities for ecological research, *Trends in Ecology and Evolution*, **2**, 224–7.
417. Vitousek, P.M. *et al.* (1987) Biological invasion by *Myrica faya* alters ecosystem development in Hawaii, *Science*, **238**, 802–4.
418. Vivrette, N.J. and C.H. Muller (1977) Mechanisms of invasion and dominance of coastal grasslands by *Mesembryanthemum crystallinum*, *Ecological Monographs*, **47**, 301–18.
419. Waage, J.K. (1990) Ecological theory and the selection of biological control agents, in *Critical Issues in Biological Control*, (ed. M. Mackauer, L.E. Ehler and J. Roland), Intercept, Andover, pp. 135–57.
420. Wace, N. (1986) The arrival, establishment and control of alien plants on Gough Island, *South African Journal of Antarctic Research*, **16**, 95–101.
421. Wager, V.A. (1927) The structure and life history of South African *Lagarosiphons*, *Transactions of the Royal Society of South Africa*, **16**, 191–212.
422. Wagner, W.L., D.R. Herbst and R.S.N. Yee (1984) Status of the native flowering plants of the Hawaiian Islands, in *Hawaii's Terrestrial Ecosystems: preservation and management*, (ed. C.P. Stone and J.M. Scott), Cooperative National Park Resources Studies Unit, University of Hawaii, Honolulu, pp. 23–74.
423. Walter, H. (1968) *Die vegetation der Erde*, Gustav Fischer Verlag, Stuttgart.
424. Walter, H. and H. Lieth (1960) *Klimmadiagramm-Weltatlas*, Gustav Fischer Verlag GmbH, Jena.
425. Warshauer, F.R. *et al.* (1983) The Distribution, Impact and Potential Management of the Introduced Vine, *Passiflora mollissma* (Passifloraceae) in Hawaii, Cooperative National Park Resources Studies Unit, Hawaii, Report No. 48.
426. Waterhouse, B.M. (1988) Broom (*Cytisus scoparius*) at Barrington tops New South Wales, *Australian Geographical Studies*, **26**, 239–48.
427. Watson, A.K. and M. Clement (1986) Evaluation of rust fungi as biological control agents of weedy centaurea in North America, *Weed Science*, **34**(Suppl. 1), 7–10.
428. Webb, C.J., W.R. Sykes and P.J. Garnock-Jones (1988) *Flora of New Zealand: naturalised pteridophytes, gymnosperms, dicotyledons*, Vol. 4, DSIR, Christchurch.
429. Weiss, P.W. and I.R. Noble (1984) Interactions between seedlings of *Chrysanthemoides monilifera* and *Acacia longifolia*, *Australian Journal of Ecology*, **9**, 107–15.
430. Weiss, P.W. and I.R. Noble (1984) Status of coastal dune communities invaded by *Chrysanthemoides monilifera*, *Australian Journal of Ecology*, **9**, 93–8.

431. Wells, M.J. (1980) Nassella Tussock, in *Plant Invaders: beautiful but dangerous*, 2nd ed, (ed. C.H. Stirton), The Department of Nature and Environmental Conservation of the Cape Provincial Administration, Cape Town, pp. 140–3.

432. Wells, R.D.S. and J.S. Clayton (1991) Submerged vegetation and spread of *Egeria densa* Planchon in Lake Rotorua, central North Island, New Zealand, *New Zealand Journal of Marine and Freshwater Research*, **25**, 63–70.

433. West, C.J. (1991) *Literature Review of the Biology of* Clematis vitalba *(Old Man's Beard)*, *Vegetation Report*, DSIR Land Resources, Report No. 725, New Zealand.

434. West, R.G. (1988) A commentary on Quaternary cold stage floras in Britain, *Journal of Biogeography*, **15**, 523–8.

435. Wester, L.L. and H.B. Wood (1977) Koster's curse (*Clidemia hirta*), a weed pest in Hawaiian forests, *Environmental Conservation*, **4**, 35–41.

436. Westman, W.E. (1990) Park management of exotic plant species: problems and issues, *Conservation Biology*, **4**, 251–60.

437. Whiteaker, L.D. and D.E. Gardner (1985) *The Distribution of* Myrica faya Ait. *in the State of Hawaii, Technical Report No. 55*, Cooperative National Park Resources Studies Unit, University of Hawaii at Manoa, Honolulu.

438. Whiteaker, L.D. and D.E. Gardner (1992) Firetree (*Myrica faya*) distribution in Hawaii, in *Alien Plant Invasions in Native Ecosystems of Hawaii: management and research*, (ed. C.P. Stone, C.W. Smith and J.T. Tunison), University of Hawaii Cooperative National Park Resources Studies Unit, Honolulu.

439. Whiteman, J.B. and P.M. Room (1991) Temperatures lethal to *Salvinia molesta* Mitchell, *Aquatic Botany*, **40**, 27–35.

440. Whitmore, T.C. (1991) Invasive woody plants in perhumid tropical climates, in *Ecology of Biological Invasion in the Tropics*, (ed. P.S. Ramakrishnan), International Scientific Publications, New Delhi, pp. 35–40.

441. Williams, P.A. (1981) Aspects of the ecology of broom (*Cytisus scoparius*) in Canterbury, New Zealand, *New Zealand Journal of Botany*, **19**, 31–43.

442. Williams, P.A. (1983) Secondary vegetation succession on the Port Hills Banks Peninsula, Canterbury, New Zealand, *New Zealand Journal of Botany*, **21**, 237–47.

443. Williams, P.A. (1984) Woody weeds and native vegetation – a conservation problem, in *Protection and Parks. Essays in the Preservation of Natural Values in Protected Areas*, (ed. P.R. Dingwall), Proceedings of Section A4e, 15th Pacific Science Congress, Dunedin, February 1983, Department of Lands and Survey, Wellington, NZ, pp. 61–6.

444. Williams, P.A. and R.P. Buxton (1985) Hawthorn (*Crataegus monogyna*) populations in mid-Canterbury, *New Zealand Journal of Ecology*, **9**, 11–17.

445. Williams, P.A. and S.M. Timmins (1990) *Weeds in New Zealand Protected Natural Areas: a Review for the Department of Conservation*, Science and Research Series, Report No. 14, Department of Conservation, Wellington.

446. Williamson, M.H. and K.C. Brown (1986) The analysis and modeling of British invasions, *Philosophical Transactions of the Royal Society, London, Series B*, **314**, 505–21.

447. Willson, B.W. (1985) The biological control of *Acacia nilotica* in Australia, in *Proceedings of the VI International Symposium on Biological Control of Weeds*, Agriculture Canada, Ottawa, pp. 849–53.

448. Wilson, C.G. and G.J. Flanagan (1991) Establishment of *Acanthoscelides quadridentatus* (Schaeffer) and *A. puniceus* Johnson (Coleoptera: Bruchidae) on *Mimosa pigra* in northern Australia, *Journal of the Australian Entomological Society*, **30**, 279–80.

449. Wilson, J.B. and M.T. Sykes (1988) Some tests for niche limitation by examination of species diversity in the Dunedin area, New Zealand, *New Zealand Journal of Botany*, **26**, 237–44.

450. Witkowski, E.T.F. (1991) Effects of invasive alien acacias on nutrient cycling in the coastal lowlands of the Cape Fynbos, *Journal of Applied Ecology*, **28**, 1–15.

451. Witkowski, E.T.F. (1991) Growth and competition between seedlings of *Protea repens*

(L.) L. and the alien invasive *Acacia saligna* (Labill.) Wendl. in relation to nutrient availability, *Functional Ecology*, **5**, 101–10.

452. Wriggley, J.W. and M. Fagg (1979) *Australian Native Plants: a manual for their propagation, cultivation, and use in landscaping*, Collins, Sydney.

453. Zimmerman, H.G. (1980) Prickly pear, in *Plant Invaders: beautiful but dangerous*, 2nd ed, (ed. C.H. Stirton), The Department of Nature and Environmental Conservation of the Cape Provincial Administration, Cape Town, pp. 112–15.

INDEX